CÉSAR VALLEJO

César Vallejo in the summer of 1929

CÉSAR VALLEJO
The Complete Posthumous Poetry

×

×　×

Translated by
Clayton Eshleman
&
José Rubia Barcia

×　×
×

UNIVERSITY OF CALIFORNIA PRESS

Berkeley　•　Los Angeles　•　London

University of California Press
Berkeley and Los Angeles, California
University of California Press, Ltd.
London, England
First Paperback Printing 1980
ISBN 0-520-04099-6
Library of Congress Catalog Card Number 77-93472
Copyright © 1978 by The Regents of the University of California
Designed by Bob Cato
Printed in the United States of America

1 2 3 4 5 6 7 8 9

Dedicated to Maureen Ahern and Juan Larrea,
for their tremendous dedication to Vallejo.

ACKNOWLEDGMENTS

Some of these translations, in semifinal drafts,
have appeared in: Text, Boundary 2, River Styx,
Impact, Bezoar, Ecuatorial, and Pequod. Several of the poems
translated in the Notes section, plus the entire Appendix,
was published by The Black Sparrow Press as "Sparrow #65."
"Paris, October 1936" was published by The Bellevue
Press as a broadside. Eight of the translations appeared in
a special issue of Oasis (London), #19, on Clayton
Eshleman's poetry and translations. Several of the
final drafts first appeared in Eshleman's essay,
"Vallejo, 1978," published in Montemora #4.

INDICE

CONTENTS

ESPAÑA, APARTA DE MÍ ESTE CÁLIZ (1937–1938)

SPAIN, TAKE THIS CUP FROM ME (1937–1938)

INTRODUCTION

According to most recent scholarship, César Vallejo appears to have written five books of poetry. The first two, *Los heraldos negros* (1918) and *Trilce* (1922), were published in Peru during his lifetime. The latter three first appeared in 1939, the year after the poet's death, in an edition of two hundred and fifty copies edited by the poet's widow and her friend, the historian Raúl Porra Barrenechea. Published in Paris by Georgette Vallejo herself, the first edition of the posthumous poetry bore the title *Poemas humanos*, and contained 108 poems, approximately half of which were dated in the fall of 1937 and half of which were not dated. The collection seemed to be without any conscious order, except for the last fifteen poems under the title *España, aparta de mí este cáliz*. It is now known that Vallejo worked feverishly on his poetry during the last months of his life, but was able only to complete a final draft of the complete text of *España, aparta de mí este cáliz*, a copy of which was sent to Spain for publication. The edition was to be under the care of the Spanish poet Emilio Prados and published by a cultural unit attached to the Loyalist army at the Aragon front. The book was printed in September 1938, but could not be bound and distributed, and not a single copy survived the defeat of the Spanish Republic a few months later. On February 9, 1940, *España, aparta de mí este cáliz* was published in Mexico, by Editorial Séneca, under the care of the same Emilio Prados, with some preliminary words by Juan Larrea entitled ''Profecía de América'' and a portrait in ink of Vallejo by Picasso.

Between 1942 and 1961 a number of poorly produced editions of the remaining *Poemas humanos* appeared in Argentina and Perú. Then in 1968, an expensive weighty tome billed as the *Obra Poética Completa* appeared, published by Francisco Moncloa Editores in Lima, which offered not only typeset pages for all of Vallejo's poetry that appeared in book form (although it did not include a number of early poems published in magazines and newspapers), but facsimile reproductions of the hand-corrected typescripts for all but several of the posthumously published poems. While typeset pages unaccountably repeated errors from previous editions and appeared in an even more arbitrary order, the presence of the facsimiles enabled Vallejo's old friend and his most dedicated scholar, the poet Juan Larrea, to establish a rational order for the undated poems, and to confirm my hunch that the dated poems made up a separate manuscript and that Vallejo intended for them to be published in their dated order.[1] Larrea has also made a convincing case for Vallejo's having a title for the undated poems and has another probable title for the dated ones. Since 1939, two poems have been added to these books. Thus, it now appears that since there is no evidence whatsoever that

---

[1] Juan Larrea, ''Los poemas póstumos de Vallejo a la luz de su edición facsimilar,'' *Aula Vallejo* 11–12–13 (Córdoba, Argentina, 1974), pp. 55–171.

Vallejo himself even contemplated such a title as *Poemas humanos*, his posthumous poetry can be more sensibly presented in three books:

Nómina de huesos, forty-one poems and prose poems (1923–1936), the undated poems and prose poems in the first edition of *Poemas humanos*.

Sermón de la barbarie, fifty-four poems (1936–1938), the dated poems in *Poemas humanos*.[2]

España, aparta de mí este cáliz, fifteen poems (1937–1938), originally included in *Poemas humanos* and since 1940 published as a separate book.

As many of the readers of this book will know, in 1968 Grove Press published my translation of Vallejo's first two posthumous collections of poetry, under the title *Poemas Humanos/Human Poems*, and in 1974, brought out José Rubia Barcia's and my version of *España, aparta de mí este cáliz* as *Spain, Take This Cup From Me*. At a later point in this essay I will explain why Barcia and I have thoroughly retranslated all the work I did in the sixties as well as revise and augment the work we did together in the early seventies. Before doing so, I would like again, as I did for the 1968 translation, to provide the reader with some biographical information on Vallejo, adding some material that has come to light since that time, and also to describe the sixteen year journey of my involvement in these translations. I think that others might be curious to know what effect a poet central to another poet's life has had on him and, in the case of a translating relationship, to understand its psychic as well as its linguistic ramifications. Vallejo got into every corner of my Being so thoroughly that I now understand this period, 1962–1978, as that of my apprenticeship to poetry, with the central task being to do accurate and engaging translations of Vallejo's posthumously published poetry.

Since I am going to write in detail about the year to year translating process, I will acknowledge those who worked with me for longer periods of time when they appear in the narrative. Unfortunately, I have forgotten the names of a few people with whom I spent brief periods of checking versions. When I was in Kyoto, between 1962 and 1964, doing my first drafts, I was so desperate that I corraled any Spanish speaker who passed through. Luis Vinholes, a Brazilian poet, then serving with the Brazilian Embassy in Tokyo, helped me every time he visited Kyoto, and introduced me to Fernando Lemos, a Portuguese sculptor, who also for a short time tried to help. Then there was Sidney Wright, a Mexican-born American Buddhist who was in Kyoto briefly—I once gave him a version of Vallejo's poem "Panteón" to go over and made an appointment to meet him at the American Cultural Center a few days later. I got there a little before he did, and will never forget the expression on his face as he came through the door and, shaking, told me: "This poem has been written by a man who has been dead five days!" When I was in the Peruvian Andes in 1966, I spent several evenings with a schoolteacher who gave me interpretations for some of Vallejo's obscure lines in the poem, "Telúrica y magnética," claiming that they were Andean slang. Since that time, I have discovered that in regard to that particular poem she is incorrect, but I still warmly remember sitting with her by a kerosene lamp, late at night, on the roof of the world, discussing Vallejo. I should also like to acknowledge the two persons responsible for the only financial assistance I have received while working on the translations: in 1966 Keith Botsford

---

[2]Larrea adds two undated poems to *Sermón de la barbarie*. He explains why on p. 103, ibid.

arranged for me to receive a $500 award from the National Translation Center at Austin, Texas, and in 1969, José Guillermo Castillo arranged a $700 grant from the Center for Inter-American Relations in New York City.

*

César Abraham Vallejo was born on March 16, 1892, in Santiago de Chuco, an Andean town of 14,000 inhabitants, in north central Perú. The journey at that time to the provincial capital, Trujillo, took four days by horseback to the nearest railhead at Menocucho and then another day by train to the coast. Vallejo's grandmothers were Chimu Indians and both of his grandfathers, by a strange coincidence, were Catholic Spanish priests. He was the youngest of eleven children, and grew up in a home saturated in religious devotion. His father, a notary who served as a district official in the town, hoped that he would become a priest. Although Vallejo's life took a much deeper turn, the weight and rigidity of "the family," based on "The Holy Family" and daily reinforced by prayer, was to haunt him for the rest of his life. Juan Espejo Asturrizaga, who has written on Vallejo's Peruvian years,[3] speaks of the profound anguish in Vallejo caused by the conflict between the spiritual and the worldly—especially in regard to his erotic experience—which had its roots in the deep idealism, the sense of sin, good, and evil, of such a Catholic upbringing.

Vallejo completed his secondary schooling in 1908 in Huamachuco, a town even more remote than Santiago de Chuco, and entered the School of Philosophy and Letters at Trujillo University in 1910, but had to drop out for lack of money. Between 1908 and 1913, he started and stopped a college education several times, as his family was unable to support him and he could not find a job to support himself while studying. In 1911 he worked as a tutor to the children of a mine owner in the region of Huanuco in central Perú. In 1912 he worked in the accounts department on a large sugar estate, the hacienda Roma, in the Chicama valley. At Roma, Vallejo saw thousands of peons arrive in the courtyard at dawn, to go off into the fields to work, for a few cents a day, on a fistful of rice, until nightfall. He saw how their lives were dominated by alcohol sold to them on credit, and how, hopelessly in debt, in a few weeks they would become insolvent, their debt rapidly covering years beyond which they themselves would live. Seeing this hideous process devastated him and lit a fuse that burned until 1928, the year he suffered the implosion that resulted in his inability to conform with social conditions for the rest of his life.

One of Vallejo's hacienda Roma roommates, a Salomón Mendoza, relates that on Sunday, their only day off, Vallejo would go for walks and read instead of getting drunk with the other employees, and that occasionally he would show Mendoza his first attempts at poetry.[4] It was not, however, until after he enrolled again in the School of Philosophy and Letters at Trujillo University in 1913, and began to study for a degree in literature that he started to read seriously and was introduced by Antenor Orrego, a journalist and the local intellectual guide, to others his own age, some of whom were to become nationally famous in literature, journalism, and politics. Orrego, who was then working for the newspaper, *La Reforma*, recalls: "Along about November or December of 1914, Vallejo approached me with a notebook of poems. I can't remember how many, certainly no more than twenty-five or thirty poems. It was then that I became aware of

---

[3]Juan Espejo Asturrizaga, *César Vallejo: Itinerario del hombre* (Lima, 1965).
[4]Ibid., p. 30.

all the reading he was doing on his own, of all Spanish literature from the Golden Age on, and that his poetic imitations went back as far as Gonzalo de Berceo. There were magnificent imitations of Quevedo as well as Lope, Tirso, and many others."[5] During his student years, in which he alternated between literature and law, Vallejo supported himself teaching part-time in Trujillo. He first taught botany and economics at the Centro Escolar de Varones, and later he taught the first grade in the elementary school at the Colegio Nacional de San Juan. It was also during these years that Vallejo began to publish his first poems, gave public lectures and readings, and studied material on determinism, mythology, and evolution. He received the equivalent of a Master's Degree in Spanish literature in 1915 with a thesis on *Romanticism in Spanish Poetry*. He continued his studies in law up to 1917, the year he left Trujillo to move to Lima. His life in Trujillo had become complicated by a series of tortured love affairs, one involving a young woman (addressed as "Mirtho" in his poetry) over whom he contemplated suicide. A photo taken in 1917 shows his high Indian cheekbones and heavy, long black hair—a very handsome face.

Once established in Lima, Vallejo found work as a regular teacher and became the principal of the prestigious Colegio Barros and later Assistant Professor at the Colegio Nacional de Nuestra Señora de Guadalupe. At night he hung out in the Bohemian cafes and visited opium dens in Chinatown. He also began to meet the important literary figures of the time, such as Abraham Valdelomar, who died as a result of an accident before he completed an introduction to *Los heraldos negros*, and Manual Gonzalez Prada, then director of the National Library and one of Perú's leading leftists. Prada praised Vallejo's poetry for its audacity and may have started him thinking about social reform and revolution.

When *Los heraldos negros* appeared in the summer of 1919, it was received enthusiastically. The impression is that at that time Vallejo had filled to brimming the antiquated forms the literary "establishment" found acceptable—to continue to push his talent in its own directions would soon bring him almost complete silence. He soon lost his teaching post at Colegio Barros partially because he refused to marry a young woman with whom he was having an affair, whose brother-in-law taught there too. His mother died, and after losing a second teaching job early in 1920, he decided to visit home.

Traveling with his friend, Juan Espejo Asturrizaga, he passed through Huaman-chuco, where he had been graduated from high school, and visited with one of his brothers. While there, he and Espejo edited a law paper, and with their pay they went off to a saloon—and came back drunk. Vallejo had been invited that evening to a theatrical performance in his old high school. The play was badly received by the audience and Vallejo got up on stage and said: "Trotting along, trotting along on my sorrel colt, my mane disheveled, resembling a nomad's hut lost in the desert, I return to this Athens of the Andes. If Santiago de Chuco gave me the raw material, the amorphous block, Huamanchuco polished this block and made of it a work of art." He then recited three poems; the third was from *Trilce* and did not receive any applause. He then became angry and told the audience: "Since you don't applaud me, I don't give a damn for your applause, for the intellectuals in the country now *are* applauding me. One day my poetry will make me greater than even Rubén Darío, and I will have the pleasure of seeing America prostrated before my feet."[6] This caused a scandal in town,

---

[5]Orrego's remarks occur during a symposium transcribed in *César Vallejo: Poeta Trascendental de Hispanoamérica/Su Vida, Su Obra, Su Significado,* the title of *Aula Vallejo 2–3–4* (Córdoba, 1962), p. 118.
[6]Espejo Asturrizaga, *CV: Itinerario del hombre,* p. 92.

during which Vallejo rode off for Santiago de Chuco to attend the annual festival of the patron saint, Saint James, or in Spanish, Santiago, also the patron saint of Spain.

He rode into a town feud that had been smoldering since the last elections. On the last Sunday of the festival, violence broke out: one of the subprefect's aides was shot and the general store, owned by a family whose political ties were opposed to those of the Vallejo family, was burned to the ground. Vallejo, who was actually helping the subprefect write up the legal information about the shooting, was blamed as an accomplice in the store burning and later, in court, as the "intellectual instigator." In spite of protest telegrams from intellectuals and newspaper editors, he was held in a Trujillo jail for 105 days, after which he was freed on parole on February 26, 1921. He left for Lima on March 30. The whole business embittered him and was the catalyst for his leaving Perú two years later.

Before being arrested, Vallejo had hidden out for three months in a country house in Mansiche near Trujillo owned by Orrego. There he began the book that for most readers places Latin American poetry in the center of Western cultural tradition. In 1922 he submitted a manuscript—to be printed with his own funds—called "Cráneos de bronce," under the name of "César Perú." Chided by his friends who said he was affecting an imitation of Anatole France, he decided to use his own name. He was then told—so the story goes—that the first pages of the book had been printed and that a name change would cost him "tres libras" extra. Perhaps he didn't even have the equivalent of three dollars, for Espejo relates: "Vallejo felt mortified. Several times he repeated *tres, tres, tres,* with that insistence he had for repeating words and deforming them, *tresss, trisss, trieesss, tril, trilssss.* He stammered and in the lisp *trilsssce* came out . . . *trilce? trilce?* He hesitated for a moment, then exclaimed: 'Ok, I'll use my own name, but the book will be called *Trilce.*' "[7] As a neologism, an opinion sustained by Larrea and probably closer to the facts, "trilce" could be thought of as based on "tres" (three), in which Vallejo always seemed to remember the Trinity, and "dulce" (sweet), in which he also must have heard "duo" (a pair as opposed to "three"). The neologism might be translated in English as "thleet" or "threet."[8]

The book contains seventy-seven poems and to anyone who has read Latin American poetry written before it, not only does it seem to come out of nowhere but also to *inhabit* nowhere as well. André Coyné, one of Vallejo's most astute commentators, states: "In *Trilce,* there is no universe, no objects, except those furtively introduced across the unadorned and familiar world of the hearth and love; we are presented solely with rapid sensations, glimpsed in a semi-conscious or semi-vigilant state, and (now that the eye hardly has a role) received like shocks and indicated solely by a painful resonance always without resolution—a resonance that is internal, visceral. . . . Poems that hardly are poems, traced on the birthlike and insistent talk of childhood or fever, each stanza organizing on the basis of a separate intuition, for the poet is always at the mercy of the sudden attack of this or that term or the pressing in of anxiety."[9]

After the publication of *Trilce,* Vallejo continued to teach in Lima, but in the spring of 1923 he was notified that his position had been eliminated. At the same time, he still felt in danger of being forced to go back to jail in Trujillo and decided to accept the invitation of his friend, Julio Gálvez, a nephew of Antenor Orrego, to go to Paris together, sharing the money that Gálvez had received as an inheritance. It seems that

[7]Ibid., p. 109.
[8]Juan Larrea, *César Vallejo: heroe y mártir indohispano* (Montevideo, 1973), p. 83.
[9]André Coyné, *César Vallejo y su obra poética* (Lima, 1958), p. 125.

Gálvez had a first-class ticket which he exchanged for two thirdclass tickets. Both embarked June 17 on the steamship *Oroya* for France. Vallejo never returned to Peru.

Vallejo nearly starved in Paris. In 1923 he and Gálvez walked the streets looking for bottles to cash in. The following year, on March 24, his father died in Santiago de Chuco. The Costa Rican sculptor, Max Jiménez, left them his studio. Vallejo was briefly hospitalized for a bleeding hemorrhoid. He translated a book on Perú into Spanish for 1000 francs and met the Spaniards, Juan Gris and Larrea, and the Chilean, Vicente Huidobro. In 1925 he found his first stable job in a newly opened press agency, "Les Grands Journaux Ibèro-Americains" and began to contribute articles to two Lima periodicals, *Mundial* and *Variedades*. He also got a monthly grant of 330 pesetas from the Spanish government to continue his interrupted law studies at the University of Madrid. He made a first visit to Madrid to enroll at the university in the fall of 1925, but since he was not required to remain on campus, he returned immediately to Paris where he continued to receive the grant for two years. The grant, plus the income from articles, seems to have enabled him to become involved in the Parisian artistic milieu.

In 1926 he moved into the Hotel Richelieu, went to exhibitions, concerts, and cafés. He met Artaud, the composer Satie, Picasso, and Cocteau. He received news from home that on June 7 the Trujillo Tribunal in charge of his old case had given orders to arrest him, which confirmed his intuition to leave Perú. He also made the acquaintance this year of a young woman, Georgette Philipart, who he began to live with three years later and married in 1934. With Larrea he coedited two issues of a magazine called *Favorables-Paris-Poema*, in which appeared the last poems he would publish during his lifetime. He began to contribute a weekly column to *Variedades*, and at the Café de la Regence met Henriette Maisse, with whom he would live for two and a half years. With the exception of two pieces dated in the fall of 1937, Vallejo wrote the prose poems that open *Nómina de huesos* between 1924 and 1929. These extremely somber, straightforward, and deeply felt works form a bridge between *Trilce* and the poetry that Vallejo would write in the thirties when, having committed himself to Marxist ideology, he forced the teeth of revolution into the gums of his personal life and wrote the densely compassionate and bitter work for which he is most famous.

In 1927 he left his post at the press agency and refused to continue receiving the Spanish grant. His economic situation became very bad. That year he also published an essay in *Variedades* called "Contra el secreto profesional," in which he discussed the double failure of South American poets to use European influences and to find an expression indigenous to their own people. He attacked the "pseudo-new" in poetry and declared that poets became avant-garde out of cowardice or poverty.

By 1928 he was reading Marxist literature and attending lectures on dialectical materialism. It was in this year that he went through the crisis of conscience that led him to believe that his lack of direction up to that time was due to his distance from the social and economic problems of enslaved humanity. It is difficult to determine whether he came to the conclusion that Marxism was a solution to these problems. Chances are he remained divided, for while his political activities in the years that followed would lead us to believe that at least until 1933 he was an actively committed Communist, the poetry he had been writing since 1923 and would continue to write until his death in 1938, identifies with and embraces suffering humanity, but never argues any doctrine or solution. That September he made the first of three trips to Russia, returning in November to form, with other expatriots, the Peruvian Socialist party. The stated goals were, through adoption of Marxism and Leninism, to train cadres and maintain contact with comrades in Peru.

In January 1929, Vallejo and Georgette Philipart started living together, after Georgette's mother died and she became economically independent. His Marxist studies continuing, Vallejo began to teach in worker cells and decided no longer to publish poetry, believing that the artist's role was, for the time being, to work for the revolution. He made his second trip to Russia, interviewed Mayakovsky in Moscow, and on the way back to Paris traveled through Berlin, Vienna, Florence, Rome, and Nice. That November found him working on a book of Marxist theory and its application to the Soviet Union which eventually became *Rusia en 1931*.

In 1930 Vallejo wrote his first drama, *Mampar* (later retitled *Cancerbero* and then probably destroyed), and we are told that he continued to write dramas (including one screenplay) for the rest of his life, leaving nearly 600 pages of such material unpublished at his death. To date, only a couple of plays have been published in magazines. The rest, I presume, remain in the hands of his widow.[10] In 1930 he again traveled to Spain and met the Spanish poets Salinas and Alberti, as well as Unamuno and Gerardo Diego. The well-known Spanish writer and editor, José Bergamin, wrote an introduction to the second edition of *Trilce* and Pierre Lagarde, reviewing the book in Paris, wrote: "Vallejo has invented Surrealism before the Surrealists." In June, Vallejo returned to Paris and began his second play, *Moscú contra Moscú*. In the first days of December, he was arrested by the police in a Paris railroad station while awaiting a Peruvian communist delegation that was arriving from Moscow. He was ordered to leave France in three days. Again he returned to Madrid where, in 1931, he wrote his only novel, *El tungsteno*, and translated two novels by Marcel Aymé and one by Henri Barbusse. The Monarchy had just fallen and the Republic had been proclaimed. It was now that Vallejo officially joined the Spanish Communist party and, once *Rusia en 1931* was published and went through three editions rapidly, was even temporarily famous. He made his third trip to Russia to attend the International Congress of Writers. He arrived back in Madrid a couple of months later, penniless, with a second book on Russia underway. He also wrote another play, *Lock-out,* and some stories. In spite of his success with *Rusia en 1931,* he could not find a publisher for the other material.

When Georgette, who had been with Vallejo in Spain, returned to Paris in January 1932 to try to arrange for his return, she found their apartment sacked by the police. Meanwhile, Vallejo was desperately trying to establish publishing connections in Madrid: within the space of a couple of months he submitted his collection of essays, *El arte y la revolución*, to a publisher and it was rejected; he submitted *Moscú contra Moscú* and *Lock-out* which met the same fate; Lorca offered to read *Mampar* himself at the Cervantes Theatre but before the reading could take place, the theater was closed down; Vallejo offered "Rusia ante el segundo plan quinquenal," still being written, to two publishers and both rejected it; Lorca read *Moscú contra Moscú* to the Argentine actress and director Camila Quiroga who claimed it could not be staged; then Lorca proposed to present it to other directors, but Vallejo, upon hearing that a resident permit had been obtained in Paris, took off, arriving in mid-February 1933 with nothing but the clothes he was wearing. The conditions of the permit forbade him to engage in any political activity whatsoever, and he seems to have accepted such conditions, for from the time he returned until the Spanish civil war broke out in 1936, he gave up all political activity. The years 1933 to 1936 are the least documented in Vallejo's adult life and may very well have been his darkest.

---

[10]In July 1978 we were informed that Editorial Laia, in Barcelona, Spain, is publishing Vallejo's *Obras Completas*, and that so far nine volumes have appeared.

In 1934 he wrote a play satirizing Peruvian political life, *Los hermanos Colacho,* and since we now know that in 1936 he made an attempt to publish *Nómina de huesos,* it is reasonable to assume that much of the writing of the book was done during this year. Apparently, his precarious financial situation became worse and worse. I was told that the Vallejos lived on rice and potatoes during these years and that Vallejo himself spent most of his time in a darkened apartment. By 1935 the couple could no longer afford the Hotel Garibaldi and took a room on Boulevard Raspail.

In early 1936 he found some Spanish language teaching and published "El hombre y dios en la escultura incaica" in *Beaux-Arts* magazine, one of a number of indications that his interest in pre-Hispanic Peruvian history increased toward the end of his life. He and Georgette were still moving from place to place and they finally settled in the Hotel du Maine. The Fascist uprising in Spain that July seems to have been the exterior goad for his spectacular display of sustained creativity for the next year and a half. He renewed his political life, attended meetings and assemblies, canvassed the streets collecting money, and at night waited in Montparnasse Station for telegrams from Madrid. In December he was given permission to visit Barcelona and Madrid for two weeks; while there he had a chance to observe at first hand the people's reaction to the war. He returned to Paris completely absorbed in the Loyalist anti-Fascist cause, following the battles from day to day. At this point it is possible to watch Vallejo build what might be called a "popular poetry," incorporating war reportage, while at the same time another branch of his poetry was becoming more hermetic than ever before. He began, in *Los heraldos negros,* struggling within the straitjacket of rhymed verse and exploded these bindings in the short-circuited associative webs of *Trilce.* In *Nómina de huesos* and especially *Sermón de la barbarie,* the backdrop ceases to be the childhood hearth, as it still is in *Trilce,* and becomes that of the world of twentieth-century man, at the center of which Vallejo portrays himself conceiving his own death. By the time the *España* manuscript was completed, the elitist tradition of many of the Modernist and Postmodernist poets had been turned inside out.

In 1937 he founded, with others, the Comité Ibero-americano para la defensa de la República Española, and its publicity bulletin, "Nuestra España." To raise money he wrote a film script, *Charlot contra Chaplin.* In July he left again for Spain, which was now deep in civil war, and took part in the Segundo Congreso Internacional de Escritores para la Defensa de la Cultura that met in Valencia on the fourth, then in Madrid on the eighth, holding another session in Barcelona and closing in Paris on the sixteenth of the month. Among the 200 writers attending from 28 countries, Vallejo was elected the Peruvian representative. On this last trip to Spain, Vallejo visited the front briefly and saw with his own eyes some of the horror. Back in Paris he wrote a fifteen-scene tragedy, *La piedra cansada* (set in Incan Peru), and then in one sustained push, from approximately early September to early December, fifty-two of the fifty-four poems that make up *Sermón de la barbarie* along with the fifteen poems of *España, aparta de mí este cáliz.*

It now appears that he had a final typescript for all the posthumously published poetry by the beginning of 1938, and that during January and February he made the thousands of handwritten corrections that cover these typescripts. In early March the years of strain and deprivation, compounded by heartbreak over Spain, as well as exhaustion from the pace of the previous year, finally took their toll. X-rays and other analysis showed no cause for alarm, but a fever he had contracted lingered and by late March he could not get out of bed. The Peruvian Embassy had him moved to the Aragó Clinic where, despite medical attention, his condition worsened. No one involved in his case knew what was killing him or how to heal him. At one point, Mme Vallejo had him propped up in bed so as to receive the ministrations of astrologers and wizards. On April 14, he lost consciousness, with still no diagnosis as to the cause of his illness. His prose poem, "Voy a hablar de la esperanza," while written years before, is a searing prophecy of all of this. There he writes:

I ache now without any explanation. My pain is so deep, that it never had a cause nor does it lack a cause now. What could have been its cause? Where is that thing so important, that it might stop being its cause? Its cause is nothing; nothing could have stopped being its cause. . . . If life were, in short, different, my pain would be the same. Today I suffer from further above. Today I am simply in pain.

On the morning of April 15, having swept down the Ebro valley, the Fascists finally reached the Mediterranean, cutting the Loyalist territory in two. At more or less the same moment, Vallejo cried out in delirium, "I am going to Spain! I want to go to Spain!" and at 9:20 A.M. he died. It was Good Friday. The clinic record states that he died of an "acute intestinal infection." His body was buried April 19 at Montrouge, the "Communist" cemetery in southern Paris. In the sixties, Mme Vallejo, who has been living in Lima on a government pension for many years, had his remains removed to Montparnasse and a new headstone made. I visited the tomb in 1973, to find the following words chipped in:

J'ai tant neigé
pour que tu dormes
Georgette

The source of this "French haiku" is unknown and will probably remain so. To anyone who has read Vallejo's body of poetry, such an epitaph seems odd indeed.[11]

*

While I was a student at Indiana University in 1957, a painter friend, Bill Paden, gave me a copy of the New Directions *Latin American Poetry* anthology and I was particularly impressed with the poetry of Pablo Neruda and César Vallejo. At the same time, I read Angel Flores's translation of Neruda's *Residencia en la tierra,* and upon comparing his version with those of Hays and Fitts in the anthology, I was intrigued with the differences. Without knowing any Spanish, I began to tinker with the versions and that summer, with a pocket Spanish-English dictionary and two hundred dollars, I hitch-hiked to Mexico. The following summer I again returned to Mexico, rented a room in the back of a butcher's home in Chapala, and spent the summer with Neruda's poetry, as well as writing most of the poems that were to appear in my first book, *Mexico & North.*
    The following school year, I edited the English Department sponsored literary tri-quarterly, *Folio,* where I printed three Neruda versions, collectively done by Walter

[11]Since Larrea has shown how Mme Vallejo mixed up the chronology of Vallejo's posthumously published poetry so as to present the sole two poems in which she figures, at the end—one might conclude, looking at the new headstone, that she felt the world should be led to believe *all* of Vallejo's last thoughts revolved about her. Larrea discusses this matter in *Aula Vallejo* 11–12–13, pp. 67–69.

Compton, Al Pérez, Cecilia Ugarte, and myself, and four Vallejo versions, translated by Maureen Lahey, and myself. Behind my inspiration to be involved in foreign poetries was "Babel," Jack and Ruth Hirschman's program of bilingual readings of poetry and prose. I had participated in the series, reading Louise Varèse's versions of St.-John Perse's *Eloges*. Through the Hirschmans, I had become aware of poetry in translation almost as soon as I became aware in 1956 that poetry existed at all.

I finished a Master's Degree in 1961, and took a job with the University of Maryland's Far Eastern Division, teaching English to military personnel in Japan, Korea, and Taiwan. Before leaving, almost as an afterthought, I packed the copy of *Poesía de América*, featuring Vallejo,[12] which I had found in a Mexico City bookstore the first summer I was there. The following year my first wife and I moved to Kyoto where for the next two years I mainly studied and wrote. By this time I had around forty pages of Neruda translations and having been encouraged by Paul Blackburn to publish them, I arranged with George Hitchcock for a small edition to be brought out by The Amber House Press, a book series that never got beyond the Neruda title, sponsored by the editors of the old *San Francisco Review*. Before the book was produced, I showed my manuscript to Cid Corman who said the translations were too wordy, and convinced me that I should take out many of the articles and conjunctions—which I did, again mailing the poems to Blackburn, who wrote me that I had ruined the translation. I finally ended up compromising, the book was published, and the translations have never interested me again. I tell this anecdote to point out the way one can be buffeted by differing opinions (Corman did not care for Neruda's poetry and this influenced the way he felt about my English versions), until one develops not only a translation viewpoint but also a feel for both languages and how they work in poetry.

I continued to translate Neruda in 1962 and at one point planned to do a selection of his *Odas*. But, having left my comfortable "bohemian" student life, I was feeling the pressure to make poetry into something that would sustain me, and I was going through a period of finding that those poets who had first excited me were not weighty enough for continued learning. By early 1963 part of me was still cleverly trying to avoid what it knew it had to do and part of me wanted to *be* a translator so as not to have to face the part of me that was frightened to come forth as a poet. There were many days that I would get up early in the morning to work on my poetry, type out one line and then block—I did not know how to push it on without sounding "unpoetic." I gradually taught myself to sit before the problem for hours, but translation was the big temptation, the easiest escape to rationalize. But, was it an escape? What was I learning by staring at a line for hours?

The first poem of Vallejo's that I tried to read in Kyoto was "Me viene, hay días, una gana ubérrima, política . . ." It was as if a hand of wet sand came out of the original and "quicked" me in—I was quicksanded, over my head, or was it a spar Vallejo threw me? Each move I made, or tried to make, drew me farther in or farther out. I could not tell where the focus lay, between Vallejo's poetry and my desire to write poetry, or in that part of me that wanted to evade the hard work of doing my own poetry. And how much of this difficulty had to do with my inability to read literary Spanish? I had been able to read Neruda with the help of a dictionary; with Vallejo I was lost. Yet to turn away from him was to be more lost, found out by my inability to express anything that was "my own," as well as to express myself in the most simple ways with others. I had no voice. I merely wanted.

---

[12]*Poesía de América*, #5, "Homenaje a César Vallejo" (México DF, 1954).

For several days, I have felt an exuberant, political need
to love, to kiss affection on its two cheeks,
and I have felt from afar a demonstrative
desire, another desire to love, willingly or by force,
whoever hates me, whoever rips up his paper, a little boy,
the woman who cries for the man who was crying,
the king of wine, the slave of water,
whoever hid in his wrath,
whoever sweats, whoever passes, whoever shakes his person in my soul.
And I want, therefore, to adjust
the braid of whoever talks to me; the hair of the soldier;
the light of the great one; the greatness of the little one.
I want to iron directly
a handkerchief for whoever is unable to cry
and, when I am sad or happiness hurts me,
to mend the children and the geniuses.

Vallejo was claiming that he desired to love—not that he did not love, but that he desired to, and that his desire for desire led him to imagine, later in the same poem, all sorts of "interhuman" acts he would like to perform, like kissing a singer's muffler, or kissing a deaf man on his cranial murmur. He wanted to help everyone achieve his goal, no matter what it was, even to help the killer kill, and—he wanted to be kind to himself in everything. These were thoughts that, had I had them myself, I would have either dismissed or so immediately repressed that they would have evaporated. But I now realized that there was a whole wailing cathedral of desires, half-desires, mad-desires, anti-desires, all of which, in the Vallejo poem, seemed caught on the edge of no-desire. And if so, what made him reach desiring desire? The need to flee his body? A need to enter his body? To enter another body? I did not know what he meant, but trying to read him made me feel that I was in the presence of a mile-thick spirit. So I kept at it.

In the afternoon I would ride my motorcycle downtown and work on translations in the Yorunomado ("Night Window") café. I would always sit by the carp pond on the patio. There I discovered the following words of Vallejo: "Then where is the other flank of this cry of pain if, to estimate it as a whole, it breaks now from the bed of a man?" I saw Vallejo in a birth bed in that line, not knowing how to give birth, which indicated to me a totally other realization, that artistic bearing and fruition were physical as well as mental, a matter of one's total energy. I knew that I had to learn to become a physical traveler as well as a mental one. For most of 1963 and the first half of 1964, everything I saw and felt clustered about this feeling; it seemed to be in a phrase from the I Ching, "the darkening of the light," as well as in the Kyoto sky, which was gray and overcast yet mysteriously luminous.

As I struggled to get Vallejo's involuted Spanish into English, I increasingly had the feeling that I was struggling with a man more than with a text, and that this struggle was a matter of my becoming or failing to become a poet. The man I was struggling with not only did not want his words changed from one language to another but it seemed as if he did not want to be changed himself. I began to realize that in working on Vallejo I had ceased merely to be what I was before coming to Japan, that I had a glimpse now of another life, a life I was to create rather than be given, and that this other man I was struggling with was the old Clayton who was resisting change. The old Clayton wanted to continue living in his white Presbyterian world of "light"—not really light, but the "light" of man associated with day/clarity/good and woman associated with night/ opaqueness/bad. The darkness that was beginning to make itself felt in my sensibility could be viewed as the breaking up of that "light."

In giving birth to myself, William Blake's poetry also became very important. I wanted to converse with Blake and knew I could not do this in the sense of Clayton talking with William, but that I might be able to do it if I created a figure of my imagination. It was really not Blake himself I sought, but his imagination which he created and named Los. In the last half of the only poem I completed to any satisfaction while living in Japan,[13] I envisioned myself as a kind of angelless Jacob wrestling with a figure from an alien alphabet, trying to take its meaning from him; I lose the struggle and find mysef on a harakiri platform in medieval Japan, being condemned by Vallejo (now playing the role of a *karo*, or overlord) to disembowel myself. I do so, cutting my ties to the "given life," and releasing a Los-like figure, named Yorunomado (in honor of my working place), who had been to that point chained to an altar in my solar plexus. In early 1964 the fruit of my struggle with Vallejo was not a successful linguistic translation, but an imaginative advance in which a third (or allowing Blake's role in the process) or fourth figure emerged from my intercourse with the text. Had I consumed Vallejo in a final English version at that time, Yorunomado would not have been unlocked. He became my guide in the ten-year process of developing a "created life," recorded in the book-length poem, *Coils*.

I was close to completing a first draft of the translation around March 1963 when I had a strange experience. After working all afternoon in Yorunomado, I cycled over to a pottery manufacturer where I taught English as a foreign language once a week. Whenever I had things to carry on the cycle, I would strap them with a stretch-cord to the platform in back of the seat. That evening, as usual, I did so, and re-strapped the poem-filled notebook, my dictionary, and a copy of *Poemas humanos*, when I left the company. It was now dark and the alley was poorly lit. I had gone about 100 yards when I heard a voice, in Japanese, cry "Hey, you dropped something!" I swerved around—the platform was empty—even the stretch-cord gone. I stopped and retraced my direction on foot. Nothing. I looked for the person who had called. No one was there. While I was walking around in the dark, a large skinny dog began to follow me very closely—I was reminded of the Mexican pariah dogs and that gave an eerie sort of identity with this dog. Was it Peruvian? Was it—Vallejo? I went back the next morning when it was light and of course there was not a trace of the things I had lost.

In the following twelve months, I completed three more drafts of the book. Rafael Squirru, an Argentine scholar who was then one of the editors of *Américas* magazine at the OAS in Washington, D.C., went over the first of these line by line and mailed me his corrections, queries, and bafflements every week. Cid Corman went over a great deal of the second and third drafts, and to Cid I owe a special debt, not only for the time he put in on the manuscript but for what I learned about the art of translation from his comments and his own translations of Basho and Eugenio Montale on which he was working at the time. Previous to working with Corman, I thought a literal translation was, in effect, a first draft, which followed the original almost word by word. I thought that the goal of a translating project was to take the literal draft and interpret everything that was not acceptable English. By interpret, I mean to monkey with words, phrases, punctuation, line breaks, even stanza breaks, turning the literal into something that was not an original poem in English but—and here is the rub—something that because of the

[13]"The Book of Yorunomado," in *Indiana* (Los Angeles, 1969). This poem was later reworked and appeared as "Webs of Entry" in *Coils* (Los Angeles, 1973).

liberties taken was also not accurate to the original itself. MacIntyre's Rilke, Belitt's Neruda, or Lowell's *Imitations* come to mind as examples of interpretive translations. Corman taught me to respect the original at every point, to check everything (including words that I thought I knew), and to work toward a goal in which the meaning of every bit of the original is preserved as literally as possible and in such a way that an engaging poem in English has been made. Such a translation is not literal (in the way that word is crudely used) nor is it interpretative (meaning one in which liberties have been taken). Certainly it is both in the most ample sense. I have found over the years that precise literal translations, done with grace, are not only terribly difficult to do but nearly impossible. There are impulsive urges in every translator to fill in, pad out, to make something strong that more literally would fall flat, to *explain* a word rather than to *translate it*, to shade this or that to give a "heightened tone," and so on. I recall Kafka's story, "The Penal Colony," where the condemned is strapped to a torture device that murders him by inscribing, with a steel needle, his sentence in his back. As if translators, the victim text in their heads, sentence it on the basis of what it has done, and carry this sentence out, in the name of "poetic justice," by killing the original, pen in hand.

Often when poets translate, they depend on a "pony" or someone else's literal version to work off. This manner of working seems natural enough if an interpretational translation is the goal. I tried to avoid this trap by only checking my drafts with others and never asking anyone to do a draft that I would rework. In the course of translating Vallejo, I am aware of one exception to this rule: in 1965, Octavio Corvalán, then a professor of Spanish at Indiana University, prepared a first draft of *Spain, Take This Cup From Me.*

I had returned to Bloomington, Indiana, the fall of 1964 and lived there until the following summer, at which time I went to Peru. I supported myself by translating an anthology of Latin American poetry (in which neither Neruda or Vallejo were included), commissioned by Squirru for the OAS, and completed a fourth draft of *Human Poems* which I checked, line for line, with Olga Villagarcía, a Peruvian woman doing graduate work at the university, and a fifth draft that I went over with Corvalán. On the basis of his first draft of *Spain*, I prepared two more, both of which Corvalán commented on. I then decided to do nothing more with *Spain* until I finished *Human Poems.*

At this point some textual details should be mentioned. As I noted before, the poems that made up the manuscript were left by Vallejo in a heavily corrected typescript, from which Mme Vallejo made a clean copy for publication. There are many errors in the first edition which were repeated in subsequent editions and new errors made (principally, I have been told, because Mme Vallejo refused most of these publishers permission, and the pirated editions were done off the first or some other edition without being checked against Vallejo's worksheets, which were not available to anyone, to my knowledge, until a facsimile of them was published in 1968). In the first and subsequent editions, Vallejo's seemingly intentional misspellings were corrected, neologisms were eliminated, periods and commas left out (or put in where they did not exist), stanzas were inverted, and in one case one poem made of two, and in another, two poems made into one.

By the spring of 1965 I was working from four fundamentally the same but differing editions of *Poemas humanos*,[14] having seen neither a copy of the first edition nor the

[14]These are: a 1959 and a 1961 edition published by Perú Nuevo (Lima), a 1959 edition published Nuevo Mundo (Lima), and a 1949 edition published by Losada (Buenos Aires). These books, along with other materials relating to the two Grove Press translations, are part of the Eshleman/Vallejo Archive at the University of California, San Diego, library.

worksheets. And, as I mentioned before, the order in which the poems were printed made no sense whatsoever. The only information about this was several pages of notes by Mme Vallejo which appeared in the 1959 Perú Nuevo edition. There she claimed that the prose poems actually belonged to a separate collection called "Código Civil" which had been written in the twenties. Yet, without explanation, she had not only published these poems in *Poemas humanos* but had included them at the end, after poems dated in 1937. In the 1959 Perú Nuevo edition she also eliminated the dates on the previously dated poems, claiming that the dates were meaningless because they indicated when a poem was *finished*, not when it was *written*. But such a statement made no sense either, for she herself had published the dates in the first edition. Furthermore, even if they did represent completion points, why should they not be respected? Many writers only date a work when it is completed. Finally, the idea of a "finished" as opposed to "written" poem was suspect, since she had also stated that the text of the first edition had been based on worksheets that Vallejo had left unfinished at the time of his death. To even further add to these complications, she did not change the order of the poems in the 1959 edition! The book ended, as had all other editions, with the longest of the prose poems, "Las ventanas se han estremecido . . ." at the end of which, given its placement, the author presumably dies.

Instead of shaping up as I worked along, the whole project was becoming a nightmare. I was having dreams in which Vallejo's corpse, fully dressed, with muddy shoes, was laid out in bed between Barbara and myself. By this time I had gotten in touch with Mme Vallejo and explained that I did not see how I could complete the translation unless I came to Perú and examined the worksheets. I hired a lawyer to draw up a contract, and mailed it to her along with samples from the fourth draft. I must have written her a half dozen letters to which I received one reply that did not respond to any of my requests. But I was determined to go, and with Barbara several months pregnant, we left in August. By this time, I had also completed one of the central pieces in *Coils*, a long poem called "Niemonjima," in which I had tried to bring my psychic involvement with Vallejo up to date.

Before I went to Perú, I also found out that Mme Vallejo had refused New Directions permission to publish a collection of Vallejo translations by H. R. Hays, the first person, to my knowledge, to publish Vallejo translations in English. I was in a very tricky position with the woman, because I not only needed to see the first edition and worksheets, but also, on the basis of the drafts I had sent, needed her permission to be able to get a publisher's contract and advance on the book-to-be. I had not been in her apartment fifteen minutes when she told me that my translations were full of "howlers," that Vallejo was untranslatable in the first place, and that neither the first edition nor the worksheets were available to be seen.

Georgette Vallejo was then a small wiry middle-class French woman in her late sixties. She lived rather spartanly, yet not uncomfortably, in a small apartment, appointed with pre-Incan pottery and weavings, in Miraflores, one of the wealthiest districts in Lima. She possessed an awesome dedication to Vallejo and to his writing. At the same time, she would not entertain any questions concerning the way she had refused not only to re-edit published work but to allow unpublished work to appear. When I asked her why she had not published Vallejo's dramas (she had, as a matter of fact, translated a few scenes from *La piedra cansada* and published them in a French magazine, without allowing the drama to be published in Spanish),[15] she said that she

---

[15]Although I have not seen it, I have been told that *La piedra cansada* appeared in *Visión del Perú* #4 (Lima, 1969), the entire issue of which was devoted to Vallejo.

did not think they were of much interest and, even if they were, she had not yet found the right publisher.

Near the end of 1965, I met Maureen Ahern, an American woman with a Ph.D from San Marcos University, who was then married and living with her family on a chicken farm in Cieneguilla, about twenty miles outside Lima. During the last few months that I was in Perú, I checked my sixth draft with Maureen, going out to the farm several evenings each week. When we returned to the States in the spring of 1966 and moved to New York City, Grove Press expressed interest in the translation. I prepared a seventh draft and Grove had it checked by "readers." I was offered a contract—contingent upon Mme Vallejo's signature. I wrote Maureen and asked her if there was anything she could do. She offered to go and meet Georgette. For the next six months Maureen must have seen Georgette a couple of times a week and she did this while taking care of her kids, teaching fulltime, battling illness and trying to save a floundering marriage.

While Richard Seaver, then the senior editor at Grove, was sending letter after letter to Georgette, trying to convince her that the translation Grove had accepted was not the one I set her from Bloomington in 1964, Maureen and her husband Johnny were inviting her out to the farm for holiday weekends. Since Seaver was getting nowhere, Maureen eventually had to mention that she was a friend of mine and that she had worked on the translation. Georgette protested that she had been betrayed and once again it looked as if everything was off. But Maureen kept after her and one day Américo Ferrari, a scholar who had written on Vallejo, appeared at the Grove offices and told Seaver that Mme Vallejo had asked him to check the translation. Apparently he wrote her that it was all right, for a week or so later, she wrote Seaver and said that she would sign a contract if Grove included the following clause: when and if she found a translation that she considered to be better than mine, Grove must destroy mine and publish the other one. Seaver told me that he had had it with her. So I wrote Maureen that unless a signed contract appeared within the next month, the whole project would be off. Maureen continued to plead with her. Once again, she seemed to change her mind: she would sign a Grove contract if they would ask for world English rights on all of Vallejo's poetry (instead of American rights on *Human Poems* alone). Her rationale was that she never wanted to be bothered with having to deal with other publishers on other Vallejo books.

By this time, everyone involved at Grove was so irritated and confused that no new contract was prepared. I saw myself within an inch of getting a contract and at the same time within half an inch of losing everything. I cabled Maureen to make one more attempt to get Georgette to sign the last contract that Grove had sent here. So Maureen and Johnny went over to reason with her. After several hours Georgette said that if Johnny would sit down and type up the contract that she wanted, she would sign it then and there. He did, she signed it, and a week later Seaver called me and said that while it was not their contract, Grove found it acceptable and their lawyer had determined it was legal. He wrote Georgette, enclosing her part of the advance. Subsequently, Maureen wrote that Georgette had just called her on the phone, extremely upset, saying that she thought the contract Johnny had typed out was "only a gesture," and that she had signed it so Maureen would not be disappointed, and that she had never intended, at any point, to sign a legal contract! I should add that at an earlier stage in the negotiations, Maureen had gone over my seventh draft with Georgette, and that on the basis of a few corrections I had prepared an eighth and a ninth version. Grove went ahead and the book was published in the spring of 1968. I ended my Translator's Foreword with: "I will elaborate no further. My work is done."

In 1970 my present wife Caryl and I moved to California, and while completing *Coils*, I decided to finish other projects I had begun in the sixties. I made a fourth draft of *Spain, Take This Cup From Me*, and once again found myself looking for someone to check it with. I was introduced to José Rubia Barcia, a Spanish poet and essayist, in exile since the Spanish civil war, who has been teaching at UCLA for years. While going over the draft with Barcia, I was so impressed with his honesty, scrupulosity, and literary intelligence, that I suggested we work together, as co-translators. This is not to imply that the people who had helped me before were not honest and scrupulous. All, without exception, gave the work their best. The main reason a co-translation did not occur before is that in the sixties none of us really understood what Vallejo had written and thus all translating and all checking took place in the dark. I think of alchemy in this connection, as if in taking up Vallejo's book I had begun a "Vallejo Working" and the 1968 version represents a kind of putrefaction, which I mistook at the time for incombustible sulphur. The persistent working in the dark had resulted in a translation that was on the "right path," so to speak, and no other person could really work on a one-to-one basis with me until this right path had been achieved.

While Barcia and I were working on the Spanish civil war poems, I showed him the 1968 translation of *Poemas humanos*, which he carefully went over and penciled around 2,000 queries and suggestions for change in the margins. He felt that what I had accomplished was meaningful, but that we could do it much better working together. In the fall of 1972, using the 1968 translation as a base, we began to work toward the present translation. We did one draft which I took to Paris with me in the fall of 1973 and then tried to work through the mail. It was terribly time consuming, as we had so many questions to ask each other and after I completed what would be the eleventh draft (taking the entire translation from the beginning into consideration) and Barcia compiled a one hundred page commentary on material that possibly should be annotated, we decided to wait until my return to California to continue. At this time, I did another piece of my own writing on Vallejo, a poem called "At the Tomb of Vallejo" (which Barcia translated into Spanish), occasioned by some visits to the new resting place in Montparnasse. Grove published *Spain, Take This Cup From Me* in the spring of 1974, and once I returned that fall we went ahead, and over the next three and a half years, did seven more drafts. Relative to my experiences in the sixties, these years were rather calm and scholarly.

In 1977, while working on the eighteenth draft, one of Vallejo's crossed out lines, literally, "I will call him at the margin of his name of encased (encajonado) river," leaped up at me; I heard "encanyoned" in "encajonado" and came to "The Name Encanyoned River," a long poem that meanders through the walls of apprenticeship and, other than this Introduction, culminates the relationship. In several cases, I have counted the number of changes made in a poem between 1968 and 1978: there are 139 in "Telluric and magnetic," and 83 in "Good sense." I would guess that there are around 8,000 in the entire book. We have also done more work on our 1974 *Spain* translation, though in that case, it is more in the nature of revision than retranslation.

There are several good reasons for the retranslation. First of all, Vallejo's posthumous poetry is extraordinarily difficult, perhaps the most complex collection of poems ever to be written in the Spanish language. Vallejo appears to be the first Spanish language poet to approach the language as if it were steel to be bent and reshaped into a sculpture that bears not only his imprint but also the record of the kinetic tension involved at all the stages of giving the sculpture its final shape. When traditional syntax is sufficient to carry what he wants to say, he allows it and works within it. But when it is incapable of yielding a point or meaning, he bends it to suit needs of the poem in progress, risking obscurity to say at moments what feels ineffable. While the poetry that results is not traditional, neither could it be called experimental. Rather, both of these forces are present as agents in composition, and the task for a Vallejo translator becomes to deal with both of these poles. It is as if Antonin Artaud's spider alphabet had dropped onto William Butler Yeats while the latter was working on a quatrain. If one can imagine the result of the struggle that might ensue from such a conjunction, he will have a useful "glyph" of the nature of Vallejo's mature poetry.

If my description of this poetry makes it sound opaque, I should point out that relative to *Trilce* it is accessible. Comparing the posthumously published poetry with the former book, Américo Ferrari has written: "The language has become cleaner, without smudges. The breath more ample and sustained, attains, here and there, the solemn tone of a hymn. One no longer finds certain technical methods of *Trilce*, blank spaces, deliberately incorrect spellings, onomatopoeic gratings, the capital letters that underline the weight of a word. Thus, the poet's thought becomes more transparent, more accessible; the emotion runs in waves following meanders of a free and spontaneous language, but the poet, more than ever, controls and directs. This language, at one moment limpid, at another, desperately obscure, has, like a river, its sweeping rapids, its whirlpools, its falls."[16]

Another reason for retranslation has to do with scholarship. Along with the facsimile material, we have been fortunate to have the fruits of Larrea's years with Vallejo's work, much of which is presented in the "11-12-13" issue of *Aula Vallejo*.[17] Besides establishing a rational ordering of the undated poems, by coordinating them with dated letters from the six typewriters Vallejo used while in Europe, Larrea convincingly demonstrates that what has heretofore been called *Poemas humanos* is two separate manuscripts. As early as 1956, Mme Vallejo told André Coyné that the title *Poemas humanos* had not been chosen by the poet himself, but "indicated, in the opinion of the editors, the universal meaning of his poetry."[18] Larrea suggests that such a title may have occurred to Mme Vallejo as a slight variation on the title of a Gerardo Diego book, *Versos humanos*. Whether this is true or not is impossible to tell—there is no connection between Vallejo's poetry and Diego's. According to Larrea, in 1936 Vallejo put together a manuscript for publication of all the poetry and prose poetry that he had written since coming to Europe, and called it *Nómina de huesos*, based on the title of the first poem, in the same way that *Los heraldos negros* was based on the opening poem's title. Vallejo submitted this manuscript to a Madrid publisher who apparently accepted it but the word never reached Vallejo. Before he could do anything else with the manuscript, the Spanish civil war broke out, and his attention was turned not only there but to writing new poems, the dated versions of which were typed out in the fall of 1937. Since *Nómina de huesos* has many handwritten corrections, we assume that while working on the dated poems Vallejo went back to this manuscript and did more work on it. Handwritten corrections were added to both manuscripts probably in December 1937 and January/February 1938; for example, we know he was making corrections in 1938 because in the typed lines "My friend, you are

[16]Américo Ferrari, "Trajectoire Du Poète," *César Vallejo/Poètes d'aujourd'hui* #168 (Paris, 1967), p. 29. However, Ferrari is wrong about the lack of deliberate misspellings and capital letters in the posthumously published poetry. There are less of them than in *Trilce*, but they certainly exist. Ferrari's error is probably due to the fact that he had not seen the worksheets when he wrote his essay.

[17]In addition to this material, we should add that Larrea's latest book was recently published in April 1978: *César Vallejo/Poesía completa* (Barcelona), 932 pp. A second volume is announced which will examine one by one all of Vallejo's poems.

[18]Larrea records and discusses Coyné's conversation with Mme Vallejo in *Aula Vallejo* 11–12–13, pp. 319–321.

completely, / up to your hair, in the 37th year," (from "The soul that suffered from being its body"), he hand-corrected the "7" to an "8;" surely "38th" refers to 1938 and not to Vallejo's own age (46) at the time. Vallejo became sick in March and probably stopped working on these manuscripts (but not *España*) at that time. Thus there is no "final version," or if one wants to call the corrected worksheets a final version, the phrase must be qualified: all we know is that Vallejo stopped working on the poems sometime in 1938 before he died. We do not know if he considered the dated poems in *Sermón de la barbarie* completed or not. Had he lived longer, he might very well have made a clean typescript, at which time he might have made more changes.

As for the dated poems, no title can be found. Larrea makes a plausible, if not convincing, case for *Sermón de la barbarie*, arguing that it is the key phrase in the last dated poem, "Sermón sobre la muerte," and suggests that "la barbarie" was a metaphor for "Babel," the Word (*bab-ilu*), the "Gate of God" that Vallejo engaged in the central book of his career. Having spent twenty-one years with this poetry, I respect Larrea's imaginative findings based on his much longer acquaintanceship. I have a strong feeling that Vallejo himself did not title the dated manuscript, and given the option to either go along with Larrea or to conclude that the lack of a title is in itself significant—to assume that Vallejo consciously did *not* title this manuscript—I prefer accepting Larrea's sense of things. If a so-called true title is found in the future, let it be added, in the same spirit that *Poemas humanos* is now erased.

My final justification for a retranslation has to do with my own relation to the text, which should be implicit by now. I began translating Vallejo when I was a young man who wanted to be a poet. In ways that do not cease to amaze me, César Vallejo became my poetic university and, on one level, our retranslation represents a resolution of knots and frustrations of my own which can be felt at times in the 1968 version. I have, as a poet, come up through Vallejo, and am now proud to offer a translation of his work that has my own poetic growth not only buried but overcome in it. I feel that the retranslation presents a clearer and, at the same time, a more obscure Vallejo than before. We have tried very hard not to make him any more clear in English than he is in Spanish. When his language is obscure, it always represents an effort to realize a reality in which nothing is clear, a sensing that in the heart of Being there is a wound, that in the "lesion of the response," is the "lesion mentally of the unknown."

Our method in this retranslation has been to constantly work off the literal edge of what Vallejo is saying and to be as uninterpretative as possible. We do not see ourselves recreating a text in English; rather, we hope to be making one in Spanish visible to an English reader. Our goal has been to achieve a translation that reads as great poetry in English while at the same moment it is exactly what Vallejo is saying in Spanish. Obviously, this is not purely possible. Our desire to be responsible, first of all, to Vallejo's exact word and meaning will not allow us to distort the handful of rhymed poems so as to rhyme them in English. Also, there are hundreds of situations in which a choice must be made, such as between "skull," "helmet," and "hoof," in the case of "casco." In such a situation, the context helps, but we realize that it is not a matter of finding the word that duplicates Vallejo's meaning in Spanish, but of selecting one layer of meaning from a word that Vallejo probably chose to use because it meant many things.

Because of the number of difficult words, neologisms, and intentional misspellings, and too, because of the thousands of handwritten changes that Vallejo made on the typescript, we decided that a section of Notes was called for. We have not tried to comment on everything that is puzzling, for if we did the Notes section would be several hundred pages long. What we have done is to translate material that Vallejo has crossed out, to try to give the reader a sense of the process he used in "completing" the manuscript. We have not translated all the crossed out material; in some cases it is illegible and in others it is without interest. Since we are sure that earlier versions exist for at least some of the poems,[19] and also since several of the posthumously published poems are without facsimile in the *Obra Poética Completa*, we must point out that when we note that Vallejo "originally" wrote such and such, we are referring to the first typed version of a poem on a worksheet reproduced in the Moncloa edition. Most of Vallejo's corrections definitely improve poems, especially in the first two posthumously published books—much less so in *España*. The tendency of the corrections is to move away from predictable associations to more elliptic, imaginative and, at times, obscure ones.

In *España*, there are two poems that seem significantly stronger before handwritten corrections and additions/subtractions were made: we have presented these pieces in a translation based on the uncorrected typescript in our Notes. Also in regard to *España*, we have created an Appendix to make available one sequence of eight Roman numeraled poems (I—VIII) that were finally distributed throughout the manuscript in a different order with some of the best writing eliminated (section II was completely suppressed, as were nearly half of III, and a half dozen lines of IV, V, and VII). We feel that the essence of this book is in these eight sections.

In regard to neologisms and misspellings: we have consulted Giovanni Meo Zilio's study[20] and made use of some of his suggestions. His study is unfortunately not based on the worksheets (it came out in 1967), and contains some misreadings based on the earlier error riddled and falsely standardized editions. We have also corresponded with Larrea concerning difficult and/or made-up words, and have checked some problematic Peruvianisms with Irene Vegas-García, a young Peruvian scholar, specializing in Vallejo, at UCLA. We have gone so far as to restore Vallejo's worksheet indentations, titles (in the Contents as well as in the text), and title "signs," to the extent that certain pages will look more like a typescript than a typeset page. At all points our present Spanish text is based on the facsimilies themselves and not on the typeset text in the *Obra Poética Completa*. In order to indicate to the reader some of the difficulties involved in establishing a clean text, we have reproduced several pages of Vallejo's worksheets from the 1968 Moncloa edition.

Clayton Eshleman / July 1978, Los Angeles.

---

[19]For example, in the *Poètes d'aujourd'hui* translation of Vallejo's poetry into French, facing p. 128, is a reproduction of a worksheet for the poem beginning "Ello es que el lugar donde me pongo . . ." dated the same day as the one in the *Obra Poética Completa* and most probably written earlier

[20]Geovanni Meo Zilio, "Neologismos en Vallejo," *Lavori della Sezione Fiorentina del Gruppo Ispanistico* (Florence, 1967).

NÓMINA DE HUESOS

(1923–1936)

PAYROLL OF BONES

Nómina de huesos

Se pedía a grandes voces:
—Que muestre las dos manos a la vez.
Y esto no fué posible.
—Que, mientras llora, le tomen la medida de sus pasos.
Y esto no fué posible.
—Que piense un pensamiento idéntico, en el tiempo en que un cero permanece inútil.
Y esto no fué posible.
—Que haga una locura.
Y esto no fué posible.
—Que entre él y otro hombre semejante a él, se interponga una muchedumbre de hombres como él.
Y esto no fué posible.
—Que le comparen consigo mismo.
Y esto no fué posible.
—Que le llamen, en fin, por su nombre.
Y esto no fué posible.

Payroll of bones

*

They demanded shouting:
—Let him show both hands at the same time.
And this was not possible.
—While he cries, let them take the measure of his steps.
And this was not possible.   5
—Let him think an identical thought, in the time that a zero   *
remains useless.
And this was not possible.
—Let him do something crazy.
And this was not possible.   10
—Let a crowd of men like him, come between him and another
man just like him.
And this was not possible.
—Let them compare him with himself.
And this was not possible.   15
—Let them call him, finally, by his name.
And this was not possible.

La violencia de las horas

Todos han muerto.

Murió doña Antonia, la ronca, que hacía pan barato en el burgo.

Murió el cura Santiago, a quien placía le saludasen los jóvenes y las mozas, respondiéndoles a todos, indistintamente: ¡"Buenos días, José! ¡Buenos días, María!"

Murió aquella joven rubia, Carlota, dejando un hijito de meses, que luego también murió, a los ocho días de la madre.

Murió mi tía Albina, que solía cantar tiempos y modos de heredad, en tanto cosía en los corredores, para Isidora, la criada de oficio, la honrosísima mujer.

Murió un viejo tuerto, su nombre no recuerdo, pero dormía al sol de la mañana, sentado ante la puerta del hojalatero de la esquina.

Murió Rayo, el perro de mi altura, herido de un balazo de no se sabe quién.

Murió Lucas, mi cuñado en la paz de las cinturas, de quien me acuerdo cuendo llueve y no hay nadie en mi experiencia.

Murió en mi revólver mi madre, en mi puño mi hermana y mi hermano en mi víscera sangrienta, los tres ligados por un génnero triste de tristeza, en el mes de agosto de años sucesivos.

Murió el músico Méndez, alto y muy borracho, que solfeaba en su clarinete tocatas melancólicas, a cuyo articulado se dormían las gallinas de mi barrio, mucho antes de que el sol se fuese.

Murió mi eternidad y estoy velándola.

Violence of the hours

All are dead.
Doña Antonia died, the hoarse one, who made cheap bread in the
village.

The priest Santiago died, who liked to be greeted by the young men
and the girls, acknowledging everyone indiscriminately: "Good morning,
José! Good morning, Maria!"

That young blonde, Carlota, died, leaving a very small child, who
then also died, eight days after his mother.

My Aunt Albina died, who used to sing inherited tenses and moods,
while she sewed in the interior corridors, for Isadora, the servant by
profession, that very honorable woman.

An old one-eyed man died, I don't remember his name, but he
slept in the morning sun, seated before the corner tinsmith's door.

Rayo died, the dog with my height, shot by lord-knows-who.

Lucas died, my brother-in-law in the peace of the waists, who I
remember when it rains and there is no one in my experience.

My mother died in my revolver, my sister in my fist and my brother
in my bloody viscera, the three bound by a sad kind of sadness, in the
month of August of successive years.

The musician Méndez died, tall and very drunk, who sol-faed
melancholy toccatas on his clarinet, at whose articulation the hens
in my neighborhood went to sleep, long before the sun went down.

My eternity has died and I am waking it.

El buen sentido

—Hay, madre, un sitio en el mundo, que se llama París.
Un sitio muy grande y lejano y otra vez grande.

Mi madre me ajusta el cuello del abrigo, no por que
empieza a nevar, sino para que empiece a nevar.

La mujer de mi padre está enamorada de mí, viniendo y
avanzando de espaldas a mi nacimiento y de pecho a mi muer-
te. Que soy dos veces suyo: por el adiós y por el regreso. La
cierro, al retornar. Por eso me dieran tánto sus ojos, justa de
mí, infraganti de mí, aconteciéndose por obras terminadas, por
pactos consumados.

¿Mi madre está confesa de mí, nombrada de mí. ¿Cómo
no da otro tanto a mis otros hermanos? A Víctor, por ejemplo,
el mayor, que es tan viejo ya, que las gentes dicen: ¡Parece
hermano menor de su madre! ¡Fuera porque yo he viajado
mucho! ¡Fuera porque yo he vivido más!

Mi madre acuerda carta de principio colorante a mis re-
latos de regreso. Ante mi vida de regreso, recordando que
viajé durante dos corazones por su vientre, su ruboriza y se
queda mortalmente lívida, cuando digo, en el tratado del alma:
Aquella noche fuí dichoso. Pero más se pone triste; más se pusiera triste.

—Hijo, ¡cómo estás viejo!

Y desfila por el color amarillo a llorar, porque me halla
envejecido, en la hoja de espada, en la desembocadura de mi
rostro. Llora de mí, se entristece de mí. ¿Qué falta hará mi
mocedad, si siempre seré su hijo? ¡Porqué las madres se
duelen de hallar envejecidos a sus hijos, si jamás la edad de
ellos alcanzará a la de ellas? ¿Y por qué, si los hijos, cuanto
más se acaban, más se aproximan a los padres? Mi madre
llora porque estoy viejo de mi tiempo y porque nunca llegaré
a envejecer del suyo!

Mi adiós partió de un punto de su sér, más externo que
el punto de su sér al que retorno. Soy, a causa del excesivo
plazo de mi vuelta, más el hombre ante mi madre que el hijo
ante mi madre. Allí reside el candor que hoy nos alumbra
con tres llamas. Le digo entonces hasta que me callo:

Hay, madre, en el mundo, un sitio que se llama París.
Un sitio muy grande y muy lejano y otra vez grande.

La mujer de mi padre, al oírme, almuerza y sus ojos mor-
tales descienden suavemente por mis brazos.

Good sense

—There is, mother, a place in the world called Paris. A very
big place and far off and once again big.
   My mother turns up the collar of my overcoat, not because it is
beginning to snow, but so it can begin to snow.
   My father's wife is in love with me, coming and advancing back-   5
ward toward my birth and chestward toward my death. For I am hers
twice: by the farewell and by the return. I close her, on coming back.
That is why her eyes had given so much to me, brimming with me,
caught red-handed with me, making herself happen through finished
works, through consummated pacts.   10*
   Is my mother confessed by me, named by me. Why doesn't she
give as much to my other brothers? To Victor, for example, the
eldest, who is so old now, that people say: He looks like his mother's
younger brother! Perhaps because I have traveled so much! Perhaps
because I have lived more!   15
   My mother grants a charter of colorful beginning to my stories of
return. Before my returning life, remembering that I traveled during
two hearts through her womb, she blushes and remains mortally livid,
when I say, in the treatise of the soul: That night I was happy. But
more often she becomes sad; more often she could become sad.   20*
   —My son, you look so old!
   And files along the yellow color to cry, for she finds me aged, in
the swordblade, in the rivermouth of my face. She cries from me, becomes
sad from me. What need will there be for my youth, if I am always to
be her son? Why do mothers ache finding their sons old, if the age of   25
the sons never reaches that of their mothers? And why, if the sons,
the more they approach death, the more they approach their parents?
My mother cries because I am old from my time and because never
will I grow old from hers!
   My farewell set off from a point in her being, more external than   30
the point in her being to which I return. I am, because of the excessive
time-limit of my return, more the man before my mother than the son
before my mother. There resides the candor which today makes us glow   *
with three flames. I say to her then until I hush:
   —There is, mother, in the world, a place called Paris. A very big   35
place and very far off and once again big.
   My father's wife, on hearing me, eats her lunch and her mortal eyes
descend softly down my arms.

El momento más grave de la vida

Un hombre dijo:
—El momento más grave de mi vida estuvo en la batalla
del Marne, cuando fuí herido en el pecho.
Otro hombre dijo:
—El momento más grave de mi vida, ocurrió en un mare-
moto de Yokohama, del cual salvé milagrosamente, refugiado
bajo el alero de una tienda de lacas.
Y otro hombre dijo:
—El momento más grave de mi vida acontece cuando
duermo de día.
Y otro dijo:
—El momento más grave de mi vida ha estado en mi
mayor soledad.
Y otro dijo:
—El momento más grave de mi vida fué mi prisión en
una cárcel del Perú.
Y otro dijo:
—El momento más grave de mi vida es el haber sorprendido
de perfil a mi padre.
Y el último hombre dijo:
—El momento más grave de mi vida no ha llegado todavía.

The gravest moment in life

*

A man said:
—The gravest moment in my life took place in the battle of
the Marne, when they wounded me in the chest.
Another man said:
—The gravest moment in my life, occurred during a Yokohama   5
seaquake, from which I was miraculously saved, sheltered under the
eaves of a lacquer shop.
And another man said:
—The gravest moment in my life happens when I sleep during
the day.   10
And another said:
—The gravest moment of my life has taken place in my greatest
loneliness.
And another said:
—The gravest moment in my life was my imprisonment in a   15
Peruvian jail.
And another said:
—The gravest moment in my life is having surprised my father
in profile.
And the last man said: 20
—The gravest moment in my life is yet to come.

Las ventanas se han estremecido, elaborando una metafísica del
universo. Vidrios han caído. Un enfermo lanza su queja: la mitad
por su boca lenguada y sobrante, y toda entera, por el ano de su
espalda.
Es el huracán. Un castaño del jardín de las Tullerías habráse
abatido, al soplo del viento, que mide ochenta metros por segundo.
Capiteles de los barrios antiguos, habrán caído, hendiendo, matando.
¿De qué punto interrogo, oyendo a ambas riberas de los océanos,
de qué punto viene este huracán, tan digno de crédito, tan honrado
de deuda, derecho a las ventanas del hospital? ¡Ay las direcciones
inmutables, que oscilan entre el huracán y esta pena directa de
toser o defecar! ¡Ay las direcciones inmutables, que así prenden
muerte en las entrañas del hospital y despiertan células clandes-
tinas, a deshora, en los cadáveres!
¿Qué pensaría de sí el enfermo de enfrente, ése que está durmien-
do, si hubiera percibido el huracán? El pobre duerme, boca arriba,
a la cabeza de su morfina, a los pies de toda su cordura. Un adarme
más o menos en la dosis y le llevarán a enterrar, el vientre roto,
la boca arriba, sordo al huracán, sordo a su vientre roto, ante el
cual suelen los médicos dialogar y cavilar largamente, para, al fin,
pronunciar sus llanas palabras de hombres.

La familia rodea al enfermo agrupándose ante sus sienes regre-
sivas, indefensas, sudorosas. Ya no existe hogar sino en torno al
velador del paciente enfermo, donde montan guardia impaciente, sus
zapatos vacantes, sus cruces de repuesto, sus píldoras de opio.
La familia rodea la mesita por espacio de un alto dividendo. Una
mujer acomoda en el borde de la mesa, la tasa, que casi se ha caído.
Ignoro lo que será del enfermo esta mujer, que le besa y no puede
sanarle con el beso, le mira y no puede sanarle con los ojos, le ha-
bla y no puede sanarle con el verbo. ¿Es su madre? ¿Y cómo, pues,
no puede sanarle? ¿Es su amada? ¿Y cómo, pues, no puede sanarle?
¿Es su hermana? ¿Y cómo, pues, no puede sanarle? ¿Es, simplemente,
una mujer? ¿Y cómo, pues, no puede sanarle? Por que esta mujer le
ha besado, le ha mirado, le ha hablado y hasta le ha cubierto mejor
el cuello al enfermo y, ¡cosa verdaderamente asombrosa! no le ha
sanado.

El paciente contempla su calzado vacante. Traen queso. Llevan
tierra. La muerte se acuesta al pie del lecho, a dormir en sus tran-
quilas aguas y se duerme. Entonces, los libres pies del hombre en-
fermo, sin menudencias ni pormenores innecesarios, se estiran en acen-
to circunflejo, y se alejan, en una extensión de dos cuerpos de no-
vios, del corazón.

The windows shuddered, elaborating a metaphysic of the universe.   *
Glass fell. A sick man utters his complaint: half of it through his tonguish
and excessive mouth, and the whole thing, through the anus in his back.
It is a hurricane. A chestnut tree in the Tuileries garden must have
been toppled, by the blowing of the wind, which attained 80 meters a second.   5
Capitals in the old quarters, must have fallen, splitting, killing.
From what point do I question, listening to both shores of the oceans,
from what point does this hurricane come, so worthy of credit, so honest
in debt, straight at the hospital windows? Ay the immutable directions,   *
that oscillate between the hurricane and this direct embarrassment to   10
cough or to defecate! Ay those immutable directions, that thus attach
death to the entrails of the hospital and awaken clandestine cells, at off
hours, in the cadavers!
What would the sick man in front of me, the one sleeping, think of
himself if he had heard the hurricane? The poor guy sleeps, on his back,   15
at the head of his morphine, at the foot of all his sanity. A half of drachm
more or less in the dose and they will carry him away to be buried, belly
torn open, face upward, deaf to the hurricane, dead to his torn belly,
over which the doctors are used to debating and pondering at great
lengths, to, finally, pronounce their plain and human words.   20

The family surrounds the sick man clustering before his regressive,
defenseless, sweaty temples. Home no longer exists except around the
night table of the sick relative, where his vacant shoes, his spare crosses,
his opium pills impatiently mount guard. The family surrounds the night
table during a high dividend. A woman sets back at the edge of the table,   25
the cup, which had almost fallen.
I don't know who this woman could be to this sick man, who kisses
him and cannot heal him with her kiss, who looks at him and cannot heal
him with her eyes, who talks to him and cannot heal him with her word.
Is she his mother? And why, then, can't she heal him? Is she his be-   30
loved? And why, then, can't she heal him? Is she his sister? And why,
then, can't she heal him? Is she, simply, a woman? And why, then,
can't she heal him? For this woman has kissed him, has watched over
him, has talked to him and has even carefully covered the sick man's
neck and, the truly astonishing thing is! she has not healed him.   35

The patient contemplates his vacant shoes. They bring in cheese. They
carry out dirt. Death lies down at the foot of the bed, to sleep in its
quiet waters and goes to sleep. Then, the freed feet of the sick man,
without trifles or unnecessary details, stretch out, in a circumflex
accent, and pull away, the distance of two sweethearts' bodies, from   40
his heart.

El cirujano ausculta a los enfermos horas enteras. Hasta donde sus manos cesan de trabajar, y empiezan a jugar, las lleva a tientas, rozando la piel de los pacientes, en tanto sus párpados científicos vibran, tocados por la indocta, por la humana flaqueza del amor. Y he visto a esos enfermos morir precisamente del amor desdoblado del cirujano, de los largos diagnósticos, de las dosis exactas, del riguroso análisis de orinas y excrementos. Se rodeaba de improviso un lecho con un biombo. Médicos y enfermeros cruzaban delante del ausente, pizarra triste y próxima, que un niño llenara de números, en un gran monismo de pálidos miles. Cruzaban así, mirando a los otros, como si más irreparable fuese morir de apendicitis o neumonía, y no morir al sesgo del paso de los hombres.

Sirviendo la causa de la religión, vuela con éxito esta mosca, a lo largo de la sala. Ciertamente, a la hora de visita de los cirujanos, sus zumbidos nos perdonan pecho, pero desarrollándose luego se adueñan del aire, para saludar con genio de mudanza, a los que van a morir. Unos enfermos oyen a esa mosca hasta durante el dolor y de ellos depende, por eso, el linaje del disparo en las noches tremebundas.

¿Cuánto tiempo ha durado la anestesia, que llaman los hombres? ¡Ciencia de Dios, Teodicea! si se me echa a vivir en tales condiciones, anestesiado totalmente, volteada mi sensibilidad para adentro! ¡Ah doctores de las sales, hombres de las esencias, prójimos de las bases! Pido se me deje con mi tumor de conciencia, con mi irritada lepra sensitiva, ocurra lo que ocurra, aunque me muera. Dejadme dolerme, si lo queréis, mas dejadme despierto de sueño, con todo el universo metido, aunque fuese a las malas, en mi temperatura polvorosa.

En el mundo de la salud perfecta, se reirá por esta perspectiva en que padezco, pero, en el mismo plano y cortando la baraja del juego, percute aquí otra risa de contrapunto.
En la casa del dolor, la queja asalta síncopes de gran compositor, golletes de carácter, que nos hacen cosquillas de verdad, atroces, arduas, y, cumpliendo lo prometido, nos hielan de espantosa incertidumbre.
En la casa del dolor, la queja arranca frontera excesiva. No se reconoce en esta queja de dolor, a la propia queja de la dicha en éxtasis, cuando el amor y la carne se eximen de azor y cuando al regresar, hay discordia bastante para el diálogo.
¿Dónde está, pues, el otro flanco de esta queja de dolor, si, a estimarla en conjunto, parte ahora del lecho de un hombre?
De la casa del dolor parten quejas tan sordas e inefables y tan colmadas de tánta plenitud, que llorar por ellas sería poco, y sería ya mucho sonreír.

The surgeon auscultates the patients for hours on end. Up to the
point when his hands quit working, and begin to play, he uses them
gropingly, grazing the patients' skin, while his scientific eyebrows
vibrate, touched by the untaught, by the human weakness of love. And   45
I have seen these patients die precisely from the unfolded love of the
surgeon, from the lengthy diagnoses, from the exact doses, from the
rigorous analysis of urine and excrement. A bed was suddenly encircled
with a folding screen. Doctors and nurses were crossing in front of the
absent one, sad and nearby blackboard, that a child had filled with num-   50
bers, in a great monism of pallid thousands. They kept on crossing,
looking at the others, as if it were more inevitable to die from appen-
dicitis or pneumonia, than to die obliquely to the passing of man.

Serving the cause of religion, this fly zooms successfully all
around the hospital ward. Certainly, during the surgeon's visiting   55
hours, her buzzings forgive us chest, but growing then they take over   *
the air, to salute in the spirit of change, those who are about to die.
Some of the sick hear this fly even in their pain and on them depends,
for this reason, the lineage of the gunshot in the dreadful nights.

How long has anesthesia, as men call it, lasted? Science of God,   60
Theodicy! if I am forced to live under such conditions, totally anes-
thetized, my sensitivity turned outside in! O doctors of the salts,
men of the essences, fellowmen of the bases! I beg to be left with my
tumor of consciousness, with my irritated sensitive leprosy, no matter
what happens, even though I may die! Allow me to feel pain, if you   65
wish, but leave me aroused from sleep, with all the universe embedded,
even if by force, in my dusty fever.

In the world of perfect health, the perspective on which I suffer
will be mocked, but, on the same level and cutting the deck for the game,
another laugh percusses here in counterpoint.   70
In the house of pain, the moans assault syncopes of a great composer,
gullets of character, which make us feel real, arduous, atrocious
tickles, and, fulfilling what they promised, freeze us in terrifying
uncertainty.
In the house of pain, the moans uproot excessive frontier. In this   75
moan of pain, one cannot recognize one's own moan of happiness in ec-
stacy, when love and flesh are free from embarrassment and when upon   *
coming back, there is enough discord for dialogue.
Where, then, is the other flank of this moan of pain, if, to con-
sider it as a whole, it now comes from the bed of a man?   80
From the house of pain there come moans so muffled and ineffable
and so overflowing with so much fullness, that to weep for them would
be too little, and yet to smile would be too much.

Se atumulta la sangre en el termómetro.
¡No es grato morir, señor, si en la vida nada se deja y si en
la muerte nada es posible, sino sobre lo que se deja en la vida!
¡No es grato morir, señor, si en la vida nada se deja y si en la
muerte nada es posible, sino sobre lo que se deja en la vida!
¡No es grato morir, señor, si en la vida nada se deja y si en la
muerte nada es posible, sino sobre lo que pudo dejarse en la vida!

Blood runs wild in the thermometer.   *
It is not pleasant to die, lord, if one leaves nothing in life and if   85
nothing is possible in death, except on top of what is left in life!
It is not pleasant to die, lord, if one leaves nothing in life and if
nothing is possible in death, except on top of what is left in life!
It is not pleasant to die, lord, if one leaves nothing in life and if
nothing is possible in death, except on top of what could have been left   90
in life!

Voy a hablar de la esperanza

Yo no sufro este dolor como César Vallejo. Yo no me duelo ahora como artista, como hombre ni como simple ser vivo siquiera. Yo no sufro este dolor como católico, como mahometano ni como ateo. Hoy sufro solamente. Si no me llamase César Vallejo, también sufriría este mismo dolor. Si no fuese artista, también lo sufriría. Si no fuese hombre ni ser vivo siquiera, también lo sufriría. Si no fuese católico, ateo ni mahometano, también lo sufriría. Hoy sufro desde más abajo. Hoy sufro solamente.

Me duelo ahora sin explicaciones. Mi dolor es tan hondo, que no tuvo ya causa ni carece de causa. ¿Qué sería su causa? ¿Dónde está aquello tan importante, que dejase de ser su causa? Nada es su causa; nada ha podido dejar de ser su causa. ¿A qué ha nacido este dolor, por sí mismo? Mi dolor es del viento del norte y del viento del sur, como esos huevos neutros que algunas aves raras ponen del viento. Si hubiese muerto mi novia, mi dolor sería igual. Si me hubieran cortado el cuello de raíz, mi dolor sería igual. Si la vida fuese, en fin, de otro modo, mi dolor sería igual. Hoy sufro desde más arriba. Hoy sufro solamente.

Miro el dolor del hambriento y veo que su hambre anda tan lejos de mi sufrimiento, que de quedarme ayuno hasta morir, saldría siempre de mi tumba una brizna de yerba al menos. Lo mismo el enamorado. ¡Qué sangre la suya más engendrada, para la mía sin fuente ni consumo!

Yo creía hasta ahora que todas las cosas del universo eran, inevitablemente, padres e hijos. Pero he aquí que mi dolor de hoy no es padre ni es hijo. Le falta espalda para anochecer, tanto como le sobra pecho para amanecer y si lo pusiesen en una estancia oscura, no daría luz y si lo pusiesen en una estancia luminosa, no echaría sombra. Hoy sufro suceda lo que suceda. Hoy sufro solamente.

$$\times$$
$$\times \quad \times$$

I am going to speak of hope

I do not suffer this pain as César Vallejo. I do not ache now as
an artist, as a man or even as a simple living being. I do not suffer
this pain as a Catholic, as a Mohammedan or as an atheist. Today
I am simply in pain. If my name were not César Vallejo, I would still
suffer this very same pain. If I were not an artist, I would still suffer   5
it. If I were not a man or even a living being, I would still suffer it.
If I were not a Catholic, atheist or Mohammedan, I would still suffer
it. Today I am in pain from further below. Today I am simply in pain.

I ache now without any explanation. My pain is so deep, that it
never had a cause nor does it lack a cause now. What could have been   10
its cause? Where is that thing so important, that it might stop being
its cause? Its cause is nothing; nothing could have stopped being its
cause. For what has this pain been born, for itself? My pain
comes from the north wind and from the south wind, like those neuter eggs
certain rare birds lay in the wind. If my bride were dead, my pain   15
would be the same. If they had slashed my throat all the way through,
my pain would be the same. If life were, in short, different, my pain
would be the same. Today I suffer from further above. Today I am
simply in pain.   *

I look at the hungry man's pain and see that his hunger is so far   20
from my suffering, that if I were to fast unto death, at least a blade of
grass would always sprout from my tomb. The same with the lover!
How engendered his blood is, in contrast to mine without source or use!

I believed until now that all the things of the universe were, in-
evitably, parents or sons. But behold that my pain today is neither   25
parent nor son. It lacks a back to darken, as well as having too much
chest to dawn and if they put it in a dark room, it would not give light
and if they put it in a brightly lit room, it would cast no shadow. Today
I suffer no matter what happens. Today I am simply in pain.   *

×
×   ×

Tendríamos ya una edad misericordiosa, cuando mi padre ordenó nuestro ingreso a la escuela. Cura de amor, una tarde lluviosa de febrero, mamá servía en la cocina el yantar de oración. En el el corredor de abajo, estaban sentados a la mesa mi padre y mis hermanos mayores. Y mi madre iba sentada al pie del mismo fuego del hogar. Tocaron a la puerta.

—Tocan a la puerta!—mi madre.

Tocan a la puerta—mi propia madre.

—Tocan a la puerta—dijo toda mi madre, tocándose las entrañas a trastos infinitos, sobre toda la altura de quien viene.

—Anda, Nativa, la hija, a ver quien viene.

Y, sin esperar la venia maternal, fuera Miguel, el hijo, quien salió a ver quien venía así, oponiéndose a lo ancho de nosotros.

Un tiempo de rúa contuvo a mi familia. Mamá salió, avanzando inversamente y como si hubiera dicho: las partes. Se hizo patio afuera. Nativa lloraba de una tal visita, de un tal patio y de la mano de mi madre. Entonces y cuando, dolor y paladar techaron nuestras frentes.

Porque no le dejé que saliese a la puerta,—Nativa, la hija,—me ha echado Miguel al pavo. A su paVO.

¡Qué diestra de subprefecto, la diestra del padrE, revelando, el hombre, las falanjas filiales del niño! Podía así otorgarle la ventura que el hombre deseara más tarde. Sin embargo:

—Y mañana, a la escuela,—disertó magistralmente el padre, ante el público semanal de sus hijos.

—Y tal, la ley, la causa de la ley. Y tal también la vida.

Mamá debió llorar, gimiendo apenas la madre. Ya nadie quiso comer. En los labios del padre cupo, para salir rompiéndose, una fina cuchara que conozco. En las fronteras bocas, la absorta amargura del hijo, quedó atravesada.

Mas, luego, de improviso, salió de un albañal de aguas llovedizas y de aquel mismo patio de la visita mala, una gallina, no ajena ni ponedora, sino brutal y negra. Cloqueaba en mi garganta. Fué una gallina vieja, maternalmente viuda de unos pollos que no llegaron a incubarse. Origen olvidado de ese instante, la gallina era viuda de sus hijos. Fueron hallados vacíos todos los huevos. La clueca después tuvo el verbo.

Nadie la espantó. Y de espantarla, nadie dejó arrullarse por su gran calofrío maternal.

—¿Dónde están los hijos de la gallina vieja?

—¿Dónde están los pollos de la gallina vieja?

¡Pobrecitos! ¡Dónde estarían!

We probably already were of a compassionate age, when my father   *
commanded us to enter school. A priestess of love, one rainy February after-   *
noon, mama served in the kitchen the viands of prayer. In the downstairs
interior corridor, my father and older brothers were seated at the table. And my
mother went sitting by the very fire of the hearth. Someone knocked at the   5*
door.

    —Someone's knocking at the door!—my mother.

    —Someone's knocking at the door—my own mother.

    —Someone's knocking at the door—said all of my mother, playing   *
her entrails with infinite frets, over all the height of whoever was coming.   10

    Go, Nativa, the daughter, see who's there.

    And, without waiting for maternal permission, it was Miguel, the
son, who went out to see who had come like this, in opposition to the width of
all of us.

    A street time held my family. Mama went out, advancing inversely   15
and as if she might have said: the parts. The outside became a patio. Nativa
was crying from such a visit, from such a patio and from her mother's hand.
Then and when, pain and palate roofed our foreheads.

    —Because I didn't let him go to the door,—Nativa, the daughter,
—Miguel has made me blush. With his bluSH.   20*

    What a sub-prefectural right hand, the right hand of the fatheR,   *
revealing, the man, the filial phalanges of the child! He could thus grant him
the felicity that the man would desire later on. However:

    —And tomorrow, to school,—father magisterially lectured,
before the weekly public of his children.   25

    —And thus, the law, the cause of the law. And thus also life.

    Mama probably cried, mother hardly moaning. Now no one wanted
to eat. A delicate spoon, known to me, fit in father's lips, to emerge breaking.
In the brotherly mouths, the entranced bitterness of the son, got stuck.

    But, afterwards, unexpectedly, neither alien nor egg-laying, but brutal   30
and black, a hen came out of a rainwater sewer and from the very same patio
of the bad visitor. She clucked in my throat. She was an old hen, maternally
widowed from some chicks that did not get to be incubated. Forgotten origin
of that instant, the hen was the widower of her children. All the eggs were   *
found empty. The brooder afterward had the word.   35

    No one frightened her. And in case she was frightened, no one allowed
himself to be lulled by her great maternal chill.

    —Where are the old hen's children?

    —Where are the old hen's chickens?

    Poor things! Where could they be!   40

Hallazgo de la vida

¡Señores! Hoy es la primera vez que me doy cuenta de la presencia de la vida. ¡Señores! Ruego a ustedes dejarme libre un momento, para saborear esta emoción formidable, espontánea y reciente de la vida, que hoy, por la primera vez, me extasía y me hace dichoso hasta las lágrimas.

Mi gozo viene de lo inédito de mi emoción. Mi exultación viene de que antes no sentí la presencia de la vida. No la he sentido nunca. Miente quien diga que la he sentido. Miente y su mentira me hiere a tal punto que me haría desgraciado. Mi gozo viene de mi fe en este hallazgo personal de la vida, y nadie puede ir contra esa fe. Al que fuera, se le caería la lengua, se le caerían los huesos y correría el peligro de recoger otros, ajenos, para mantenerse de pie ante mis ojos.

Nunca, sino ahora, ha habido vida. Nunca, sino ahora, han pasado gentes. Nunca, sino ahora, ha habido casas y avenidas, aire y horizontes. Si viniese ahora mi amigo Peyriet, le diría que no le conozco, y que debemos empezar de nuevo. ¿Cuando, en efecto, le he conocido a mi amigo Peyriet? Hoy sería la primera vez que nos conocemos. Le diría que se vaya y regrese y entre a verme, como si no me conociera, es decir, por la primera vez.

Ahora yo no conozco a nadie ni nada. Me advierto en un país extraño, en el que todo cobra relieve de nacimiento, luz de epifanía inmarcesible. No, señor. No hable usted a ese caballero. Usted no lo conoce y le sorprendería tan inopinada parla. No ponga usted el pie sobre esa piedrecilla: quién sabe no es piedra y vaya usted a dar en el vacío. Sea usted precavido, puesto que estamos en un mundo absolutamente inconocido.

¡Cuán poco tiempo he vivido! Mi nacimiento es tan reciente, que no hay unidad de medida para contar mi edad. ¡Si acabo de nacer! ¡Se aún no he vivido todavía! Señores: soy tan pequeñito, que el día apenas cabe en mí.

Nunca, sino ahora, oí el estruendo de los carros, que cargan piedras para una gran construcción del boulevard Haussmann. Nunca, sino ahora, avancé paralelamente a la primavera, diciéndola: "Si la muerte hubiera sido otra . . ." Nunca, sino ahora, vi la luz áurea del sol sobre las cúpulas del Sacré-Coeur. Nunca, sino ahora, se me acercó un niño y me miró hondamente con su boca. Nunca, sino ahora, supe que existía una puerta, otra puerta y el canto cordial de las distancias.

¡Dejadme! La vida me ha dado ahora en toda mi muerte.

Discovery of life

Gentlemen! Today is the first time that I realize the presence of
life! Gentlemen! I beg you to leave me alone for a moment, so I can
savor this formidable, spontaneous and recent life emotion, which today,
for the first time, enraptures me and makes me happy to the point of
tears.

My joy comes from what is unexperienced of my emotion. My
exultation comes from the fact that before I did not feel the presence of
life. I have never felt it. If anyone says that I have felt it he is lying. He
is lying and his lie hurts me to such a degree that it would make me mis-
erable. My joy comes from my faith in this personal discovery of life,
and no one can go against this faith. If anyone would try, his tongue
would fall out, his bones would fall out and he would risk picking up
others, not his own, to keep himself standing before my eyes.

Never, except now, has life existed. Never, except now, have
people walked by. Never, except now, have there been houses and
avenues, air and horizons. If my friend Peyriet came over right now,
I would tell him that I do not know him and that we must begin anew.
When, in fact, have I met my friend Peyriet? Today would be the first
time we became acquainted. I would tell him to go away and come back
and drop in on me, as if he did not know me, that is, for the first time.

Now I do not know anyone or anything. I notice I am in a strange
country where everything acquires a Nativity relief, a light of unfading
epiphany. No, sir. Do not speak to that gentleman. You do not know
him and such unexpected chatter would surprise him. Do not put your
foot on that tiny stone: who knows it is not a stone and you will plunge
into empty space. Be cautious, for we are in a totally inknown world.

What a short time I have lived! My birth is so recent,
there is no unit of measure to count my age. I have just been born! I
have not even lived yet! Gentlemen: I am so tiny, the day hardly fits
inside me.

Never, except now, did I hear the racket of the carts,
that carry stone for a great construction on boulevard Haussmann. Never,
except now, did I advance parallel to the spring, saying to it: "If death
had been something else . . ." Never, except now, did I see the golden
light of the sun on the cupolas of Sacré-Coeur. Never, except now, did
a child approach me and look at me deeply with his mouth. Never, except
now, did I know a door existed, and another door and the cordial song
of the distances.

Let me alone! Life has now struck me in all my death.

Una mujer de senos apacibles, ante los que la lengua de la vaca resulta una glándula violenta. Un hombre de templanza, mandibular de genio, apto para marchar de a dos con los goznes de los cofres. Un niño está al lado del hombre, llevando por el revés, el derecho animal de la pareja.

¡Oh la palabra del hombre, libre de adjetivos y de adverbios, que la mujer declina en su único caso de mujer, aún entre las mil voces de la Capilla Sixtina! ¡Oh la falda de ella, en el punto maternal donde pone el pequeño las manos y juega a los pliegues, haciendo a veces agrandar las pupilas de la madre, como en las sanciones de los confesonarios!

Yo tengo mucho gusto de ver así al Padre, al Hijo y al Espíritusanto, con todos los emblemas e insignias de sus cargos.

A woman with peaceful breasts, before which a cow's tongue becomes a violent gland. A temperate man, mandibular in character, able to march side by side with the coffer's hinges. A child is next to the man, carrying in reverse, the animal right of the couple.

Oh the word of man, free from adjectives and adverbs, which woman declines in her singular case of woman, even among the thousand voices of the Sistine Chapel! Oh her skirt, at the maternal place where the child puts his hands and plays with the pleats, sometimes making his mother's pupils dilate, as in the sanctions of the confessionals!

I derive a great pleasure from seeing the Father, the Son and the Holyghost like this, with all the emblems and insignia of their offices.

Cesa el anhelo, rabo al aire. De súbito, la vida se amputa, en seco. Mi propia sangre me salpica en líneas femeninas, y hasta la misma urbe sale a ver esto que se pára de improviso.

—Qué ocurre aquí, en este hijo del hombre? —clama la urbe, y en una sala del Louvre, un niño llora de terror a la vista del retrato de otro niño.

—Qué ocurre aquí, en este hijo de mujer? —clama la urbe, y a una estatua del siglo de los Ludovico, le nace una brizna de yerba en plena palma de la mano.

Cesa el anhelo, a la altura de la mano enarbolada. Y no me escondo detrás de mí mismo, a aguaitarme si paso por lo bajo o merodeo en alto.

Longing ceases, ass in the air. Suddenly, life amputates itself, abruptly. My own blood splashes me in feminine lines, and even the city itself comes out to see what it is that stops unexpectedly.

—What's going on here, inside this son of man?—the city shouts, and in a hall of the Louvre, a child cries in terror at the sight of another child's portrait.

—What's going on here, inside this son of woman?—the city shouts, and in a statue from the Ludwigian century, a blade of grass is born right in the palm of its hand.

Longing ceases, at the height of the raised hand. And I hide behind myself, to spy upon myself if I slip through below or if I maraud up high.

×
× ×

—No vive ya nadie en la casa—me dices—; todos se han ido. La
sala, el dormitorio, el patio, yacen despoblados. Nadie ya queda,
pues que todos han partido.

Y yo te digo: Cuando alguien se va alguien queda. El punto por
donde pasó un hombre, ya no está solo. Unicamente está solo, de so-
ledad humana, el lugar por donde ningún hombre ha pasado. Las ca-
sas nuevas están más muertas que las viejas, por que sus muros son
de piedra o de acero, pero no de hombres. Una casa viene al mundo,
no cuando la acaban de edificar, sino cuando empiezan a habitarla.
Una casa vive únicamente de hombres, como una tumba. De aquí esa
irresistible semejanza que hay entre una casa y una tumba. Sólo que
la casa se nutre de la vida del hombre, mientras que la tumba se nu-
tre de la muerte del hombre. Por eso la primera está de pie, mien-
tras que la segunda está tendida.

Todos han partido de la casa, en realidad, pero todos se han
quedado en verdad. Y no es el recuerdo de ellos lo que queda, sino
ellos mismos. Y no es tampoco que ellos queden en la casa, sino
que continúan por la casa. Las funciones y los actos, se van de la
casa en tren o en avión o a caballo, a pie o arrastrándose. Lo que
continúa en la casa es el órgano, el agente en gerundio y en círcu-
lo. Los pasos se han ido, los besos, los perdones, los crímenes.
Lo que continúa en la casa es el pie, los labios, los ojos, el co-
razón. Las negaciones y las afirmaciones, el bien y el mal, se han
dispersado. Lo que continúa en la casa, es el sujeto del acto.

×
×   ×

  —No one lives in the house anymore—you tell me—; all have gone.
The living room, the bedroom, the patio, are deserted. No one remains
any longer, since everyone has departed.
  And I say to you: When someone leaves someone remains. The point
through which a man passed, is no longer empty. The only place that is   5
empty, with human solitude, is that through which no man has passed.
New houses are deader than old ones, for their walls are of stone or steel,
but not of men. A house comes into the world, not when people finish
building it, but when they begin to inhabit it. A house lives only off men,
like a tomb. That is why there is an irresistible resemblance between a   10
house and a tomb. Except that the house is nourished by the life of man,
while the tomb is nourished by the death of man. That is why the first is
standing, while the second is laid out.
  All have departed from the house, in fact, but all have remained in
truth. And it is not their memory that remains, but they themselves.   15
Nor is it that they remain in the house, but that they continue about the
house. Functions and acts, leave the house by train or by plane or on
horseback, walking or crawling. What continues in the house is the organ,
the agent in gerund and in circle. The steps have left, the kisses, the
pardons, the crimes. What continues in the house are the foot, the lips,   20
the eyes, the heart. Negations and affirmations, good and evil, have
dispersed. What continues in the house, is the subject of the act.

×
× ×

Existe un mutilado, no de un combate sino de un abrazo, no de la
guerra sino de la paz. Perdió el rostro en el amor y no en el odio.
Lo perdió en el curso normal de la vida y no en un accidente. Lo per-
dió en el orden de la naturaleza y no en el desorden de los hombres.
El coronel Piccot, Presidente de "Les Gueules Cassées," lleva la bo-
ca comida por la pólvora de 1914. Este mutilado que conozco, lleva
el rostro comido, por el aire inmortal e inmemorial.

Rostro muerto sobre el tronco vivo. Rostro yerto y pegado con
clavos a la cabeza viva. Este rostro resulta ser el dorso del crá-
neo, el cráneo del cráneo. Ví una vez un árbol darme la espalda y
ví otra vez un camino que me daba la espalda. Un árbol de espaldas
sólo crece en los lugares donde nunca nació ni murió nadie. Un cami-
no de espaldas sólo avanza por los lugares donde ha habido todas las
muertes y ningún nacimiento. El mutilado de la paz y del amor, del
abrazo y del orden y que lleva el rostro muerto sobre el tronco vi-
vo, nació a la sombra de un árbol de espaldas y su existencia tras-
curre a lo largo de un camino de espaldas.

Como el rostro está yerto y difunto, toda la vida psíquica, to-
da la expresión animal de este hombre, se refugia, para traducirse
al exterior, en el peludo cráneo, en el tórax y en las extremida-
des. Los impulsos de su ser profundo, al salir, retroceden del
rostro y la respiración, el olfato, la vista, el oído, la palabra,
el resplandor humano de su ser, funcionan y se expresan por el pe-
cho, por los hombros, por el cabello, por las costillas, por los
brazos y las piernas y los pies.

Mutilado del rostro, tapado del rostro, cerrado del rostro, este
hombre, no obstante, está entero y nada le hace falta. No tiene
ojos y ve y llora. No tiene narices y huele y respira. No tiene
oídos y escucha. No tiene boca y habla y sonríe. No tiene frente
y piensa y se sume en sí mismo. No tiene mentón y quiere y subsis-
te. Jesús conocía al mutilado de la función, que tenía ojos y no
veía y tenía orejas y no oía. Yo conozco al mutilado del órgano,
que ve sin ojos y oye sin orejas.

×
× ×

×
× ×

There is a man mutilated not from combat but from an embrace, not from war but from peace. He lost his face through love and not through hate. He lost it in the normal course of life and not in an accident. Lost it in the order of nature and not in the disorder of men. Colonel Piccot, President of "Les Gueules Cassées," lives with his mouth eaten away by the gunpowder of 1914. This mutilated man I know, has his face eaten away by the immortal and immemorial air.

A dead face above the living torso. A stiff face fastened with nails to the living head. This face turns out to be the backside of the skull, the skull of the skull. I once saw a tree turn its back on me and another time I saw a road that turned its back on me. A back turned tree only grows where no one ever died or was born. A back turned road only advances through places where there have been all deaths and no births. The man mutilated by peace and by love, by an embrace and by order and who lives with a dead face above his living torso, was born in the shadow of a back turned tree and his existence takes place along a back turned road.

As his face is stiff and dead, all his psychic life, all the animal expression of this man, takes refuge, to translate itself outwardly, in his hairy skull, in his thorax and in his extremities. The impulses of his profound being, on going out, back away from his face and his breathing, his sense of smell, his sight, his hearing, his speech, the human radiance of his being, function and are expressed through his chest, through his shoulders, through his hair, through his ribs, through his arms and his legs and his feet.

Face mutilated, face covered, face closed, this man, nevertheless, is whole and lacks nothing. He has no eyes and he sees and cries. He has no nose and he smells and breathes. He has no ears and he listens. He has no mouth and he talks and smiles. No forehead and he thinks and withdraws into himself. No chin and he desires and subsists. Jesus knew the man whose mutilation left him functionless, who had eyes and could not see and had ears and could not hear. I know the man whose mutilation left him organless, who sees without eyes and hears without ears.

×
× ×

Me estoy riendo

Un guijarro, uno solo, el más bajo de todos,
controla
a todo el médano aciago y faraónico.

El aire adquiere tensión de recuerdo y de anhelo,
y bajo el sol se calla
hasta exigir el cuello a las pirámides.

Sed. Hidratada melancolía de la tribu errabunda
gota
a
gota
del siglo al minuto.

Son tres. Treses paralelos,
barbados de barba inmemorial,
en marcha   3   3   3

Es el tiempo este anuncio de gran zapatería,
es el tiempo, que marcha descalzo
de la muerte   hacia   la muerte.

I am laughing

A pebble, only one, the lowest of all,   *
controls
the whole ill-fated Pharaonic sand bank.

The air acquires tension of memories and yearnings,
and under the sun it keeps quiet   5
until it demands the pyramids' necks.

Thirst. Hydrated melancholy of the tribe wandering
drop
by
drop,   10
from century to minute.

They are three. Parallel threes,
bearded with immemorial beards,
marching   3   3   3

It is time this advertisement of a great shoestore,   15
it is time, that marches barefoot
from death   toward   death.

He aquí que hoy saludo, me pongo el cuello y vivo,
superficial de pasos insondable de plantas.
Tal me recibo de hombre, tal más bien me despido
y de cada hora mía retoña una distanciA.

¿Queréis más? encantado.
Políticamente, mi palabra
emite cargos contra mi labio inferior
y económicamente,
cuando doy la espalda a Oriente,
distingo en dignidad de muerte a mis visitas.

Desde ttttales códigos regulares saludo
al soldado desconocido
al verso perseguido por la tinta fatal
y al saurio que Equidista diariamente
de su vida y su muerte,
como quien no hace la cosa.

El tiempo tiene hun miedo ciempiés a los relojes.

(Los lectores pueden ponder el título que quieran a este poema.)

Behold that today I salute, I fix on my collar and I live,
superficial in steps fathomless in soles.
So do I graduate as a man, or rather so do I take leave
and from each of my hours sprouts a distAnce.   *

You want more? with pleasure.   5
Politically, my word
spreads charges against my lower lip
and economically,
when I turn my back to the Orient,
I distinguish my visitors with mortal dignity.   10

From ssssuch regular codes I salute
the unknown soldier
the poetic line pursued by the fatal ink
and the saurian that Equidists daily
from its life and its death,   15
as one who doesn't give a damn.

Time has aa centipedal fear of clocks.   *

(The readers can give whatever title they like to this poem.)

Lomo de las sagradas escrituras

Sin haberlo advertido jamás exceso por turismo
y sin agencias
de pecho en pecho hacia la madre unánime.

Hasta París ahora vengo a ser hijo. Escucha
Hombre, en verdad te digo que eres el HIJO ETERNO,
pues para ser hermano tus brazos son escasamente iguales
y tu malicia para ser padre, es mucha.

La talla de mi madre, moviéndome por índole de movimiento
y poniéndome serio, me llega exactamente al corazón:
pesando cuanto cayera de vuelo con mis tristes abuelos,
mi madre me oye en diámetro, callándose en altura.

Mi metro está midiendo ya dos metros,
mis huesos concuerdan en género y en número
y el verbo encarnado habita entre nosotros
y el verbo encarnado habita, al hundirme en el baño,
un alto grado de perfección.

Spine of the scriptures

Without ever having realized it excess through tourism   *
and without agencies
from chest on chest toward the unanimous mother.   *

As far as Paris now I come to be a son. Listen
Man, verily I say unto thee thou art the ETERNAL SON,   5
because to be a brother thy arms are hardly equal
and thy malice to be a father, is abundant.

My mother's size, moving me for the sake of movement
and making me serious, reaches me exactly at my heart:
weighing how low I have fallen from my sad grandparents,   10
my mother hears me in diameter, keeping quiet on high.

My meter is now measuring two meters,
my bones agree in gender and in number
and the word made flesh dwells among us
and the word made flesh dwells, as I sink into the bathtub,   15
on a high degree of perfection.

altura y pelos

¿Quién no tiene su vestido azul?
¿Quién no almuerza y no toma el tranvía,
con su cigarrillo contratado y su dolor de bolsillo?
¡Yo que tan sólo he nacido!
¡Yo que tan sólo he nacido!

¿Quién no escribe una carta?
¿Quién no habla de un asunto muy importante,
muriendo de costumbre y llorando de oído?
¡Yo que solamente he nacido!
¡Yo que solamente he nacido!

¿Quién no se llama Carlos o cualquier otra cosa?
¿Quién al gato no dice gato gato?
¡Ay! yo que sólo he nacido solamente!
¡Ay! yo que sólo he nacido solamente!

height and hair   *

  Who doesn't own a blue suit?
Who doesn't eat lunch and board the streetcar,
with his bargained for cigarette and his pocket-sized pain?
I who was born so alone!
I who was born so alone!   5

  Who doesn't write a letter?
Who doesn't talk about something very important,
dying from habit and crying by ear?
I who solely was born!
I who solely was born!   10

  Who isn't called Carlos or any other thing?
Who to the kitty doesn't say kitty kitty?
Aie! I who alone was solely born!
Aie! I who alone was solely born!

×
× ×

¡Cuatro conciencias
simultáneas enrédanse en la mía!
¡Si viérais cómo ese movimiento
apenas cabe ahora en mi conciencia!
¡Es aplastante! Dentro de una bóveda
pueden muy bien
adosarse, ya internas o ya externas
segundas bóvedas, más nunca cuartas;
mejor dicho, sí,
mas siempre y, a lo sumo, cual segundas.
No puedo concebirlo; es aplastante.
Vosotros mismos a quienes inicio en la noción
de estas cuatro conciencias simultáneas,
enredadas en una sola, apenas os tenéis
de pie ante mi cuadrúpedo intensivo.
¡Y yo, que le entrevisto (Estoy seguro)!

×
×   ×

      Four consciousnesses are
simultaneously snarled in my own!
If you could only see how that movement
hardly fits now in my consciousness!
It's crushing! Inside a vault   5
they can easily
lean back to back, now internal now external
second vaults, but never fourths;
better said, yes,
but always and, at most, as seconds.   10
I cannot conceive it; it's crushing.
Those of you who I initiate into the notion
of these four simultaneous consciousnesses,
snarled in only one, barely remain
standing before my intense quadruped.   15
And I, who interview him (Am sure)!

×
× ×

Entre el dolor y el placer median tres criaturas,
de las cuales la una mira a un muro,
la segunda usa de ánimo triste
y la tercera avanza de puntillas;
pero, entre tú y yo,
sólo existen segundas criaturas.

Apoyándose en mi frente, el día
conviene en que, de veras,
hay mucho de exacto en el espacio;
pero, si la dicha, que, al fin, tiene un tamaño,
principia, ¡ay! por mi boca,
¿quién me preguntará por mi palabra?

Al sentido instantáneo de la eternidad
corresponde
este encuentro investido de hilo negro,
pero a tu despedida temporal,
tan sólo corresponde lo inmutable,
tu criatura, el alma, mi palabra.

×
× ×

    Between pain and pleasure there are three
creatures. One looks at a wall,
the second puts on a sad disposition
and the third advances on tiptoes;
but, between you and me,   5
only second creatures exist.

    Leaning on my forehead, the day
agrees that, in truth,
there is much accuracy in space;
but, if the happiness, that, after all, has size,   10
begins, alas! in my mouth,
who is going to ask me for my word?

    To the instantaneous meaning of eternity   *
corresponds
this encounter vested with black thread,   15
but to your temporal farewell,
corresponds solely what is immutable,
your creature, the soul, my word.

En el momento en que el tenista lanza magistralmente
su bala, le posee una inocencia totalmente animal;
en el momento
en que el filósofo sorprende una nueva verdad,
es una bestia completa.
Anatole France afirmaba
que el sentimiento religioso
es la función de un órgano especial del cuerpo humano,
hasta ahora ignorado y se podría
decir también, entonces,
que, en el momento exacto en que un tal órgano
funciona plenamente
tan puro de malicia está el creyente,
que se diría casi un vegetal.
¡Oh alma! ¡Oh pensamiento! ¡Oh Marx! ¡Oh Feüerbach!

The moment the tennis player masterfully serves
his bullet, a totally animal innocence possesses him;
the moment
the philosopher surprises a new truth,
he is an absolute beast.   5
Anatole France affirmed
that religious feeling
is the function of a special organ in the human body,
until now unrecognized and one could
also say, then,   10
that, the exact moment when such an organ
fully functions
the believer is so clear of malice,
he could almost be considered a vegetable.
Oh soul! Oh thought! Oh Marx! Oh Feüerbach!   15

sombrero, abrigo, guantes

Enfrente a la Comedia Francesa, está el Café
de la Regencia; en él hay una pieza
recóndita, con una butaca y una mesa.
Cuando entro, el polvo inmóvil se ha puesto ya de pie.

Entre mis labios hechos de jebe, la pavesa
de un cigarrillo humea, y en el humo se ve
dos humos intensivos, el tórax del Café,
y en el tórax, un óxido profundo de tristeza.

Importa que el otoño se injerte en los otoños,
importa que el otoño se integre de retoños,
la nube, de semestres; de pómulos, la arruga.

Importa oler a loco postulando
¡qué cálida es la nieve, que fugaz la tortuga,
el cómo qué sencillo, qué fulminante el cuándo!

hat, overcoat, gloves

In front of the French Comedy, is the Café
Regency; in it is a room
set apart, with an armchair and a table.
When I enter, the unmoving dust has already arisen.

Between my lips made of rubber, the ember   5*
of a cigarette smokes, and in the smoke one sees
two intense smokes, the thorax of the Café,
and in the thorax, a profound oxide of sadness.

It is important that autumn graft itself to autumns,
important that autumn integrate itself with sprouts,   10
the cloud, with half-years; with cheekbones, the wrinkle.

It is important to smell like a madman postulating
how warm the snow is, how fleeting the turtle,
the how how simple, how fulminant the when!

salutación angélica

Eslavo con respecto a la palmera,
alemán de perfil al sol, inglés sin fin,
francés en cita con los caracoles,
italiano ex profeso, escandinavo de aire,
español de pura bestia, tal el cielo
ensartado en la tierra por los vientos,
tal el beso del límite en los hombros.

Mas solo tú demuestras, descendiendo
o subiendo del pecho, bolchevique,
tus trazos confundibles,
tu gesto marital,
tu cara de padre,
tus piernas de amado,
tu cutis por teléfono,
tu alma perpendicular
a la mía, tus codos de justo
y un pasaporte en blanco tu sonrisa.

Obrando por el hombre, en nuestras pausas,
matando, tú, a lo largo de tu muerte
y a lo ancho de un abrazo salubérrimo,
ví que cuando comías después, tenías gusto,
ví que en tus sustantivos creció yerba.

Yo quisiera, por eso,
tu calor doctrinal, frío y en barras,
tu añadida manera de mirarnos
y aquesos tuyos pasos metalúrgicos,
aquesos tuyos pasos de otra vida.

Y digo, bolchevique, tomando esta flaqueza
en su feroz linaje de exhalación terrestre:
hijo natural del bien y del mal
y viviendo talvez por vanidad, para que digan,
me dan tus simultáneas estaturas mucha pena,
puesto que tú no ignoras en quién se me hace tarde diariamente,
en quién estoy callado y medio tuerto.

angelic salutation

Slav in regard to the palm tree,
German with profile to the sun, English with no limits,
French in a rendezvous with the snails,
Italian on purpose, Scandinavian made of air,
purely brutal Spaniard, thus the sky   5
strung to the earth by the winds,
thus the kiss limited to the shoulders.

But you alone, Bolshevik, demonstrate,
descending or rising from your chest,
your confusable characteristics,   10
your marital gesture,
your paternal face,
your legs of the beloved,
your complexion by telephone,
your soul perpendicular   15
to mine, your elbows of a just man
and a blank passport in your smile.

Working for man, during our pauses,
killing, you, along your death
and abreast a most salubrious embrace,   20
I saw that when you ate afterwards, you had taste,
I saw that in your substantives the grass grew.

Therefore, I would like
your doctrinal warmth, cold and in bars,
your added way of looking at us   25
and those your metallurgic steps,
those your steps of another life.

And I speak, Bolshevik, taking this weakness
in its ferocious lineage of earthly exhalation:
natural son of good and evil   30
and living perhaps by vanity, to have others speak,
your simultaneous statures make me very sad,
because you know in whom I am late daily,
in whom I am silent and almost one-eyed.

epístola a los transeuntes

Reanudo mi día de conejo,
mi noche de elefante en descanso.

Y, entre mí, digo:
ésta es mi inmensidad en bruto, a cántaros,
éste mi grato peso, que me buscara abajo para pájaro;
éste es mi brazo
que por su cuenta rehusó ser ala,
éstas son mis sagradas escrituras,
éstos mis alarmados compañones.

Lúgubre isla me alumbrará continental,
mientras el capitolio se apoye en mi íntimo derrumbe
y la asamblea en lanzas clausure mi desfile.

Pero cuando yo muera
de vida y no de tiempo,
cuando lleguen a dos mis dos maletas,
éste ha de ser mi estómago en que cupo mi lámpara en pedazos,
ésta aquella cabeza que expió los tormentos del círculo en mis pasos,
éstos esos gusanos que el corazón contó por unidades,
éste ha de ser mi cuerpo solidario
por el que vela el alma individual; éste ha de ser
mi hombligo en que maté mis piojos natos,
ésta mi cosa cosa, mi cosa tremebunda.

En tanto, convulsiva, ásperamente
convalece mi freno,
sufriendo como sufro del lenguaje directo del león:
y, puesto que he existido entre dos potestades de ladrillo,
convalezco yo mismo, sonriendo de mis labios.

epistle to the transients

I resume my day of a rabbit,   *
my night of an elephant in repose.

And, to myself, I say:
this is my immensity in the raw, in jugfuls,
this my graceful weight, that sought me below to become a bird;   5
this is my arm
that on its own refused to be a wing,
these are my scriptures,
these my alarmed cullions.   *

A lugubrious island will illuminate me continental,   10
while the capitol leans on my intimate collapse
and the lance-filled assembly adjourns my parade.

But when I die
from life and not from time,
when my two suitcases become two,   15
this will be my stomach in which my lamp fit in pieces,
this that head that atoned for the torments of the circle in my steps,
these those worms that my heart counted one by one,
this will be my solidary body
over which the individual soul is watching; this will be   20
my navell in which I killed my innate lice,   *
this my thing thing, my dreadful thing.

Meanwhile, convulsively, harshly,   *
my bit convalesces,
suffering like I suffer the direct language of the lion: 25
and, because I have existed between two brick potentates,
I too convalesce, smiling at my lips.

Y no me digan nada,
que uno puede matar perfectamente,
ya que, sudando tinta,
uno hace cuanto puede, no me digan . . .

Volveremos, señores, a vernos con manzanas;
tarde la criatura pasará,
la expresión de Aristóteles armada
de grandes corazones de madera,
la de Heráclito injerta en la de Marx,
la del suave sonando rudamente . . .
Es lo que bien narraba mi garganta:
uno puede matar perfectamente.

Señores,
caballeros, volveremos a vernos sin paquetes;
hasta entonces exijo, exigiré de mi flaqueza
el acento del día, que,
según veo, estuvo ya esperándome en mi lecho.
Y exijo del sombrero la infausta analogía del recuerdo,
ya que, a veces, asumo con éxito mi inmensidad llorada,
ya que, a veces, me ahogo en la voz de mi vecino
y padezoo
contando en maíces los años,
cepillando mi ropa al son de un muerto
o sentado borracho en mi ataúd . . .

And don't say another word to me,   *
since one can kill perfectly,
and because, sweating blood,
one does what one can, don't say another . . .

We will see each other again, gentlemen, with apples;   5
late the creature will pass,
the expression of Aristotle armed
with great wood hearts,
that of Heraclitus grafted on that of Marx,
that of the gentle sounding roughly . . .   10
This is what was well narrated by my throat:
one can kill perfectly.

Gentlemen,
sirs, we will see each other again without packages;
until then I demand, I shall demand of my frailty   15
the accent of the day, that,
as I see it, was already awaiting me in my bed.
And I demand of my hat the fatal analogy of remembrance,
since, at times, I assume successfully my wept immensity,
since, at times, I drown in my neighbor's voice   20
and endure
counting on kernels the years,
brushing my clothes to the tune of a corpse
or sitting up drunk in my coffin . . .

GLEBA

Con efecto mundial de vela que se enciende,
el prepucio directo, hombres a golpes,
funcionan los labriegos a tiro de neblina,
con alabadas barbas,
pie práctico y reginas sinceras de los valles.

Hablan como les vienen las palabras,
cambian ideas bebiendo
orden sacerdotal de una botella;
cambian también ideas tras de un árbol, parlando
de escrituras privadas, de la luna menguante
y de los ríos públicos. (¡Inmenso! ¡Inmenso! ¡Inmenso!)

Función de fuerza
sorda y de zarza ardiendo,
paso de palo,
gesto de palo,
acápites de palo,
la palabra colgando de otro palo.

De sus hombros arranca, carne a carne, la herramienta florecida,
de sus rodillas bajan ellos mismos por etapas hasta el cielo,
y, agitando
y
agitando sus faltas en forma de antiguas calaveras,
levantan sus defectos capitales con cintas,
su mansedumbre y sus
vasos sanguíneos, tristes, de jueces colorados.

Tienen su cabeza, su tronco, sus extremidades,
tienen su pantalón, sus dedos metacarpos y un palito;
para comer vistiéronse de altura
y se lavan la cara acariciándose con sólidas palomas.

Por cierto, aquestos hombres
cumplen años en los peligros,
echan toda la frente en sus salutaciones;
carecen de reloj, no se jactan jamás de respirar
y, en fin, suelen decirse: Allá, las putas, Luis Taboada, los ingleses;
¡allá ellos, allá ellos, allá ellos!

GLEBE   *

With the universal effect of a candle that lights up,
their prepuce direct, hacked out men,   *
the peasants function within fog range,   *
with extolled beards,
practical feet and sincere queens of the valley.   5*

    They speak as the words come,
they exchange ideas drinking
priestly order from a bottle;
they also exchange ideas behind a tree, chatting
about private legal papers, about the waning moon   10
and about the public rivers! (Immense! Immense! Immense!)

    Function of silent
strength and of burning bush,
stick step,
stick gesture,   15
stick paragraph signs,
the word hanging from another stick.

    From their shoulders the flowered tool, flesh to flesh, tears forth,
from their knees they descend themselves by stages unto heaven,
and, agitating   20
and
agitating their shortcomings in the shape of ancient skulls,
they raise their deadly flaws with ribbons,
their meekness and their
sad, blood vessels, of flushed judges.   25

    They have their head, their trunk, their extremities,
they have their pants, their metacarpal fingers and a little stick;
to eat they dressed themselves in height
and they wash their faces caressing them with solid doves.

    Certainly, these men   30
put on years in risks,
they fling out all their forehead in their salutations;
they know no clock, at no time do they brag about breathing
and, in short, they always say: To hell with the whores, Luis Taboada, the English;   *
t'hell with'm, t'hell with'm, t'hell with'm!   35

PRIMAVERA TUBEROSA

Esta vez, arrastrando briosa sus pobrezas
al sesgo de mi pompa delantera,
coteja su coturno con mi traspié sin taco,
la primavera exacta de picotón de buitre.

La perdí en cuanto tela de mis despilfarros,
juguéla en cuanto pomo de mi aplauso;
el termómetro puesto, puesto el fin, puesto el gusano,
contusa mi doblez del otro día,
aguardéla al arrullo de un grillo fugitivo
y despedíla uñoso, somático, sufrido.

Veces latentes de astro,
ocasiones de ser gallina negra,
entabló la bandida primavera
con mi chusma de aprietos,
con mis apocamientos en camisa,
mi derecho soviético y mi gorra.

Veces las del bocado lauríneo,
con símbolos, tabaco, mundo y carne,
deglusión translaticia bajo palio,
al són de los testículos cantores;
talentoso torrente el de mi suave suavidad,
rebatible a pedradas, ganable con tan sólo suspirar . . .
Flora de estilo, plena,
citada en fangos de honor por rosas auditivas . . .
Respingo, coz, patada sencilla,
triquiñuela adorada . . . Cantan . . . Sudan . . .

TUBEROUS SPRING

This time, vigorously dragging its misery
oblique to my foremost pomp,
the exact spring with its vulture stab   *
compares its cothurnus to my heelless stumble.

I lost it as fabric of my squanderings,   5
I gambled it away as flask of my applause;
the thermometer placed, the end placed, the worm placed,
my duplicity of the other day bruised,
I awaited it to the lull of a fugitive cricket
and discharged it naily, somatic, long-suffering.   10

Latent times of a star,
occasions of being a black hen,
were joined by the bandit spring
with my mob of hassles,
with my bashfulness in shirtsleeves,   15
my soviet law and my cap.

Those were the times of the lauraceous bite,
with symbols, tobacco, world and flesh,
translatory deglutision under pallium   *
to the sound of singing testicles;   20
talented torrent that of my gentle gentleness,
refutable by stonings, gainable with just a sigh . . .
Flora of style, complete,
cited in swamps of honor by auditory roses . . .
Buck, hoofblow, simple kick,   25
adored little trick . . . They sing . . . They sweat . . .

Piedra negra sobre una piedra blanca

Me moriré en París con aguacero,
un día del cual tengo ya el recuerdo.
Me moriré en París—y no me corro—
talvez un jueves, como es hoy, de otoño.

Jueves será, porque hoy, jueves, que proso
estos versos, los húmeros me he puesto
a la mala y, jamás como hoy, me he vuelto,
con todo mi camino, a verme solo.

César Vallejo ha muerto, le pegaban
todos sin que él les haga nada;
le daban duro con un palo y duro

también con una soga; son testigos
los días jueves y los huesos húmeros,
la soledad, la lluvia, los caminos . . .

Black stone on a white stone

I will die in Paris with a sudden shower,
a day I can already remember.
I will die in Paris—and I don't budge—
maybe a Thursday, like today is, in autumn.

Thursday it will be, because today, Thursday, when I prose
these poems, the humeri that I have put on
by force and, never like today, have I turned,
with all my road, to see myself alone.

César Vallejo has died, they beat him,
everyone, without him doing anything to them;
they gave it to him hard with a stick and hard

also with a rope; witnesses are
the Thursday days and the humerus bones,
the loneliness, the rain, the roads . . .

¡Dulzura por dulzura corazona!
Dulzura a gajos, eras de vista,
esos abiertos días, cuando monté por árboles caídos!
Así por tu paloma palomita,
por tu oración pasiva,
andando entre tu sombra y el gran tezón corpóreo de tu sombra.

 Debajo de ti y yo,
tú y yo, sinceramente,
tu candado ahogándose de llaves,
yo ascendiendo y sudando
y haciendo lo infinito entre tus muslos.
(El hotelero es una bestia,
sus dientes, admirables; yo controlo
el orden pálido de mi alma:
señor, allá distante . . . paso paso . . . adiós, señor . . .)

 Mucho pienso en todo esto conmovido, perduroso
y pongo tu paloma a la altura de tu vuelo
y, cojeando de dicha, a veces,
repósome a la sombra de ese árbol arrastrado.

 Costilla de mi cosa,
dulzura que tú tapas sonriendo con tu mano;
tu traje negro que se habrá acabado,
amada, amada en masa,
¡qué unido a tu rodilla enferma!

 Simple ahora te veo, te comprendo avergonzado
en Letonia, Alemania, Rusia, Bélgica, tu ausente,
tu portátil ausente
hombre convulso de la mujer temblando entre sus vínculos.

¡Amada en la figura de tu cola irreparable,
amada que yo amara con fósforos floridos,
quand on a la vie et la juenesse,
c'est déjà tellement!

Cuando ya no haya espacio entre tu grandeza y mi postrer proyecto,
amada,
volveré a tu media, haz de besarme,
bajando por tu media repetida,
tu portátil ausente, dile así . . .

Sweetness through heartsown sweetness!   *
Sweetness in sections, eras by sight,   *
those open days, when I mounted through fallen trees!
Thus through your dove little dove,
through your passive sentence,   5
walking between your shadow and the great corporeal tenazity of your shadow.   *

  Under you and I,
you and I, in all sincerity,
your padlock choking with keys,
me ascending and sweating   10
and doing what is endless between your thighs.
(The hotel manager is a beast,
his teeth, admirable; I control
the pallid order of my soul:
sir, you way over there . . . step step . . . goodbye, sir . . .)   15

  I think a lot about all of this disturbed, foreverish   *
and place your dove at the height of your flight
and, limping with happiness, at times,
I rest in the shadow of that dragged-on tree.

  Rib of my thing,   20
sweetness that you cover smiling with your hand;
your black dress probably worn out,
beloved, beloved in mass,
how bound to your sick knee!

  Simple I see you now, ashamed I understand you   25
in Lithuania, Germany, Russia, Belgium, your absent,
your portable absent,
man convulsed from the woman trembling between his ties.

  Beloved in the figure of your irreparable tail,
beloved who I loved with flowering matches,   30
quand on a la vie et la jeunesse,   *
c'est déjà tellement!

  When there is no longer space
between your greatness and my last project,
beloved,   35
I will return to your stocking, you well kiss me,   *
going down your repeated stocking,
your portable absent, tell him this way . . .

Hasta el día en que vuelva, de esta piedra
nacerá mi talón definitivo,
con su juego de crímenes, su yedra,
su obstinación dramática, su olivo.

Hasta el día en que vuelva, prosiguiendo,
con franca rectitud de cojo amargo.
de pozo en pozo, mi periplo, entiendo
que el hombre ha de ser bueno, sin embargo.

Hasta el día en que vuelva y hasta que ande
el animal que soy, entre sus jueces,
nuestro bravo meñique será grande,
digno, infinito dedo entre los dedos.

   Until the day I will return, from this stone
my definitive heel will be born,
with its set of crimes, its ivy,
its dramatic stubbornness, its olive tree.

   Until the day I will return, continuing,   5
with the frank uprightness of a bitter cripple,
my periplus, from well to well, I understand
that man will have to be good, notwithstanding.

   Until the day I will return and until
the animal I am walks, among his judges,   10
our brave little finger will be big,
dignified, an infinite finger among fingers.

Fué domingo en las claras orejas de mi burro,
de mi burro peruano en el Perú (Perdonen la tristeza)
Mas hoy ya son las once en mi experiencia personal,
experiencia de un solo ojo, clavado en pleno pecho,
de una sola burrada, clavada en pleno pecho,
de una sola hecatombe, clavada en pleno pecho.

Tal de mi tierra veo los cerros retratados,
ricos en burros, hijos de burros, padres hoy de vista,
que tornan ya pintados de creencias,
cerros horizontales de mis penas.

En su estatua, de espada,
Voltaire cruza su capa y mira el zócalo,
pero el sol me penetra y espanta de mis dientes incisivos
un número crecido de cuerpos inorgánicos.

Y entonces sueño en una piedra
verduzca, diecisiete,
peñasco numeral que he olvidado,
sonido de años en el rumor de aguja de mi brazo,
lluvia y sol en Europa, y ¡cómo toso! ¡cómo vivo!
¡cómo me duele el pelo al columbrar los siglos semanales!
y cómo, por recodo, mi ciclo microbiano,
quiero decir mi trémulo, patriótico peinado.

It was Sunday in the clear ears of my jackass,
of my Peruvian jackass in Peru (Pardon my sadness)
But today is already eleven o'clock in my personal experience,
experience of a single eye, nailed right in the chest,
of a single asininity, nailed right in the chest,   5
of a single hecatomb, nailed right in the chest.

So do I see the portrayed hills of my country,
rich in jackasses, sons of jackasses, parents today by sight,
that now return painted with beliefs,
horizontal hills of my sorrows.   10

In his statue, with a sword,
Voltaire crosses his cape and looks at the public square,
but the sun penetrates me and frightens from my incisors
a great number of inorganic bodies.

And then I dream on a verdant   15
stone, seventeen,
numeral boulder that I have forgotten,
sound of years in the needle rumor of my arm,
rain and sun in Europe, and, how I cough! how I live!
how my hair aches me upon descrying the weekly centuries!   20
and how, on rebound, my microbial cycle,
I mean my tremulous, patriotically combed hair.

. . . .

La vida, esta vida
me placía, su instrumento, esas palomas . . .
Me placía escucharlas gobernarse en lontananza,
advenir naturales, determinado el número,
y ejecutar, según sus aflicciones, sus dianas de animales.

Encogido,
oí desde mis hombros
su sosegada producción,
cave los albañales sesgar sus trece huesos,
dentro viejo tornillo hincharse el plomo.
Sus paujiles picos,
pareadas palomitas,
las póbridas, hojeándose los hígados,
sobrinas de la nube . . . Vida! Vida! Esta es la vida!

Zurear su tradición rojo les era,
rojo moral, palomas vigilantes,
talvez rojo de herrumbre,
si caían entonces azulmente.

Su elemental cadena,
sus viajes de individuales pájaros viajeros,
echaron humo denso,
pena física, pórtico influyente.

Palomas saltando, indelebles
palomas olorosas,
manferidas venían, advenían
por azarosas vías digestivas,
a contarme sus cosas fosforosas,
pájaros de contar,
pájaros transitivos y orejones . . .

No escucharé ya más desde mis hombros
huesudo, enfermo, en cama,
ejecutar sus dianas de nimales . . . Me doy cuenta.

. . . .

Life, this life
pleased me, its instrument, those doves . . .
It pleased me to hear them steer far away,
turn out natural, in fixed numbers,
and perform, according to their afflictions, their animal reveilles.   5

  Shrugged,
in my shoulders I heard
their quiet production,
their thirteen bones slanting ner the sewers,   *
the lead swelling inside an old screw.   10
Their cashew bird beaks,
coupled dovelings,
the poorotteds, exfoliating their livers,   *
nieces of the cloud . . . Life! Life! This is life!

  To coo their tradition to them was red,   15
moral red, vigilant doves,
maybe rust red,
if they fell then bluely.   *

  Their elementary chain,
their travels of individual travelling birds,   20
sent forth dense smoke,   *
physical pain, influencial portico.

  Doves jumping, indelible
fragant doves,
forewarned they came, turning out   25*
along hazardous digestive tracks,
to tell me their phosphorescent things,
storytold birds,
transitive and Incan noble birds . . .

  No longer will I hear them from my shoulders   30
bony, sick, bedridden,
perform their nimal reveilles . . I realize that.   *

Hoy me gusta la vida mucho menos,
pero siempre me gusta vivir: ya lo decía.
Casi toqué la parte de mi todo y me contuve
con un tiro en la lengua detrás de mi palabra.

Hoy me palpo el mentón en retirada
y en estos momentáneos pantalones yo me digo:
¡Tánta vida y jamás!
¡Tántos años y siempre mis semanas! . . .
Mis padres enterrados con su piedra
y su triste estirón que no ha acabado;
de cuerpo entero hermanos, mis hermanos,
y, en fin, mi sér parado y en chaleco.

Me gusta la vida enormemente
pero, desde luego,
con mi muerte querida y mi café
y viendo los castaños frondosos de París
y diciendo:
Es un ojo éste, aquél; una frente ésta, aquélla . . . Y repitiendo:
¡Tánta vida y jamás me falla la tonada!
¡Tántos años y siempre, siempre, siempre!

Dije chaleco, dije
todo, parte, ansia, dije casi, por no llorar.
Que es verdad que sufrí en aquel hospital que queda al lado
y está bien y está mal haber mirado
de abajo para arriba mi organismo.

Me gustará vivir siempre, así fuese de barriga,
porque, como iba diciendo y lo repito,
¡tánta vida y jamás! ¡Y tántos años,
y siempre, mucho siempre, siempre, siempre!

Today I like life much less,,
but I like to live anyway: I have often said it.
I almost touched the part of my whole and restrained myself
with a shot in the tongue behind my word.

Today I touch my chin in retreat
and in these momentary trousers I tell myself: 5
So much life and never!
So many years and always my weeks! . . .
My parents buried with their stone
and their sad stiffening that has not ended;   10
full length brothers, my brothers,
and, finally, my Being standing and in a vest.

I like life enormously
but, of course,   *
with my beloved death and my café   15
and looking at the leafy chestnut trees in Paris
and saying:
This is an eye, that one too; this a forehead, that one too . . . And repeating:
So much life and the tune never fails me!
So many years and always, always, always!   20

I said vest, said
whole, part, yearning, said almost, to avoid crying.
For it is true that I suffered in that hospital close by
and it is good and it is bad to have watched
from below up my organism.   25

I would like to live always, even flat on my belly,
because, as I was saying and I say it again,
so much life and never! And so many years,
and always, much always, always, always!   *

Quisiera hoy ser feliz de buena gana,
ser feliz y portarme frondoso de preguntas,
abrir por temperamento de par en par mi cuarto, como loco,
y reclamar, en fin,
en mi confianza física acostado,
sólo por ver si quieren,
sólo por ver si quieren probar de mi espontánea posición,
reclamar, voy diciendo,
por qué me dan así tánto en el alma.

Pues quisiera en sustancia ser dichoso,
obrar sin bastón, laica humildad, ni burro negro.
Así las sensaciones de este mundo,
los cantos subjuntivos,
el lápiz que perdí en mi cavidad
y mis amados órganos de llanto.

Hermano persuasible, camarada,
padre por la grandeza, hijo mortal,
amigo y contendor, inmenso documento de Darwin:
¿a qué hora, pues, vendrán con mi retrato?
¿A los goces? ¿Acaso sobre goce amortajado?
¿Más temprano? ¿Quién sabe, a las porfías?

A las misericordias, camarada,
hombre mío en rechazo y observación, vecino
en cuyo cuello enorme sube y baja,
al natural, sin hilo, mi esperanza . . .

Today I would like to be happy willingly,
to be happy and behave leafy with questions,
to open by temperament wide open my room, as if crazy,
and to protest, in short,
reclined on my physical trust,   5
only to see if they would like,
only to see if they would like to try my spontaneous position,
to protest, I keep saying,
why they hit me like this so much in my soul.   *

For I would like in essence to be happy,   10
to get about without cane, laic humility, or black jackass.
Thus the sensations of this world,
the subjunctive songs,
the pencil that I lost in my cavity
and my beloved organs for crying.   15

Persuadable brother, comrade,
father in greatness, mortal son,
friend and opponent, immense document of Darwin:
at what hour, then, will they come with my portrait?   *
At the delights? Perhaps about delight shrouded?   20
Earlier? Who knows, at the disputations?

At the misericordias, comrade,   *
fellow man in rejection and observation, neighbor
in whose enormous neck rises and lowers,
unseasoned, without thread, my hope . . .   25

De disturbio en disturbio
subes a acompañarme a estar solo;
y lo comprendo andando de puntillas,
con un pan en la mano, un camino en el pie
y haciendo, negro hasta sacar espuma,
mi perfil su papel espeluznante.

Ya habías disparado para atrás tu violencia
neumática, otra época, mas luego
me sostienes ahora en brazo de honra fúnebre
y sostienes el rumbo de las cosas en brazo de honra fúnebre,
la muerte de las cosas resumida en brazo de honra fúnebre.

Pero, realmente, y puesto
que tratamos de la vida,
cuando el hecho de entonces eche crin en tu mano,
al seguir tu rumor como regando,
cuando sufras en suma de kanguro,
olvídame, sosténme todavía, compañero de cantidad pequeña,
azotado de fechas con espinas,
olvídame y sosténme por el pecho,
jumento que te paras en dos para abrazarme;
duda de tu excremento unos segundos,
observa cómo el aire empieza a ser el cielo levantándose,
hombrecillo,
hombrezuelo,
hombre con taco, quiéreme, acompáñame . . .

Ten presente que un día
ha de cantar un mirlo de sotana
sobre mi tonelada ya desnuda.
(Cantó un mirlo llevando las cintas de mi gramo entre su pico)
Ha de cantar calzado de este sollozo innato,
hombre con taco,
y, simultánea, doloridamente,
ha de cantar calzado de mi paso,
y no oírlo, hombrezuelo, será malo,
será denuesto y hoja,
pesadumbre, trenza, humo quieto.

Perro parado al borde de una piedra
es el vuelo en su curva;
también tenlo presente, hombrón hasta arriba.
Te lo recordarán el peso bajo, de ribera adversa,
el peso temporal, de gran silencio,
más eso de los meses y aquello que regresa de los años.

From disturbance to disturbance
you come up to accompany me to be alone;
and I realize it walking on tiptoes,
with a loaf in my hand, a road on my foot
and, black until it spills foam, my profile   5
playing its hair-raising role.

You have already fired your pneumatic violence
backwards, another epoch, but then
you now support me on an arm of memorial honor
and support the course of things on an arm of memorial honor,   10
the death of things summarized on an arm of memorial honor.

But, actually and since
we deal with life,
when the fact of that time grows mane in your hand,
upon following your rumor like watering,   15
when you suffer in short from kangaroo,   *
forget me, support me still, companion of a small amount,
whipped by dates with thorns,
forget me and support me by my chest,
donkey that stands up on two to embrace me;   20
doubt your excrement a few seconds,
observe how the air begins to be sky raising itself,
dear little man,
poor little man,
man with shoe heels, love me, keep me company . . .   25*

Keep in mind that one day
a blackbird in cassock will sing
over my ton finally naked.
(A blackbird did sing carrying the ribbons of my gram in its beak)
It will sing shod with this innate sob,   30
man with shoe heels,
and, simultaneously, grievously,
will sing shod with my step,
and not to hear it, poor little man, will be bad,
will be insult and leaf,   35
sorrow, braid, quiet smoke.

A dog standing at the edge of a stone
is the flight in its curve;
also keep that in mind, man huge to the top.
You will be reminded of this by the low weight, of an adverse shore,   40
by the temporal weight, of a great silence,
plus this of the months and that which returns from the years.

Considerando en frío, imparcialmente,
que el hombre es triste, tose y, sin embargo,
se complace en su pecho colorado;
que lo único que hace es componerse
de días;
que es lóbrego mamífero y se peina . . .

Considerando
que el hombre procede suavemente del trabajo
y repercute jefe, suena subordinado;
que el diagrama del tiempo
es constante diorama en sus medallas
y, a medio abrir, sus ojos estudiaron,
desde lejanos tiempos,
su fórmula famélica de masa . . .

Comprendiendo sin esfuerzo
que el hombre se queda, a veces pensando,
como queriendo llorar,
y, sujeto a tenderse como objeto,
se hace buen carpintero, suda, mata
y luego canta, almuerza, se abotona . . .

Considerando también
que el hombre es en verdad un animal
y, no obstante, al voltear, me da con su tristeza en la cabeza . . .

Examinando, en fin,
sus encontradas piezas, su retrete,
su desesperación, al terminar su día atroz, borrándolo . . .

Comprendiendo
que él sabe que le quiero,
que le odio con afecto y me es, en suma, indiferente . . .

Considerando sus documentos generales
y mirando con lentes aquel certificado
que prueba que nació muy pequeñito . . .

le hago una seña,
viene,
y le doy un abrazo, emocionado.
¡Qué más da! Emocionado . . . Emocionado . . .

Considering coldly, impartially,
that man is sad, coughs and, nevertheless,
takes pleasure in his reddened chest;
that the only thing he does is to compose himself
with days;
that he is a gloomy mammal and combs his hair . . .   5

Considering
that man proceeds softly from work
and reverberates boss, sounds employee;
that the diagram of time
is a constant diorama on his medals   10
and, half-open, his eyes have studied,
since distant times,
his famished mass formula . . .

Understanding without effort   15
that man pauses, occasionally thinking,
as if he wanted to cry,
and, subject to lying down like an object,
becomes a good carpenter, sweats, kills
and then sings, eats lunch, buttons himself up . . .   20

Considering too
that man is truly an animal
and, nevertheless, upon turning, hits my head with his sadness . . .

Examining, finally,
his found parts, his toilet,   25
his desperation, upon finishing his atrocious day, erasing it . . .

Understanding
that he knows I love him,
that I hate him with affection and, in short, don't care about him . . .   *

Considering his general documents   30
and scrutinizing with pince-nez that certificate
that proves he was born very tiny . . .

I signal him,
he comes,
and I embrace him, moved.
So what! Moved . . . Moved . . .   35
                                                                 *

¡Y si después de tántas palabras,
no sobrevive la palabra!
¡Si después de las alas de los pájaros
no sobrevive el pájaro parado!
¡Más valdría, en verdad,
que so lo coman todo y acabemos!

¡Haber nacido para vivir de nuestra muerte!
¡Levantarse del cielo hacia la tierra
por sus propios desastres
y espiar el momento de apagar con su sombra su tiniebla!
¡Más valdría, francamente,
que se lo coman todo y qué más da! . . .

¡Y si después de tánta historia, sucumbimos,
no ya de eternidad,
sino de esas cosas sencillas, como estar
en la casa o ponerse a cavilar!
¡Y si luego encontramos,
de buenas a primeras, que vivimos,
a juzgar por la altura de los astros,
por el peine y las manchas del pañuelo!
¡Más valdría, en verdad,
que se lo coman todo, desde luego!

Se dirá que tenemos
en uno de los ojos mucha pena
y también en el otro, mucha pena
y en los dos, cuando miran, mucha pena . . .
¡Entonces! . . . ¡Claro! . . . Entonces . . . ¡ni palabra!

And if after so many words,
the word itself does not survive!
If after the wings of the birds,
the standing bird doesn't survive!
It would be much better, really,   5
for them to blow everything and that's it!   *

To have been born to live off our death!
To raise ourselves from the sky to the earth
through our own disasters, and to watch
for the moment to extinguish our darkness with our shadow!   10
It would be much better, frankly,
for them to blow everything, who cares! . . .

And if after so much history, we die,
no longer from eternity,
but from those simple things, like being   15
at home or starting to ponder!
And if then we discover,
all of a sudden, that we are living,
judging by the height of the stars,
off the comb and the stains of a handkerchief!   20
It would be much better, really,
for them to blow everything, obviously!

It will be said that we have
in one eye much sorrow
and also in the other, much sorrow   25
and in both, when they look, much sorrow . . .
Then! . . . Of course! . . . Then . . . not a word!

Por último, sin ese buen aroma sucesivo,
sin él,
sin su cuociente melancólico,
cierra su manto mi ventaja suave,
mis condiciones cierran sus cajitas.

¡Ay, cómo la sensación arruga tánto!
¡ay, cómo una idea fija me ha entrado en una uña!

Albino, áspero, abierto, con temblorosa hectárea,
mi deleite cae viernes,
mas mi triste tristumbre se compone de cólera y tristeza
y, a su borde arenoso e indoloro,
la sensación me arruga, me arrincona.

Ladrones de oro, víctimas de plata:
el oro que robara yo a mis víctimas,
            ¡rico de mí olvidándolo!
la plata que robara a mis ladrones,
            ¡pobre de mí olvidándolo!

Execrable sistema, clima en nombre del cielo, del bronquio y la quebrada,
la cantidad enorme de dinero que cuesta el ser pobre . . .

Finally, without that good continuous aroma,
without it,
without its melancholy quotient,
my soft advantage closes its cloak,
my conditions close their little boxes.   5

Ay, how much the sensation wrinkles!
Aie! how a fixed idea has gotten under one of my nails!

Albino, acerb, open, with a trembling hectare,
my delight falls Friday,
but my sad sadoomedness mixes anger and sadness   10*
and, at its painless and sandy edge,
the sensation wrinkles me, corners me.

Thieves of gold, victims of silver:
the gold I had stolen from my victims,
            how rich I am forgetting it!   15
the silver I had stolen from my thieves,
            how poor I am forgetting it!

Abominable system, climate in the name of heaven, of the bronchus and the gorge,
the incredible amount of money that it takes to be poor . . .

Parado en una piedra,
desocupado,
astroso, espeluznante,
a la orilla del Sena, va y viene.
Del río brota entonces la conciencia,
con peciolo y rasguños de árbol ávido;
del río sube y baja la ciudad, hecha de lobos abrazados.

El parado la ve yendo y viniendo,
monumental, llevando sus ayunos en la cabeza cóncava,
en el pecho sus piojos purísimos
y abajo
su pequeño sonido, el de su pelvis,
callado entre dos grandes decisiones,
y abajo,
más abajo,
un papelito, un clavo, una cerilla . . .

¡Este es, trabajadores, aquel
que en la labor sudaba para afuera,
que suda hoy para adentro su secreción de sangre rehusada!
Fundidor del cañón, que sabe cuantas zarpas son acero,
tejedor que conoce los hilos positivos de sus venas,
albañil de pirámides,
constructor de descensos por columnas
serenas, por fracasos triunfales,
parado individual entre treinta millones de parados,
andante en multitud,
¡qué salto el retratado en su talón
y qué humo el de su boca ayuna, y cómo
su talle incide, canto a canto, en su herramienta atroz, parada,
y qué idea de dolorosa válvula en su pómulo!

También parado el hierro frente al horno,
paradas las semillas con sus sumisas síntesis al aire,
parados los petróleos conexos,
parada en sus auténticos apóstrofes la luz,
parados de crecer los laureles,
paradas en un pie las aguas móviles
y hasta la tierra misma, parada de estupor ante este paro,
¡qué salto el retratado en sus tendones!
¡qué transmisión entablan sus cien pasos!
¡cómo chilla el motor en su tobillo!

Idle on a stone,
unemployed,
scroungy, hair-raising,
at the bank of the Seine, he comes and goes.
Conscience then sprouts from the river,   5
with the petiole and scratches of an avid tree;
from the river the city rises and lowers, made of embraced wolves.

The idle one sees it coming and going,
monumental, carrying his fasts in his concave head,
on his chest his purest lice   10
and below
his little sound, that of his pelvis,
silent between two big decisions,
and below,
further down,   15
a paperscrap, a nail, a match . . .   *

This is, workers, that man
who in his work used to sweat from inside out,
who today sweats his secretion of refused blood from outside in!   *
Cannon caster, who knows how many claws are steel,   20
weaver who knows the positive threads of his veins,
mason of pyramids,
builder of descents through serene
columns, through triumphant failures,
idle individual among thirty million idle,   25
wandering in a multitude,
what a leap the one portrayed in his heel
and what a smoke the one from his fasting mouth, and how
his waist penetrates, edge to edge, his atrocious tool, idle,
and what an idea of a painful valve in his cheekbone!   30

Likewise idle the iron before the furnace,
idle the seeds with their submissive synthesis in the air,
idle the connected petroleums,
idle the light in its authentic apostrophes,
idle without growth the laurels,   35
idle on one foot the mobile waters
and even the earth itself, idle from stupor before this lock-out,
what a leap the one portrayed in his tendons!
what a transmission his hundred steps start up!
how the motor in his ankle screeches!   40

¡cómo gruñe el reloj, paseándose impaciente a sus espaldas!
¡cómo oye deglutir a los patrones
el trago que le falta, camaradas,
y el pan que se equivoca de saliva,
y, oyéndolo, sintiéndolo, en plural, humanamente,
¡cómo clava el relánpago
su fuerza sin cabeza en su cabeza!
y lo que hacen, abajo, entonces, ¡ay!
¡más abajo, camaradas,
el papelucho, el clavo, la cerilla,
el pequeño sonido, el piojo padre!

how the clock grumbles, wandering impatiently in his back!
how he hears the owners gulp down
the shot that he lacks, comrades,
and the bread that gets into the wrong saliva,   *
and, hearing it, feeling it, in plural, humanly,   45
how the lightning nails   *
its headless force into his head!
and what they do, below, then, my god!   *
further down, comrades,
the dirtypaperscrap, the nail, the match,   50
the little sound, the stallion louse!   *

Los mineros salieron de la mina
remontando sus ruinas venideras,
fajaron su salud con estampidos
y, elaborando su función mental,
cerraron con sus voces
el socavón, en forma de síntoma profundo.

¡Era de ver sus polvos corrosivos!
¡Era de oir sus óxidos de altura!
Cuñas de boca, yunques de boca, aparatos de boca (Es formidable!)

El orden de sus túmulos,
sus inducciones plásticas, sus respuestas corales,
agolpáronse al pie de ígneos percances
y airente amarillura conocieron los trístidos, tristes,
imbuídos
del metal que se acaba, del metaloide pálido y pequeño.

Craneados de labor,
y calzados de cuero de vizcacha,
calzados de senderos infinitos,
y los ojos de físico llorar,
creadores de la profundidad,
saben, a cielo intermitente de escalera,
bajar mirando para arriba,
subir mirando para abajo

¡Loor al antiguo juego de su naturaleza,
a sus insomnes órganos, a su saliva rústica!
¡Temple, filo y punta, a sus pestañas!
¡Crezcan la yerba, el líquen y la rana en sus adverbios!
¡Felpa de hierro a sus nupciales sábanas!
¡Mujeres hasta abajo, sus mujeres!
Mucha felicidad para los suyos!
¡Son algo portentoso, los mineros
remontando sus ruinas venideras,
elaborando su función mental
y abriendo con sus voces
el socavón, en forma de síntoma profundo!
¡Loor a su naturaleza amarillenta,
a su linterna mágica,
a sus cubos y rombos, a sus percances plásticos,
a sus ojazos de seis nervios ópticos
y a sus hijos que juegan en la iglesia
y a sus tácitos padres infantiles!
¡Salud, oh creadores de la profundidad! . . . (Es formidable)

The miners came out of the mine   *
climbing over their future ruins,
they girdled their health with blasts
and, elaborating their mental function,
closed with their voices   5
the shaft, in the shape of a profound symptom.

What a sight their corrosive dusts!
To have heard their high oxides!
Mouth wedges, mouth anvils, mouth apparatus (Tremendous!)

The order of their tumuli,   10
their plastic inductions, their choral replies,
crowded at the base of fiery misfortunes
and aerent yellowing was known by the saddish, sad ones,   *
imbued
with the metal that exhausts itself, the pallid and small metaloid. 15

Craniated from labor,
and shod with viscacha hide,
shod with infinite paths,
and the eyes of physical crying,
creators of the profundity,   20*
they know, from the ladder's intermittent sky,
to climb down looking up,
they know to climb up looking down.   *

Praise for the ancient works of their nature
for their sleepless organs, for their rustic saliva!   25
Temper, edge and point, for their eyelashes!
May the grass, the lichen and the frog grow in their adverbs!
Iron plush for their nuptial sheets!
Women to the depths, their women!
Lots of happiness for their people!   30
They're something prodigious, those miners
climbing over their future ruins,
elaborating their mental function
and opening with their voices
the shaft, in the shape of a profound symptom!   35
Praise for their yellowish nature,
for their magic lantern,
for their cubes and rhombs, for their plastic misfortunes,
for their huge eyes with six optical nerves
and for their children who play in the church   40
and for their silent infantile fathers!
Hail, oh creators of the profundity! . . . (Tremendous)

Pero antes que se acabe
toda esta dicha, piérdela atajándola,
tómale la medida, por si rebasa tu ademán; rebásala,
ve si cabe tendida en tu extensión.

Bien la sé por su llave,
aunque no sepa, a veces, si esta dicha
anda sola, apoyada en tu infortunio
o tañida, por sólo darte gusto, en tus falanjas.
Bien la sé única, sola
de una sabiduría solitaria.

En tu oreja el cartílago está hermoso
y te escribo por eso, te medito:
no olvides en tu sueño de pensar que eres feliz,
que la dicha es un hecho profundo, cuando acaba,
pero al llegar asume
un caótico aroma de asta muerta.

Silbando a tu muerte,
sombrero a la pedrada,
blanco, ladeas a ganar tu batalla de escaleras,
soldado del tallo, filósofo del grano, mecánico del sueño.
(¿Me percibes, animal?
¿me dejo comparar como tamaño?
No respondes y callado me miras
a través de la edad de tu palabra.)

Ladeando así tu dicha, volverá
a clamarla tu lengua, a despedirla,
dicha tan desgraciada de durar.
Antes, se acabará violentamente,
dentada, pedernalina estampa,
y entonces oirás cómo medito
y entonces tocarás cómo tu sombra es ésta mía desvestida
y entonces olerás cómo he sufrido.

But before all this
happiness ends, lose it heading it off,
take its measure, in case it exceeds your gesture; exceed it,
see if it fits stretched in your extension.

I know it well by its key,   5
even if I don't know, at times, if this happiness
walks alone, leaned on your misfortune
or drummed, just to please you, on your phalanhes.   *
I know well it is unique, alone
with a solitary wisdom.   10

In your ear the cartilage looks beautiful
and so I write you, I meditate you:
don't forget in your dream to think that you are happy,
that happiness is a profound fact, when it ends,
but upon arriving it acquires   15
the chaotic odor of a dead horn.

Whistling at your death,   *
hat rakishly tilted,   *
white, you sway to win your battle of the stairs,   *
soldier of the stalk, philosopher of the grain, mechanic of the dream.   20
(Do you perceive me, animal?
do you find my size comparable to yours?
You do not answer and silent you look at me
across the age of your word.)

Swaying your happiness like this, your tongue   25
will again cry for it, will again dismiss it,
happiness too unfortunate to last.
Instead, it will end violently,
perforated, a flintified print,
and afterwards you will hear how I meditate   30
and afterwards you will touch how your shadow is my own undressed
and afterwards you will smell how I have suffered.

Telúrica y magnética

¡Mecánica sincera y peruanísima
la del cerro colorado!
¡Suelo teórico y práctico!
¡Surcos inteligentes; ejemplo: el monolito y su cortejo!
¡Papales, cebadales, alfalfares, cosa buena!
¡Cultivos que integra una asombrosa jerarquía de útiles
y que integran con viento los mujidos,
las aguas con su sorda antigüedad!

¡Cuaternarios maíces, de opuestos natalicios,
los oigo por los pies cómo se alejan,
los huelo retornar cuando la tierra
tropieza con la técnica del cielo!
¡Molécula exabrupto! Atomo terso!

¡Oh campos humanos!
¡Solar y nutricia ausencia de la mar,
y sentimiento oceánico de todo!
¡Oh climas encontrados dentro del oro, listos!
¡Oh campo intelectual de cordillera,
con religión, con campo, con patitos!
¡Paquidermos en prosa cuando pasan
y en verso cuando páranse!
¡Roedores que miran con sentimiento judicial en torno!
¡Oh patrióticos asnos de mi vida!
¡Vicuña, descendiente nacional y graciosa de mi mono!
¡Oh luz que dista apenas un espejo de la sombra,
que es vida con el punto y, con la línea, polvo
y que por eso acato, subiendo por la idea a mi osamenta!

¡Siega en época del dilatado molle,
del farol que colgaron de la sien
y del que descolgaron de la barreta espléndida!
¡Angeles de corral,
aves por un descuido de la cresta!
Cuya o cuy para comerlos fritos
con el bravo rocoto de los temples!
(¿Cóndores? ¡Me friegan los cóndores!)
Leños cristianos en gracia
al tronco feliz y al tallo competente!
¡Familia de los líquenes
especies en formación basáltica que yo
respeto

Telluric and magnetic *

Sincere and utterly Peruvian mechanics *
those of the reddish hill! *
Theoretical and practical soil!
Intelligent furrows; example: the monolith and its retinue!
Potato fields, barely fields, lucerne fields, a wonderful thing! 5
Cultivations which integrate an astonishing hierarchy of tools
and which integrate with wind the lowings,
the waters with their muffled antiquity!

Quaternary maizes, with opposite birthdays,
I hear through my feet how they move aside, 10
I smell them return when the earth
clashes with the sky's technique!
Abruptly molecule! Terse atom!

Oh human fields! *
Solar and nutritious absence of the sea, 15
and oceanic feeling for everything!
Oh climates found inside gold, ready!
Oh intellectual field of a cordillera,
with religion, with fields, with baby ducks!
Pachyderms in prose while passing 20
and in poetry while halting!
Rodents which look with judicial feeling all around!
Oh my life's patriotic asses!
Vicuña, national and graceful descendant of my ape!
Oh light which is hardly a mirror away from the shadow, 25
which is life with a period and, with a line, dust
and that is why I revere it, climbing through the idea to my skeleton!

Harvest in the time of the spacious pepper tree, *
of the lantern hung from a human temple
and of the one taken down from the magnificent little bar! 30*
Poultry-yard angels,
birds by a slip up of the crest!
Cavess or cavy to be eaten fried *
with the wild bird pepper of the temperings! *
(Condors? Fuck the condors!) 35*
Christian logs by the grace of
a happy trunk and a competent stalk!
Family of lichens,
species in basalt formation that I
respect 40

desde este modestísimo papel!
¡Cuatro operaciones, os sustraigo
para salvar al roble y hundirlo en buena ley!
¡Cuestas en infraganti!
¡Auquénidos llorosos, almas mías!
¡Sierra de mi Perú, Perú del mundo,
y Perú al pie del orbe; yo me adhiero!
¡Estrellas matutinas si os aromo
quemando hojas de coca en este cráneo,
y cenitales, si destapo,
de un solo sombrerazo, mis diez templos!
¡Brazo de siembra, bájate y a pie!
Lluvia a base del mediodía,
bajo el techo de tejas donde muerde
la infatigable altura
y la tórtola corta en tres su trino!
¡Rotación de tardes modernas
y finas madrugadas arqueológicas!
¡Indio después del hombre y antes de él!
¡Lo entiendo todo en dos flautas
y me doy a entender en una quena!
¡Y los demás, me las pelan! . . .

from this extremely modest paper!
Four operations, I dismiss you   *
to save the oak and to destroy it properly!
Slopes caught in the act!   *
Tearful auchenia, my own souls!   45*
Sierra of my Peru, Peru of the world,
and Peru at the base of the orb; I stick with you!
Morning stars if I aromatize you
burning coca leaves in this skull,
and zenithal ones, if I uncover,   50
in one hat doff, my ten temples!
Arm sowing, get down, and on foot!
Rain on the basis of noon,
under the tile roof where the indefatigable
altitude gnaws   55
and the turtle dove cuts her trill in three.
Rotation of modern afternoons
and delicate archaeological dawns.
Indian later than man and before him!
I understand all of it on two flutes   60
and I make myself understood on a quena!   *
As for the others, they can jerk me off! . . .   *

Piensan los viejos asnos

Ahora vestiríame
de músico por verle,
chocaría con su alma, sobándole el destino con mi mano,
le dejaría tranquilo, ya que es una alma a pausas,
en fin, le dejaría
posiblemente muerto sobre su cuerpo muerto.

Podría hoy dilatarse en este frío,
podría toser; le ví bostezar, duplicándose en mi oído
su aciago movimiento muscular.
Tal me refiero a un hombre, a su placa positiva
y, ¿por qué no? a su boldo ejecutante,
aquel horrible filamento lujoso;
a su bastón con puño de plata con perrito,
y a los niños
que él dijo eran sus fúnebres cuñados.

Por eso vestiríame hoy de músico,
chocaría con su alma que quedóse mirando a mi materia . . .

¡Mas ya nunca veréle afeitándose al pie de su mañana;
ya nunca, ya jamás, ya para qué!
¡Hay que ver! ¡Qué cosa cosa!
¡qué jamás de jamases su jamás!

Old asses thinking

I would dress up now
like a musician to see him,
I would collide with his soul, feeling up his destiny with my hand,
I would leave him at peace, since he is a soul at leisure,
in short, I would leave him   5
possibly dead on his dead body.

He could expand today in this cold,
could cough; I saw him yawn, duplicating in my ear
his ominous muscular movement.
So do I talk about a man, about his positive plate   10
and, why not? about his executive boldo,
that horrible luxurious filament;
about his silver headed cane with a little dog
and about his children
he referred to as his funereal brother-in-laws.   15

That is why I would dress up today like a musician,
I would collide with his soul that kept looking at my matter . . .

But never again will I see him shaving at the foot of his morning;
never again, not ever again, now—nothing!
What a wonder! What a thing thing!   20
what a never of nevers his never!

SERMON DE LA BARBARIE

(1936–1938)

SERMON ON BARBARISM

París, Octubre 1936

De todo esto yo soy el único que parte.
De este banco me voy, de mis calzones,
de mi gran situación, de mis acciones,
de mi número hendido parte a parte,
de todo esto yo soy el único que parte.

De los Campos Elíseos o al dar vuelta
la extraña callejuela de la Luna,
mi defunción se va, parte mi cuna,
y, rodeada de gente, sola, suelta,
mi semejanza humana dase vuelta
y despacha sus sombras una a una.

Y me alejo de todo, porque todo
se queda para hacer la coartada:
mi zapato, su ojal, también su lodo
y hasta el doblez del codo
de mi propia camisa abotonada.

Paris, October 1936

From all of this I am the only one who leaves.
From this bench I go away, from my pants,
from my great situation, from my actions,
from my number split side to side,
from all of this I am the only one who leaves.   5

From the Champs Elysées or as the strange
alley of the Moon makes a turn,
my death goes away, my cradle leaves,
and, surrounded by people, alone, cut loose,
my human resemblance turns around   10
and dispatches its shadows one by one.

And I move away from everything, since everything
remains to create my alibi:
my shoe, its eyelet, as well as its mud
and even the bend in the elbow   15
of my own buttoned shirt.

La rueda del hambriento

Por entre mis propios dientes salgo humeando,
dando voces, pujando,
bajándome los pantalones . . .
Váca ini estómago, váca mi yeyuno,
la miseria me saca por entre mis propios dientes,
cogido con un palito por el puño de la camisa.

Una piedra en que sentarme
¿no habrá ahora para mí?
Aun aquella piedra en que tropieza la mujer que ha dado a luz,
la madre del cordero, la causa, la raíz,
¿ésa no habrá ahora para mí?
¡Siquiera aquella otra,
que ha pasado agachándose por mi alma!
Siquiera
la calcárida o la mala (humilde océano)
o la que ya no sirve ni para ser tirada contra el hombre,
¡ésa dádmela ahora para mí!

Siquiera la que hallaren atravesada y sola en un insulto,
¡ésa dádmela ahora para mí!
Siquiera la torcida y coronada, en que resuena
solamente una vez el andar de las rectas conciencias,
o, al menos, esa otra, que arrojada en digna curva,
va a caer por sí misma,
en profesión de entraña verdadera,
¡ésa dádmela ahora para mí!

Un pedazo de pan, ¿tampoco habrá ahora para mí?
Ya no más he de ser lo que siempre he de ser,
pero dadme
una piedra en que sentarme,
pero dadme,
por favor, un pedazo de pan en que sentarme,
pero dadme
en español
algo, en fin, de beber, de comer, de vivir, de reposarse,
y después me iré . . .
Hallo una extraña forma, está muy rota
y sucia mi camisa
y ya no tengo nada, esto es horrendo.

The hungry man's wheel

From between my own teeth I come out smoking,
shouting, pushing,
pulling down my pants . . .
My stomach empties, my jejunum empties,
misery pulls me out between my own teeth,   5
caught in my shirt cuff by a little stick.

A stone to sit down on
will now be denied to me?
Not even that stone on which the woman trips who has given birth,
the mother of the lamb, the cause, the root,   10
that one will now be denied to me?
At least that other one,
that crouching has passed through my soul!
At least
the calcarid or the evil one (humble ocean)   15*
or the one no longer even worth throwing at man,
that one give it to me now!

At least the one they could have found lying across and alone in an insult,
that one give it to me now!
At least the twisted and crowned, on which echoes   20
only once the walk of moral rectitude,
or, at least, that other one, that flung in dignified curve,
will drop by itself,
acting as a true core,
that one give it to me now!   25

A piece of bread, that too denied to me?
Now I am resigned to be what I always have to be,
but give me
a stone to sit down on,
but give me,   30
please, a piece of bread to sit down on,
but give me
in Spanish
something, in short, to drink, to eat, to live by, to rest on,
and then I will go away . . .   35
I find a strange form, my shirt very torn
and filthy
and now I have nothing, this is hideous.

×
× ×

Calor, cansado voy con mi oro, a donde
acaba mi enemigo de quererme.
¡C'est Septembre attiédi, por ti, Febrero!
Es como si me hubieran puesto aretes.

París, y 4, y 5, y la ansiedad
colgada, en el calor, de mi hecho muerto.
¡C'est Paris, reine du monde!
Es como si se hubieran orinado.
Hojas amargas de mensual tamaño
y hojas del Luxemburgo polvorosas.
¡C'est l'été, por ti, invierno de alta pleura!
Es como si se hubieran dado vuelta.

Calor, París, otoño, ¡cuánto estío
en medio del calor y de la urbe!
¡C'est la vie, mort de la Mort!
Es como si contaran mis pisadas.

¡Es como si me hubieran puesto aretes!
¡Es como si se hubieran orinado!
¡Es como si te hubieras dado vuelta!
¡Es como si contaran mis pisadas!

4 Set. 1937

×
×   ×

Heat, tired I go with my gold, where
my enemy has just finished loving me.
C'est September attiédi, for you, February!   *
It is as if they had put earrings on me.

Paris, and 4, and 5, and the anxiety   5*
hanged, in the heat, from my dead fact.
C'est Paris, reine du monde!   *
It is as if they had urinated.
Bitter leaves of monthly size
and dusty leaves from the Luxembourg.
C'est l'été, for you, winter of high pleura!   10
It is as if they had turned around.   *

Heat, Paris, autumn, so much summer
in the midst of the heat and the city!
C'est la vie, mort de la Mort!   15*
It is as if they had counted my steps.

It is as if they had put earrings on me!
It is as if they had urinated!
It is as if you yourself had turned around!
It is as if they had counted my steps!   20

×
× ×

Un pilar soportando consuelos,
pilar otro,
pilar en duplicado, pilaroso
y como nieto de una puerta oscura.
Ruido perdido, el uno, oyendo, al borde del cansancio;
bebiendo, el otro, dos a dos, con asas.

¿Ignoro acaso el año de este día,
el odio de este amor, las tablas de esta frente?
¿Ignoro que esta tarde cuesta días?
¿Ignoro que jamás se dice "nunca," de rodillas?

Los pilares que ví me están oyendo;
otros pilares son, doses y nietos tristes de mi pierna.
¡Lo digo en cobre americano,
que le debe a la plata tánto fuego!

Consolado en terceras nupcias,
pálido, nacido,
voy a cerrar mi pila bautismal, esta vidriera,
este susto con tetas,
este dedo en capilla,
corazonmente unido a mi esqueleto.

6 Set. 1937

```
    ×
  ×   ×
```

One pillar holding up consolations,
another pillar,
a duplicate pillar, pillarous   *
and like the grandchild of a dark door.
Lost noise, the one, listening, at the edge of fatigue;   5
drinking, the other, two by two, with handles.

Don't I perhaps know the year of this day,
the hatred of this love, the planks of this forehead?
Don't I know that this afternoon costs days?
Don't I know that never does one say "never," on one's knees?   10

The pillars that I saw are listening to me;
other pillars are, twos and sad grandchildren of my leg.
I say it in American copper
which owes to silver so much fire!

Consoled by third marriages,   15
pallid, born,
I am going to close my baptismal font, this showcase,   *
this fright with tits,
this finger in deathrow,
heartly tied to my skeleton.   20*

×
×   ×

Al cavilar en la vida, al cavilar
despacio en el esfuerzo del torrente,
alivia, ofrece asiento el existir,
condena a muerte;
envuelto en trapos blancos cae,
cae planetariamente,
el clavo hervido en pesadumbre; ¡cae!
(Acritud oficial, la de mi izquierda;
viejo bolsillo, en sí considerada esta derecha.)

¡Todo está alegre, menos mi alegría
y todo, largo, menos mi candor,
mi incertidumbre!
A juzgar por la forma, no obstante, voy de frente,
cojeando antiguamente,
y olvido por mis lágrimas mis ojos (Muy interesante)
y subo hasta mis pies desde mi estrella.

Tejo; de haber hilado, héme tejiendo.
Busco lo que me sigue y se me esconde entre arzobispos,
por debajo de mi alma y tras del humo de mi aliento.
Tal era la sensual desolación
de la cabra doncella que ascendía,
exhalando petróleos fatídicos,
ayer domingo en que perdí mi sábado.

Tal es la muerte, con su audaz marido.

7 Set. 1937

×
× ×

Upon reflecting on life, upon reflecting   *
slowly on the effort of the torrent,
existence feels better, settles us,
condemns to death;
wrapped in white rags it falls,   5
falls planetarily,
the nail boiled in grief; falls!
(Official bitterness, that of my left;
old pocket, in itself considered this right.)

Everything is joyful, except my joy   10
and everything, long, except my candor,
my incertitude!
To judge by the form, nevertheless, I go forward,
anciently limping,
and forget through my tears my eyes (Very interesting)   15
and climb to my feet from my star.

I weave; from having spun, I am weaving.
I search for what follows me and hides from me among archbishops,
under my soul and behind the smoke of my breathing.
Such was the sensual desolation   20
of the maiden goat that ascended
exhaling lethal petroleums,
yesterday Sunday on which I lost my Saturday.

Such is death, with her daring husband.

Poema para ser leído y cantado

Sé que hay una persona
que me busca en su mano, día y noche,
encontrándome, a cada minuto, en su calzado.
¿Ignora que la noche está enterrada
con espuelas detrás de la cocina?

Sé que hay una persona compuesta de mis partes,
a la que integro cuando va mi talle
cabalgando en su exacta piedrecilla.
¿Ignora que a su cofre
no volverá moneda que salió con su retrato?

Sé el día,
pero el sol se me ha escapado;
sé el acto universal que hizo en su cama
con ajeno valor y esa agua tibia, cuya
superficial frecuencia es una mina.
¿Tan pequeña es, acaso, esa persona,
que hasta sus propios pies así la pisan?

Un gato es el lindero entre ella y yo,
al lado mismo de su tasa de agua.
La veo en las esquinas, se abre y cierra
su veste, antes palmera interrogante . . .
¿Qué podrá hacer sino cambiar de llanto?

Pero me busca y busca. ¡Es una historia!

7 Set. 1937

Poem to be read and sung

I know there is a person   *
who looks for me in her hand, day and night,
finding me, every minute, in her shoes.
Doesn't she know that the night is buried
with spurs behind the kitchen?   5

I know there is a person made up of my parts,
who I make whole when my waist
goes galloping off on its exact little stone.
Doesn't she know that the coin
imprinted with her effigy will not return to her coffer?   10

I know the day,
but the sun has escaped me;
I know the universal act she performed on her bed
with alien courage and that tepid water, whose
superficial frequency is a gold mine.   15
Is that person, perhaps, so small
that even her own feet step on her?

A cat is the boundary between her and me,
right at the edge of her measure of water.   *
I see her on the corners, her clothing   20
opens and closes, formerly an inquiring palm tree . . .
What can she do but change crying?

But she looks and looks for me. What a story!

El acento me pende del zapato;
le oigo perfectamente
sucumbir, lucir, doblarse en forma de ámbar
y colgar, colorante, mala sombra.
Me sobra así el tamaño,
me ven jueces desde un árbol,
me ven con sus espaldas ir de frente,
entrar a mi martillo,
pararme a ver a una niña
y, al pie de un urinario, alzar los hombros.

Seguramente nadie está a mi lado,
me importa poco, no lo necesito;
seguramente han dicho que me vaya:
lo siento claramente.

¡Cruelísimo tamaño el de rezar!
¡Humillación, fulgor, profunda selva¡
Me sobra ya tamaño, bruma elástica,
rapidez por encima y desde y junto.
¡Imperturbable! ¡Imperturbable! Suenan
luego, después, fatídicos teléfonos.
Es el acento; es él.

12 Set. 1937

The accent dangles from my shoe;
I hear it succumb
perfectly, shine, fold in the shape of amber
and hang, coloring, an evil shade.
Thus my size exceeds me,   5
judges see me from a tree,
they see me with their backs walk forward,
enter my hammer,
stop to look at a girl
and, standing at a urinal, raise my shoulders.   10

Surely no one is with me,
I don't mind, I don't need anyone;
surely they have told me to go:
I feel it clearly.

Cruelest size that of prayer!   15
Humiliation, fulgor, profound forest!
My size already exceeds me, elastic mist,
rapidity superficially and since and close by.
Imperturbable! Imperturbable! Vatic
phones ring immediately, later.   20
It's the accent; it's it.

La punta del hombre,
el ludibrio pequeño de encojerse
tras de fumar su universal ceniza;
punta al darse en secretos caracoles,
punta donde se agarra uno con guantes,
punta el lunes sujeto por seis frenos,
punta saliendo de escuchar a su alma.

De otra manera,
fueran lluvia menuda los soldados
y ni cuadrada pólvora, al volver de los bravos desatinos,
y ni letales plátanos; tan sólo
un poco de patilla en la silueta.
De otra manera, caminantes suegros,
cuñados en misión sonora,
yernos por la vía ingratísima del jebe,
toda la gracia caballar andando
puede fulgir esplendorosamente!

¡Oh pensar geométrico al trasluz!
¡Oh no morir bajamente
de majestad tan rauda y tan fragante!
¡Oh no cantar; apenas
escribir y escribir con un palito
o con el filo de la oreja inquieta!

Acorde de lápiz, tímpano sordísimo,
dondoneo en mitades robustas
y comer de memoria buena carne,
jamón, si falta carne,
y un pedazo de queso con gusanos hembras,
gusanos machos y gusanos muertos.

14 Set. 1937

The tip of man,
the petty mockery of shrinking
after smoking its universal ash;
tip on yielding in secret snails,
tip where one grabs with gloves on,   5
tip Monday restrained with six bridles,
tip emerging from listening to its soul.

On the other hand,
the soldiers could have been a fine rain
and neither square gunpowder, upon returning from their brave follies,   10
nor deadly bananas; only
a bit of sideburn on the silhouette.
On the other hand, walking fathers-in-law,
brothers-in-law on a sonorous mission,
sons-in-law by the most ungrateful path of rubber,   15
all the equine grace marching
can flash resplendently!

Oh to think geometrically against the light!
Oh not to die lowly
of such swift and such fragrant majesty!   20
Oh not to sing; to barely
write and to write with a little stick
or with the edge of a restless ear!

Pencil chord, deafest eardrum,
zazhay in robust halves   25*
and to eat by heart choice meat,
ham, if there is no meat,
and a piece of cheese with female worms,
male worms and dead worms.

×
× ×

¡Oh botella sin vino! ¡oh vino que enviudó de esta botella!
Tarde cuando la aurora de la tarde
flameó funestamente en cinco espíritus.
Viudez sin pan ni mugre, rematando en horrendos metaloides
y en células orales acabando.

¡Oh siempre, nunca dar con el jamás de tánto siempre!
¡oh mis buenos amigos, cruel falacia,
parcial, penetratativa en nuestro trunco,
volátil, jugarino desconsuelo!

¡Sublime, baja perfección del cerdo,
palpa mi general melancolía!
¡Zuela sonante en sueños,
zuela
zafia, inferior, vendida, lícita, ladrona,
baja y palpa lo que eran mis ideas!

Tú y él y ellos y todos,
sin embargo,
entraron a la vez en mi camisa,
en los hombros madera, entre los fémures, palillos;
tú particularmente,
habiéndome influído;
él, fútil, colorado, con dinero
y ellos, zánganos de ala de otro peso.

¡Oh botella sin vino! ¡oh vino que enviudó de esta botella!

16 Set. 1937

<pre>
       ×
    ×   ×
</pre>

Oh bottle without wine! oh wine the widower of this bottle!
Afternoon when the dawn of the afternoon
flamed ominously in five spirits.
Widowhood without bread or filth, finishing as hideous metalloids
and ending as oral cells.   5

Oh always, never to find the never of so much always!
oh my good friends, cruel deceit,
partial, cutting into our truncated,
volatile, frolicful grief!   *

Sublime, low perfection of the pig,   10
gropes my general melancholy!
An adze sounding in dreams,
an adze
crude, inferior, sold out, just, thief,
comes down and gropes what used to be my ideas!   15

You and he and they and everyone,
nevertheless,
inserted at the same time into my shirt,
into my shoulders wood, between my femurs, little sticks;
you particularly,   20
having influenced me;
he, futile, reddish, with money
and they, winged drones of another weight.   *

Oh bottle without wine! oh wine the widower of this bottle!

×
× ×

Va corriendo, andando, huyendo
de sus pies . . .
Va con dos nubes en su nube,
sentado apócrifo, en la mano insertos
sus tristes paras, sus entonces fúnebres.

Corre de todo, andando
entre protestas incoloras; huye
subiendo, huye
bajando, huye
a paso de sotana, huye
alzando al mal en brazos, huye
directamente a sollozar a solas.

Adonde vaya,
lejos de sus fragosos, cáusticos talones,
lejos del aire, lejos de su viaje,
a fin de huir, huir y huir y huir
de sus pies—hombre en dos pies, parado
de tánto huir—habrá sed de correr.

¡Y ni el árbol, si endosa hierro de oro!
¡Y ni el hierro, si cubre su hojarasca!
Nada, sino sus pies,
nada sino su breve calofrío,
sus paras vivos, sus entonces vivos . . .

18 Set. 1937

×
× ×

He is running, walking, fleeing
from his feet . . .
He moves with two clouds on his cloud,
apocryphally seated, his sad fors,
his funereal thens, inserted in his hand.   5

He runs from everything, walking
between colorless protests; he flees
going up, flees
going down, flees
at a cassock pace, flees   10
lifting evil up in his arms, flees   *
directly to sob alone.

Wherever he goes,
far from his brambly, caustic heels,
far from the air, far from his journey,   15
in order to flee, to flee and to flee and to flee
from his feet—man on both feet, standing
from so much flight—will have a thirst for running.

And neither the tree, if it endorses iron of gold!
Nor iron, if it covers its dead foliage!
Nothing, but his feet,
nothing but his brief chill,
his fors alive, his thens alive . . .

Al fin, un monte
detrás de la bajura: al fin, humeante nimbo
alrededor, durante un rostro fijo.

Monte en honor del pozo,
sobre filones de gratuita plata de oro.

Es la franja a que arrástranse,
seguras de sus tonos de verano,
las que eran largas válvulas difuntas;
el taciturno marco de este arranque
natural, de este augusto zapatazo,
de esta piel, de este intrínseco destello
digital, en que estoy entero, lúbrico.

Quehaceres en un pie, mecha de azufre,
oro de plata y plata hecha de plata
y mi muerte, mi hondura, mi colina.

¡Pasar
abrazado a mis brazos,
destaparme después o antes del corcho!
Monte que tántas veces manara
oración, prosa fluvial de llanas lágrimas;
monte bajo, compuesto de suplicantes gradas
y, más allá, de torrenciales torres;
niebla entre el día y el alcohol del día,
caro verdor de coles, tibios asnos
complementarios, palos y maderas;
filones de gratuita plata de oro.

19 Set. 1937

At last, a hill
behind the lowness: at last, a smoking halo
around, during a fixed face.

Hill in honor of the well,
over veins of gratuitous silver of gold.   5

It is the fringe toward which drag,
sure of their summer tones,
those which were long defunct valves;
the taciturn frame of this natural
start, of this august shoesmack,   10
of this skin, of this intrinsic digital
gleam, in which I am whole, lubricious.

Chores on one foot, fuse of silver,
gold of silver and silver made of silver
and my death, my depth, my knoll.   15

To pass
embraced in my arms,
to open myself up after or before the cork!
Hill that so often flowed
prayer, fluvial prose of plain tears;   20
low hill, of supplicant steps formed
and, beyond, of torrential towers;
fog between the day and the alcohol of the day,
dear verdure of cabbages, tepid
complementary asses, sticks and timber;   25
veins of gratuitous silver of gold.

Quiere y no quiere su color mi pecho,
por cuyas bruscas vías voy, lloro con palo,
trato de ser feliz, lloro en mi mano,
recuerdo, escribo
y remacho una lágrima en mi pómulo.

Quiere su rojo el mal, el bien su rojo enrojecido
por el hacha suspensa,
por el trote del ala a pie volando,
y no quiere y sensiblemente
no quiere aquesto el hombre;
no quiere estar en su alma
acostado, en la sien latidos de asta,
el bimano, el muy bruto, el muy filósofo.

Así, casi no soy, me vengo abajo
desde el arado en que socorro a mi alma
y casi, en proporción, casi enaltézcome.
Que saber por qué tiene la vida este perrazo
por qué lloro, por qué,
cejón, inhábil, veleidoso, hube nacido
gritando;
saberlo, comprenderlo
al son de un alfabeto competente,
sería padecer por un ingrato.

¡Y no! ¡No! ¡No! ¡Qué ardid, ni paramento!
Congoja, sí, con sí firme y frenético
coriáceo, rapaz, quiere y no quiere, cielo y pájaro;
congoja, sí, con toda la bragueta.
Contienda entre dos llantos, robo de una sola ventura,
vía indolora en que padezco en chanclos
de la velocidad de andar a ciegas.

22 Set. 1937

My chest wants and does not want its color,
through whose rough paths I am going, I cry with stick,
I try to be happy, I cry in my hand,
I remember, I write
and rivet a tear into my cheekbone.   5

Evil wants its red, good its redness reddened
by the suspended ax,
by the trot of the wing flying on foot,
and man does not want, sensitively
does not want this;   10
he does not want to be lying down
in his soul, with horn throbs in his temples,
the bimanous one, the extreme brute, the extreme philosopher.

Thus, almost I am not, I fall down
from the plow on which I help my soul   15
and almost, in proportion, I almost exalt myself.
To know why life is such an utter bitch   *
why I cry, why,
browbig, unfit, fickle, I was born   *
shouting;   20
to know this, to comprehend it
to the sound of a competent alphabet
would be to suffer for an ingrate.

And no! No! No! Neither trick, nor ornament!
Anguish, yes, with a firm and frenetic yes,   25
coriaceous, rapacious, want and no want, sky and bird;
anguish, yes, with all my pants' fly.   *
Struggle between two cries, theft of a single chance,
painless path on which I endure in clogs
the velocity of walking around blindly.   30

×
×   ×

Esto
sucedió entre dos párpados; temblé
en mi vaina, colérico, alcalino,
parado junto al lúbrico equinoccio,
al pie del frío incendio en que me acabo.

Resbalón alcalino, voy diciendo,
más acá de los ajos, sobre el sentido almíbar,
más adentro, muy más, de las herrumbres,
al ir el agua y al volver la ola.
Resbalón alcalino
también y grandemente, en el montaje colosal del cielo.

¡Qué venablos y arpones lanzaré, si muero
en mi vayna; daré en hojas de plátano sagrado
mis cinco huesecillos subalternos,
y en la mirada, la mirada misma!
(Dicen que en los suspiros se edifican
entonces acordeones óseos, táctiles;
dicen que cuando mueren así los que se acaban,
¡ay! mueren fuera del reloj, la mano
agarrada a un zapato solitario.)

Comprendiéndolo y todo, coronel
y todo, en el sentido llorante de esta voz,
me hago doler yo mismo, extraigo tristemente,
por la noche mis uñas;
luego no tengo nada y hablo solo,
reviso mis semestres
y para henchir mi vértebra, me toco.

23 Set. 1937

×
× ×

This   *
happened between two eyelids; I shook
in my scabbard, choleric, alkaline,
standing by the lubricious equinox,
at the foot of the cold blaze in which I perish.   5

Alkaline slip, I keep saying,
this side of the garlic cloves, over the felt syrup,
deeper in, much deeper, than the rusts,
when the water goes and the wave comes.
Alkaline slip   10
too and greatly, in the colossal staging of the sky.   *

  What darts and harpoons I will hurl, if I die
in my skabbard; in sacred banana leaves I will give away   *
my five subordinate little bones,
and in the look, the look itself!   15
(It is said that in sighs one builds   *
then bony tactile accordions;
it is said that when those who perish die this way,
aie! they die outside the clock, the hand
clutched to a solitary shoe.)   20

  In spite of understanding it and all, cyma
and all, in the crying meaning of this word,
I make myself suffer, I extract sadly,
at night, my fingernails;
then I have nothing and talk to myself,   25
I revise my half-years   *
and in order to fill up my vertebra, touch myself.

×
×   ×

Quedéme a calentar la tinta en que me ahogo
y a escuchar me caverna alternativa,
noches de tacto, días de abstracción.

Se estremeció la incógnita en mi amígdala
y crují de una anual melancolía,
noches de sol, días de luna, ocasos de París.

Y todavía, hoy mismo, al atardecer,
digiero sacratísimas constancias,
noches de madre, días de biznieta
bicolor, voluptuosa, urgente, linda.

Y aun
alcanzo, llego hasta mí en avión de dos asientos,
bajo la mañana doméstica y la bruma
que emergió eternamente de un instante.

Y todavía
aun ahora,
al cabo del cometa en que he ganado
mi bacilo feliz y doctoral,
he aquí que caliente, oyente, tierro, sol y luno,
incógnito atravieso el cementerio,
tomo a la izquierda, hiendo
la yerba con un par de endecasílabos,
años de tumba, litros de infinito,
tinta, pluma, ladrillos y perdones.

24 Set. 1937

Clapping and guitar

Now, between ourselves, right here,
come with me, bring your body by the hand
and let's dine together and spend our life for a moment
in two lives, giving a part to our death.
Now, come with yourself, do me the favor   5
of complaining in my name and by the light of the teneblous night   *
in which you bring your soul by the hand
and we flee on tiptoes from ourselves.

Come to me, yes, and to you, yes,
in even step, to see the two of us out of step,
stepping in place to farewell.   10
Until we return! I'll see you then!
Until we read, ignoramuses!
Until we return, let's say goodbye!

What are the rifles to me,   15
listen to me;
listen to me, what's it to me
if the bullet is already circulating in my signature's rank?
What are the bullets to you,
if the rifle is already smoking in your odor?   20
This very day we will weigh
in the arms of a blindman our star
and, once you sing to me, we will cry.
This very day, beautiful woman, with your even step
and your trust reached by my alarm,   25
we will come out of ourselves, two by two.
Until we both become blind!
Until
we cry from so *much* returning!

Now,   30
between ourselves, bring
your sweet person by the hand
and let's dine together and spend our life for a moment
in two lives, giving a part to our death.
Now, come with yourself, do me the favor   35
of singing something
and playing on your soul, clapping hands.
Until we return! Until then!
Until we part, let's say goodbye!

El alma que sufrió de ser su cuerpo

Tu sufres de una glándula endocrínica, se ve,
o, quizá,
sufres de mí, de mi sagacidad escueta, tácita.
Tú padeces del diáfano antropoide, allá, cerca,
donde está la tiniebla tenebrosa.
Tú das la vuelta al sol, agarrándote el alma,
extendiendo tus juanes corporales
y ajustándote el cuello; eso se ve.
Tú sabes lo que te duele,
lo que te salta al anca,
lo que baja por ti con soga al suelo.
Tú, pobre hombre, vives; no lo niegues,
si mueres; no lo niegues,
si mueres de tu edad! ¡ay! y de tu época.
Y, aunque llores, bebes,
y, aunque sangres, alimentas a tu híbrido colmillo,
a tu vela tristona y a tus partes.
Tú sufres, tú padeces y tú vuelves a sufrir horriblemente,
desgraciado mono,
jovencito de Darwin,
alguacil que me atisbas, atrocísimo microbio.
Y tú lo sabes a tal punto,
que lo ignoras, soltándote a llorar.
Tú, luego, has nacido; eso
también se ve de lejos, infeliz y cállate,
y soportas la calle que te dió la suerte
a tu ombligo interrogas: ¿dónde? ¿cómo?

Amigo mío, estás completamente,
hasta el pelo, en el año treinta y ocho,
nicolás o santiago, tal o cual,
estés contigo o con tu aborto o con-
migo
y cautivo en tu enorme libertad,
arrastrado por tu hércules autónomo . . .
Pero si tú calculas en tus dedos hasta dos,
es peor; no lo niegues, hermanito.

¿Que nó? ¿Que sí, pero que nó?
¡Pobre mono! . . . ¡Dame la pata! . . . No. La mano, he dicho.
¡Salud! ¡Y sufre!

8 Nov. 1937

The soul that suffered from being its body

You suffer from an endocrine gland, it's obvious,
or, perhaps,
you suffer from me, from my tacit, stark sagacity.
You endure the diaphanous anthropoid, over there, nearby,   *
where the tenebrous darkness is.   5
You revolve around the sun, grabbing on to your soul,
extending your corporal juans   *
and adjusting your collar; that's obvious.
You know what aches you,
what leaps on your rump,   10
what descends through you by rope to the ground.
You, poor man, you live; don't deny it,
if you die; don't deny it,
if you die from your age! ah! and from your epoch.
And, even if you cry, you drink,   15
and, even if you bleed, you nourish your hybrid eyetooth,
your wistful candle and your private parts.
You suffer, you endure and again you suffer horribly,
miserable ape,   *
Darwin's little man,   20
bailiff prying on me, most atrocious microbe.
And you know this so well,
that you ignore it, bursting into tears.
You, then, were born; that
too is obvious at a distance, poor devil and shut up,   25
and you put up with the street that luck gave you
you question your navel: where? how?   *

My friend, you are completely,
up to your hair, in the 38th year,
nicolas or santiago, this one or that one,   30
either with yourself or with your abortion or with
me
and captive in your enormous liberty,
dragged on by your autonomous hercules . . .
But if you calculate on your fingers up to two,   35
it's worse; don't deny it, pal.

Why *no*? Why yes, but why *no*?
Poor ape! . . . Gimme your paw! . . . No. The hand, I meant.
To your health! Keep suffering!

Yuntas

Completamente. Además, ¡vida!
Completamente. Además, ¡muerte!

Completamente. Además, ¡todo!
Completamente. Además, ¡nada!

Completamente. Además, ¡mundo!
Completamente. Además, ¡polvo!

Completamente. Además, ¡Dios!
Completamente. Además, ¡nadie!

Completamente. Además, ¡nunca!
Completamente. Además, ¡siempre!

Completamente. Además, ¡oro!
Completamente. Además, ¡humo!

Completamente. Además, ¡lágrimas!
Completamente. Además, ¡risas! . . .

Completamente!

9 Nov. 1937

Couplings

Completely. Furthermore, life!
Completely. Furthermore, death!

Completely. Furthermore, everything!
Completely. Furthermore, nothing!

Completely. Furthermore, world!   5
Completely. Furthermore, dust!

Completely. Furthermore, God!
Completely. Furthermore, no one!

Completely. Furthermore, never!
Completely. Furthermore, always!   10

Completely. Furthermore, gold!
Completely. Furthermore, smoke!

Completely. Furthermore, tears!
Completely. Furthermore, laughs! . . .

Completely!   15

×
× ×

Acaba de pasar el que vendrá
proscrito, a sentarse en mi triple desarrollo;
acaba de pasar criminalmente.

Acaba de sentarse más acá,
a un cuerpo de distancia de mi alma,
el que vino en un asno a enflaquecerme;
acaba de sentarse de pie, lívido.

Acaba de darme lo que está acabado,
el calor del fuego y el pronombre inmenso
que el animal crió bajo su cola.

Acaba
de expresarme su duda sobre hipótesis lejanas
que él aleja, aún más, con la mirada.

Acaba de hacer al bien los honores que le tocan
en virtud del infame paquidermo,
por lo soñado en mí y en él matado.

Acaba de ponerme (no hay primera)
su segunda aflixión en plenos lomos
y su tercer sudor en plena lágrima.

Acaba de pasar sin haber venido.

12 Nov. 1937

×
× ×

He has just passed by, the one who will come
banished, to sit down on my triple unfolding;
he has just passed by criminally.

He has just sat down nearer,
a body away from my soul,   5
the one who came on an ass to make me gaunt;
he has just sat down standing up, livid.

He has just given me what is finished,
the heat of fire and the immense pronoun
that the animal reared under its tail.   10

He has just
expressed his doubts about remote hypotheses
which he distances, even further, with his gaze.

He has just bestowed on the good its rightful honors
by virtue of the infamous pachyderm,   15
through what is dreamed in me and in him killed.

He has just fixed (there is no first)
his second aflixion right in my shoulders   *
and his third sweat right in my tear.

He has just passed by without having come.   20*

×
×   ×

¡Ande desnudo, en pelo, el millonario!
¡Desgracia al que edifica con tesoros su lecho de muerte!
¡Un mundo al que saluda;
un sillón al que siembra en el cielo;
llanto al que da término a lo que hace, guardando los comienzos;
ande el de las espuelas;
poco dure muralla en que no crezca otra muralla;
dése al mísero toda su miseria,
pan, al que ríe;
hayan perder los triunfos y morir los médicos;
haya leche en la sangre;
añádase una vela al sol,
ochocientos al veinte;
pase la eternidad bajo los puentes!
¡Desdén al que viste,
corónense los pies de manos, quepan en su tamaño;
siéntese mi persona junto a mí!
¡Llorar al haber cabido en aquel vientre,
bendición al que mira aire en el aire,
muchos años de clavo al martillazo;
desnúdese el desnudo,
vístase de pantalón la capa,
fulja el cobre a expensas de sus láminas,
magestad al que cae de la arcilla al universo,
lloren las bocas, giman las miradas,
impídase al acero perdurar,
hilo a los horizontes portátiles,
doce ciudades al sendero de piedra,
una esfera al que juega con su sombra;
un día hecho de una hora, a los esposos;
una madre al arado en loor al suelo,
séllense con dos sellos a los líquidos,
pase lista el bocado,
sean los descendientes,
sea la codorniz,
sea la carrera del álamo y del árbol;
venzan, al contrario del círculo, el mar a su hijo
y a la cana el lloro;
dejad los áspides, señores hombres,
surcad la llama con los siete leños,
vivid,
elévese la altura,
baje el hondor más hondo,
conduzca la onda su impulsión andando,
tenga éxito la tregua de la bóveda!

×
×   ×

Let the millionaire go naked, stark naked!   *
Disgrace for whoever builds his death bed with treasures!
A world for whoever greets;
an armchair for whoever sows in the sky;
tears for whoever finishes what he does, keeping the beginnings;   5
let the spur-wearer walk;
let the wall crumble on which another wall is not growing;
let the miserable man have all his misery,
bread, for whoever laughs;
let the triumphs lose and the doctors die;   10
let milk be in our blood;
let a candle be added to the sun,
eight hundred to twenty;
let eternity pass under the bridges!
Scorn for whoever puts on clothes,   15
let our feet be crowned with hands, be fit in their size;
let my person sit next to me!
To cry having fit in that womb,
grace for whoever sees air in the air,
many years of nail for the hammer stroke;   20
let the naked man be stripped naked,
let the cape put on pants,
let the copper gleam at the expense of its plates,
magesty for whoever falls from the clay to the universe,   *
let the mouths weep, let the glances groan,   25
let us stop the steel from enduring,
thread for the portable horizons,
twelve cities for the stone path,
a sphere for whoever plays with his shadow;
a day made of an hour, for married people;   30
a mother at the plow in praise of the soil,
let the liquids be sealed with two seals,
let the mouthful call the roll,
let the descendants be,
let the quail be,   35
let the poplar and the tree have their race;
let the sea, contrary to the circle, defeat his son
and the crying, grey hair;
leave the asps alone, gentle sirs,
furrow your flame with the seven logs,   40
live,
let the height be raised,
let the deepness descend deeper,   *
let the wave drive its impulse walking,
let the vault's truce be a success!   45

¡Muramos;
lavad vuestro esqueleto cada día;
no me hagáis caso,
una ave coja al déspota y a su alma;
una mancha espantosa, al que va solo;
gorriones al astrónomo, al gorrión, al aviador!
¡Lloved, solead,
vigilad a Júpiter, al ladrón de ídolos de oro,
copiad vuestra letra en tres cuadernos,
aprended de los cónyuges cuando hablan, y
de los solitarios, cuando callan;
dad de comer a los novios,
dad de beber al diablo en vuestras manos,
luchad por la justicia con la nuca,
igualaos,
cúmplase el roble,
cúmplase el leopardo entre dos robles,
seamos,
estémos,
sentid cómo navega el agua en los océanos,
alimentaos,
concíbase el error, puesto que lloro,
acéptese, en tanto suban por el risco, las cabras y sus crías;
desacostumbrad a Dios a ser un hombre,
creced . . . !
Me llaman. Vuelvo.

19 Nov. 1937

Let us die;
wash your skeleton every day;
pay no attention to me,
let a bird grasp the despot and his soul;
an awful stain, for whoever walks around alone;   50
sparrows for the astronomer, for the sparrow, an aviator!
Give off rain, give off sun,
keep an eye on Jupiter, on the thief of your gold idols,
copy your hand-writing in three notebooks,
learn from the couples when they speak, and   55
from the lonely, when they are silent;
give food to the sweethearts,
give drink to the devil from your hands,
fight for justice with your nape,
make yourselves equal,   60
let the oak be fulfilled,
let the leopard be fulfilled between two oaks,
let us be,
let us be here,
let us feel how the water sails in the oceans,   65
take nourishment,
let the error be conceived, since I am crying,
accept it, while goats and their young climb along the cliff;
make God break the habit of being a man,
grow up . . . !   70
I am called. I am going back.

×
× ×

Viniere el malo, con un trono al hombro,
y el bueno, a acompañar al malo a andar;
dijeren "sí" el sermón, "no" la plegaria
y cortare el camino en dos la roca . . .

Comenzare por monte la montaña,
por remo el tallo, por timón el cedro
y esperaren doscientos a sesenta
y volviere la carne a sus tres títulos . . .

Sobrase nieve en la noción del fuego,
se acostare el cadáver a mirarnos,
la centella a ser trueno corpulento
y se arquearen los saurios a ser aves . . .

Faltare excavación junto al estiércol,
naufragio al río para resbalar,
cárcel al hombre libre, para serlo
y una atmósfera al cielo, y hierro al oro . . .

Mostraren disciplina, olor, las fieras,
se pintare el enojo de soldado,
me dolieren el junco que aprendí,
la mentira que inféctame y socórreme . . .

Sucediere ello así y así poniéndolo,
¿con qué mano despertar?
¿con qué pie morir?
¿con qué ser pobre?
¿con qué voz callar?
¿con cuánto comprender, y luego, a quién?

No olvidar ni recordar
que por mucho cerrarla, robáronse la puerta,
y de sufrir tan poco estoy muy resentido,
y de tánto pensar, no tengo boca.

19 Nov. 1937

×
×   ×

That the evil man might come, with a throne on his shoulder,   *
and the good man, to walk with the evil man for company;
that the sermon might say "yes," the prayer "no"
and that the path might cut the rock in two . . .

That the mountain might begin as a hill,   5
the stalk as an oar, the cedar as a tiller
and that two hundred might wait for sixty
and that the flesh might return to its three titles . . .

That there might be too much snow in the notion of fire,   *
that the corpse might lay down to watch us,   10
the flash might be corpulent thunder
and that the saurians might arch to become birds . . .

That the dung might lack an excavation nearby,   *
the river a shipwreck so to slide,
the free man a jail, so to be free   15
and the sky an atmosphere, and gold iron . . .   *

That wild beasts might show discipline, odor,
that anger might disguise itself as a soldier,
that the reed I learned might ache me,
the lie that infects and helps me . . .   20

That it might happen this way and thus stating it,
with what hand to awake?
with what foot to die?
with what to be poor?   *
with what voice to keep quiet?   25
with how much to understand, and then, whom?

Not to forget nor to remember
that from closing it too often, they stole the door,
and from suffering so little I am very resentful,
and from so *much* thinking, I have no mouth.   30*

×
×　×

Al revés de las aves del monte,
que viven del valle,
aquí, una tarde,
aquí, presa, metaloso, terminante,
vino el Sincero con sus nietos pérfidos,
y nosotros quedámonos, que no hay
más madera en la cruz de la derecha,
ni más hierro en el clavo de la izquierda,
que un apretón de manos entre zurdos.

　　Vino el Sincero, ciego, con sus lámparas.
Se vió al Pálido, aquí, bastar
al Encarnado;
nació de puro humilde el Grande;
la guerra,
esta tórtola mía, nunca nuestra,
diseñóse, borróse, ovó, matáronla.

Llevóse el Ebrio al labio un roble, porque
amaba, y una astilla
de roble, porque odiaba;
trenzáronse las trenzas de los potros
y la crin de las potencias;
cantaron los obreros; fuí dichoso.

　　El Pálido abrazóse al Encarnado
y el Ebrio, saludónos, escondiéndose.
Como era aquí y al terminar el día,
¡qué más tiempo que aquella plazoleta!
¡qué año mejor que esa gente!
¡qué momento más fuerte que ese siglo!

　　Pues de lo que hablo no es
sino de lo que pasa en esta época, y
de lo que ocurre en China y en España, y en el mundo.
(Walt Whitman tenía un pecho suavísimo y res-
piraba y nadie sabe lo que él hacía cuando lloraba en su comedor.)

×
× ×

   Contrary to the mountain birds,
that live off the valley,
here, one afternoon,   *
here, imprisoned, the Sincere,
metalous, decisive, came with his perfidious grandchildren,   5*
and we remained, because there is no
more wood in the cross to the right,
nor more iron in the nail to the left,
than a handshake between the lefthanded.

   The Sincere came, blind, with his lamps.   10
The Pale was seen, here, to be enough
for the Flesh-colored;
by sheer humbleness the Great was born;   *
the war,
this turtledove of mine, never ours,   15
sketched itself, erased itself, laid eggs, it was killed.

The Inebriated raised an oak to his lip, because
he loved, and a splinter
of oak, because he hated;
the colts' braids and the mane of the powers   20
braided themselves;
the workers sang; I was happy.

   The Pale embraced the Flesh-colored
and the Inebriated, greeted us, hiding.
Since it was here and when the day ended,   25
how much more time than that small plaza!
what year better than those people!
what moment stronger than that century!

   For what I am talking about is
nothing other than what is taking place in our time, and   30*
what is taking place in China and in Spain, and in the world.
(Walt Whitman had a very soft chest and breathed and nobody knows
what he was doing when he was crying in his dining room.)

Pero, volviendo, a lo nuestro,
y al verso que decía, fuera entonces
que ví que el hombre es malnacido,
mal vivo, mal muerto, mal moribundo,
y, naturalmente,
el tartufo sincero desespérase,
el pálido (es el pálido de siempre)
será pálido por algo,
y el ebrio, entre la sangre humana y la leche animal,
abátese, da, y opta por marcharse.

Todo esto
agítase, ahora mismo,
en mi vientre de macho entrañamente.

20 Nov. 1937

But, getting back to our subject,
and to the line that I wrote, it was then   35
I saw that man is evilborn,
evil alive, evil dead, evil dying,
and, naturally,
the sincere tartuffe despairs,
the pale (the one who is always pale)   40
will be for some reason pale,
and the inebriated, between human blood and animal milk,
slumps, gives up, and decides to take off.

    All this
stirs, right now,   45
in my male belly surprisingly.   *

×
× ×

Ello es que el lugar donde me pongo
el pantalón, es una casa donde
me quito la camisa en alta voz
y donde tengo un suelo, un alma, un mapa de mi España
Ahora mismo hablaba
de mí conmigo, y ponía
sobre un pequeño libro un pan tremendo
y he, luego, hecho el traslado, he trasladado,
queriendo canturrear un poco, el lado
derecho de la vida al lado izquierdo;
más tarde, me he lavado todo, el vientre,
briosa, dignamente;
he dado vuelta a ver lo que se ensucia,
he raspado lo que me lleva tan cerca
y he ordenado bien el mapa que
cabeceaba o lloraba, no lo sé.

Mi casa, por desgracia, es una casa,
un suelo por ventura, donde vive
con su inscripción mi cucharita amada,
mi querido esqueleto ya sin letras,
la navaja, un cigarro permanente.
De veras, cuando pienso
en lo que es la vida,
no puedo evitar de decírselo a Georgette,
a fin de comer algo agradable y salir,
por la tarde, comprar un buen periódico,
guardar un día para cuando no haya,
una noche también, para cuando haya
(así se dice en el Perú—me excuso);
del mismo modo, sufro con gran cuidado,
a fin de no gritar o de llorar, ya que los ojos
poseen, independientemente de uno, sus pobrezas,
quiero decir, su oficio, algo
que resbala del alma y cae al alma.

Habiendo atravesado
quince años; después, quince, y, antes, quince,
uno se siente, en realidad, tontillo,
es natural, por lo demás, ¡que hacer!
¿Y qué dejar de hacer, que es lo peor?
Sino vivir, sino llegar
á ser lo que es uno entre millones
de panes, entre miles de vinos, entre cientos de bocas,
entre el sol y su rayo que es de luna
y entre la misa, el pan, el vino y mi alma.

×
× ×

The fact is that the place where I put on
my pants, is a house where
I take off my shirt out loud
and where I have a ground, a soul, a map of my Spain.
Just now I was speaking   5
about me with myself and placing
on top of a little book a tremendous loaf of bread
and I have, then, made the move, I have moved,
trying to hum a little, the right
side of life to the left side;   10
later, I have washed all of me, my belly,
vigorously, with dignity;
I have turned around to see what gets dirty,
I have scraped what takes me so near
and I have properly ordered the map that   15
was nodding off or crying, I don't know.

My house, unfortunately, is a house,
a ground fortunately, where with its
inscription my beloved little spoon lives,
my dear skeleton now unlettered,   20
the pocket knife, a permanent cigar.
Truthfully, when I think
what life is,
I cannot help saying it to Georgette,   *
to be able to eat something nice and go out,   25
in the afternoon, to buy a good newspaper,
to save a day for when there isn't one,
a night too, for when there is
(that is a Peruvian saying—my apologies);
in the same way, I suffer with great care,   30
in order not to shout or cry, since our eyes
have, independent of oneself, their poverties,
I mean, their trade, something
that slips from the soul and falls to the soul.

Having gone through   35
fifteen years; fifteen years, after, and, fifteen years, before,   *
one feels, really, a little dumb,
it's natural, on the other hand, what can one do!
And what can one stop doing, that's even worse!
But to live, but to become   40
what one is among millions
of loaves, among thousands of wines, among hundreds of mouths,
between the sun and its beam, a moonbeam
and among the Mass, the bread, the wine and my soul.

Hoy es domingo y, por eso,
me viene a la cabeza la idea, al pecho el llanto
y a la garganta, así como un gran bulto.
Hoy es domingo, y esto
tiene muchos siglos; de otra manera,
sería, quizá, lunes, y vendríame al corazón la idea,
al seso, el llanto
y a la garganta, una gana espantosa de ahogar
lo que ahora siento,
como un hombre que soy y que he sufrido.

21 Nov. 1937

Today is Sunday and, for this reason,   45
the idea comes to my mind, the crying to my chest
and to my throat, something like a big lump.
Today is Sunday, and this fact
is many centuries old; otherwise,
it would be, perhaps, Monday, and the idea would have come to my heart,   50
the crying to my brain
and to my throat, an awful desire to drown
what I now feel,
like a man that I am and who has suffered.

×
× ×

Algo te identifica con el que se aleja de ti, y es la facultad
común de volver: de ahí tu más grande pesadumbre.

Algo te separa del que se queda contigo, y es la esclavitud
común de partir: de ahí tus más nimios regocijos.

Me dirijo, en esta forma, a las individualidades colectivas,
tanto como a las colectividades individuales y a los que, entre
unas y otras, yacen marchando al son de las fronteras o, simplemente,
marcan el paso inmóvil en el borde del mundo.

Algo típicamente neutro, de inexorablemente neutro, interpónese
entre el ladrón y su víctima. Esto, asimismo, puede discernirse
tratándose del cirujano y del paciente. Horrible medialuna, convexa
y solar, cobija a unos y otros. Porque el objeto hurtado tiene tam-
bién su peso indiferente, y el órgano intervenido, también su grasa
triste.

¿Qué hay de más desesperante en la tierra, que la imposibilidad
en que se halla el hombre feliz de ser infortunado y el hombre bue-
no, de ser malvado?

¡Alejarse! ¡Quedarse! ¡Volver! ¡Partir! Toda la mecánica social cabe
en estas palabras.

×
×   ×

Something identifies you with the one who leaves you, and it is
your common power to return: thus your greatest sorrow.
Something separates you from the one who remains with you,
and it is your common slavery to depart: thus your meagerest
rejoicing.   5
I address myself, in this way, to collective individualities,
as well as to individual collectivities and to those who, between them
both, lie marching to the sound of the frontiers or, simply, mark
time without moving at the edge of the world.
Something typically neuter, inexorably neuter, stands between   10
the thief and his victim. This, likewise, can be noticed in the relation
between a surgeon and his patient. A horrible halfmoon, convex and
solar, covers all of them. For the stolen object has also its indifferent
weight, and the operated on organ, also its sad fat.
What on earth is more exasperating, than the impossibility for   15
the happy man to become unhappy, and the good man to become wicked?
To leave! To remain! To return! To depart! The whole social
mechanism fits in these words.

×
×   ×

En suma, no poseo para expresar mi vida sino mi muerte.
Y, después de todo, al cabo de la escalonada naturaleza y del gorrión en
bloque, me duermo, mano a mano con mi sombra.
Y, al descender del acto venerable y del otro gemido, me repo-
so pensando en la marcha impertérrita del tiempo.
¿Por qué la cuerda, entonces, si el aire es tan sencillo? ¿Pa-
ra qué la cadena, si existe el hierro por sí sólo?
César Vallejo, el acento con que amas, el verbo con que escri-
bes, el vientecillo con que oyes, sólo saben de ti por tu garganta.
César Vallejo, póstrate, por eso, con indistinto orgullo, con
tálamo de ornamentales áspides y exagonales ecos.
Restitúyete al corpóreo panal, a la beldad; aroma los floreci-
dos corchos, cierra ambas grutas al sañudo antropoide; repara, en
fin, tu antipático venado; tente pena.
¡Que no hay cosa más densa que el odio en voz pasiva, ni más
mísera ubre que el amor!
¡Que ya no puedo andar sino en dos harpas!
¡Que ya no me conoces, sino porque te sigo instrumental, pro-
lijamente!
¡Que ya no doy gusanos, sino breves!
¡Que ya te implico tánto, que medio que te afilas!
¡Que ya llevo unas tímidas legumbres y otras bravas!
Pues el afecto que quiébrase de noche en mis bronquios, lo traje-
ron de día ocultos deanes y, si amanezco pálido, es por mi obra;
y si anochezco rojo, por mi obrero. Ello explica, igualmente, es-
tos cansancios míos y estos despojos, mis famosos tíos. Ello explica,
en fin, esta lágrima que brindo por la dicha de los hombres.
¡César Vallejo, parece
mentira que así tarden tus parientes,
sabiendo que ando cautivo,
sabiendo que yaces libre!
¡Vistosa y perra suerte!
¡César Vallejo, te odio con ternura!

25 Nov. 1937

×
× ×

In short, I have nothing with which to express my life except my   *
death.
   And, after all, at the end of graded nature and the sparrow in
bloc, I sleep, hand in hand with my shadow.
   And, upon descending from the venerable act and from the other   5
groan, I rest thinking about the inexorable march of time.
   Why the rope, then, if air is so simple? What is the chain for,
if iron exists on its own?
   César Vallejo, the accent with which you love, the language with
which you write, the soft wind with which you hear, only know of you   10
through your throat.
   César Vallejo, fall on your knees, therefore, with indistinct pride,
with a bridal bed of ornamental asps and hexagonal echoes.
   Return to the corporeal honey comb, to Beauty; aromatize the
blossomed corks, close both caves to the enraged anthropoid; mend,   15
finally, your unpleasant stag; feel sorry for yourself.
   For there is nothing denser than hate in the passive voice, no
stingier udder than love!
   For I am no longer able to walk, except on two harps!
   For you no longer know me, unless instrumentally, fastidiously   20
I follow you!
   For I no longer issue worms, but breves!
   For I now implicate you so much, you almost become sharp!
   For I now carry some timid vegetables and others that are fierce!
   Because the affection that ruptures at night in my bronchia, was brought   25
during the day by hidden deacons and, if when my morning begins I am pale,
it is because of my work; and if when my night begins I am red, because of
my worker. This equally explains this weariness of mine and these spoils, my
famous uncles. This explains, finally, this tear that I offer as a toast to the
happiness of men.   30
   César Vallejo, it is hard
to believe that your relatives are so late,
knowing that I walk imprisoned,
knowing that you lie free!
What dazzling and shitty luck!   35
César Vallejo, I hate you with tenderness!

```
      ×
   ×   ×
```

Otro poco de calma, camarada;
un mucho inmenso, septentrional, completo,
feroz, de calma chica,
al servicio menor de cada triunfo
y en la audaz servidumbre del fracaso.

Embriaguez te sobra, y no hay
tanta locura en la razón, como este
tu raciocinio muscular, y no hay
más racional error que tu experiencia.

Pero, hablando más claro
y pensándolo en oro, eres de acero.
a condición que no seas
tonto y rehuses
entusiasmarte por la muerte tánto
y por la vida, con tu sola tumba.

Necesario es que sepas
contener tu volúmen sin correr, sin afligirte,
tu realidad molecular entera
y más allá, la marcha de tus vivas
y más acá, tus mueras legendarios.

Eres de acero, como dicen,
con tal que no tiembles y no vayas
a reventar, compadre
de mi cálculo, enfático ahijado
de mis sales luminosas!

Anda, no más; resuelve,
considera tu crisis, suma, sigue,
tájala, bájala, ájala;
el destino, las energías íntimas, los catorce
versículos del pan; ¡cuántos diplomas
y poderes, al borde fehaciente de tu arranque!
¡Cuánto detalle en síntesis, contigo!
¡Cuánta presión idéntica, a tus pies!
¡Cuánto rigor y cuánto patrocinio!

×
× ×

A little more calm, comrade;
an immense much, northern, complete,
ferocious, of small calm,
at the minor service of each triumph
and in the audacious servitude of defeat.   5

You have intoxication to spare, and there is not
so much craziness in reason, as in this
your muscular reasoning, and there is no
more rational error than your experience.

But, saying it more clearly   10
and thinking it in gold, you are made of steel,
on condition that you are not
dumb and refuse
to become so enthusiastic about death
and about life, with your sole tomb.   15

It is necessary for you to learn
how to contain your volume without running, without grieving,   *
your entire molecular reality
and beyond, the march of your long live
and closer, your legendary death to.   20

You are made of steel, as it is said,
providing you do not tremble and do not start
exploding, godfather
of my calculation, emphatic godson
of my luminous salts!   25

Go right ahead; decide,
think about your crisis, add, carry,
cut it up, humble it, crumble it;
destiny, the intimate energies, the fourteen
verses of bread; how many diplomas   30
and powers, at the trustful edge of your start!
How much synthesized detail, in you!
How much identical pressure, at your feet!
How much rigor and how much patronage!

Es idiota
ese método de padecimiento,
esa luz modulada y virulenta,
si con sólo la calma haces señales
serias, características, fatales.

Vamos a ver, hombre;
cuéntame lo que me pasa,
que yo, aunque grite, estoy siempre a tus órdenes.

28 Nov. 1937

It is idiotic   35
that method of suffering,
that modulated and virulent light,
if with only calm you flash serious,
characteristic, fatal, signals.

Come on, man;   40
tell me what is happening to me,
for I, even when shouting, am always at your command.

Los desgraciados

Ya va a venir el día; da
cuerda a tu brazo, búscate debajo
del colchón, vuelve a pararte
en tu cabeza, para andar derecho.
Ya va a venir el día, ponte el saco.

Ya va a venir el día; ten
fuerte en la mano a tu intestino grande, reflexiona,
antes de meditar, pues es horrible
cuando le cae a uno la desgracia
y se le cae a uno a fondo el diente.

Necesitas comer, pero, me digo,
no tengas pena, que no es de pobres
la pena, el sollozar junto a su tumba;
remiéndate, recuerda,
confía en tu hilo blanco, fuma, pasa lista
a tu cadena y guárdala detrás de tu retrato.
Ya va a venir el día, ponte el alma.

Ya va a venir el día; pasan,
han abierto en el hotel un ojo,
azotándolo, dándole con un espejo tuyo . . .
¿tiemblas? Es el estado remoto de la frente
y la nacion reciente del estómago.
Roncan aún . . . ¡Qué universo se lleva este ronquido!
¡Cómo quedan tus poros, enjuiciándolo!
¡Con cuántos doses, ¡ay! estás tan solo!
Ya va a venir el día, ponte el sueño.

Ya va a venir el día, repito
por el órgano oral de tu silencio
y urge tomar la izquierda con el hambre
y tomar la derecha con la sed; de todos modos,
abstente de ser pobre con los ricos,
atiza
tu frío, porque en él se integra mi calor, amada víctima.
Ya va a venir el día, ponte el cuerpo.

The miserable

The day is about to come; wind
up your arm, look for yourself under
the mattress, stand again
on your head, to walk straight.
The day is about to come, put on your coat.   5

The day is about to come; grip
your large intestine tight in your hand, reflect,
before you meditate, for it is horrible
when misfortune falls on one
and one's tooth falls thoroughly.   10

You have to eat, but, I tell myself,
do not grieve, for grief and graveside
sobbing do not belong to the poor;
mend yourself, remember,
trust your white thread, smoke, call roll   15
on your chain and keep it behind your portrait.
The day is about to come, put on your soul.

The day is about to come; they go by,
they have opened an eye in the hotel,
lashing it, beating it with one of your mirrors . . .   20
are you trembling? It is the remote state of your forehead
and the recent nation of your stomach.
They're still snoring . . . What a universe is carried away by this snore!
And in what state your pores are left, on judging it!
With so many twos, my god! how alone you are!   25
The day is about to come, put on your dream.

The day is about to come, I repeat
through the oral organ of your silence
and it is urgent to take the left with your hunger
and to take the right with your thirst; in any case,   30
abstain from being poor with the rich,
stir
your cold, for my warmth becomes part of it, beloved victim.
The day is about to come, put on your body.

Ya va a venir el día;
la mañana, la mar, el meteoro, van
en pos de tu cansancio, con banderas,
y, por tu orgullo clásico, las hienas
cuentan sus pasos al compás del asno,
la panadera piensa en ti,
el carnicero piensa en ti, palpando
el hacha en que están presos
el acero y el hierro y el metal; jamás olvides
que durante la misa no hay amigos.
Ya va a venir el día, ponte el sol.

Ya viene el día; dobla
el aliento, triplica
tu bondad rencorosa
y da codos al miedo, nexo y énfasis,
pues tú, como se observa en tu entrepierna y siendo
el malo, ¡ay! inmortal,
has soñado esta noche que vivías
de nada y morías de todo . . .

Wedding March

*

At the head of my own acts,
crown in hand, battalion of gods,
the negative sign hanging from my neck,
atrocious the match and the speed, stupified
the soul and the courage, with two impacts   5

at the foot of the gaze; shouting,
the limits, dynamic, ferocious;
swallowing my inexact cryings,

I will ignite, my ant will ignite,   *
my key will ignite, the quarrel
in which I lost the cause of my track.   10

Then, making a wheat spike of the atom,
I will ignite my sickles at its foot
and the spike will finally be a spike.

×
× ×

La cólera que quiebra al hombre en niños,
que quiebra al niño en pájaros iguales,
y al pájaro, después, en huevecillos;
la cólera del pobre
tiene un aceite contra dos vinagres.

La cólera que al árbol quiebra en hojas,
a la hoja en botones desiguales
y al botón, en ranuras telescópicas;
la cólera del pobre
tiene dos ríos contra muchos mares.

La cólera que quiebra al bien en dudas,
a la duda, en tres arcos semejantes
y al arco, luego, en tumbas imprevistas;
la cólera del pobre
tiene un acero contra dos puñales.

La cólera que quiebra al alma en cuerpos;
al cuerpo en órganos desemejantes
y al órgano, en octavos pensamientos;
la cólera del pobre
tiene un fuego central contra dos cráteres.

26 Oct. 1937

         ×
       ×   ×

The anger that breaks the man into children,
that breaks the child into equal birds,
and the bird, afterward, into little eggs;
the anger of the poor
has one oil against two vinegars.   5

The anger that breaks the tree into leaves,
the leaf into unequal buds
and the bud, into telescopic grooves;
the anger of the poor
has two rivers against many seas.   10

The anger that breaks the good into doubts,
the doubt, into three similar arcs
and the arc, later on, into unforeseeable tombs;
the anger of the poor
has one steel against two daggers.   15

The anger that breaks the soul into bodies;
the body into dissimilar organs
and the organ, into octave thoughts;
the anger of the poor
has one central fire against two craters.   20

Intensidad y altura

Quiero escribir, pero me sale espuma,
quiero decir muchísimo y me atollo;
no hay cifra hablada que no sea suma,
no hay pirámide escrita, sin cogollo.

Quiero escribir, pero me siento puma;
quiero laurearme, pero me encebollo.
No hay toz hablada, que no llegue a bruma,
no hay dios ni hijo de dios, sin desarrollo

Vámonos, pues, por eso, a comer yerba,
carne de llanto, fruta de gemido,
nuestra alma melancólica en conserva.

¡Vámonos! ¡Vámonos! Estoy herido;
vámonos a beber lo ya bebido,
vámonos, cuervo, a fecundar tu cuerva.

27 Oct. 1937

Intensity and height

I want to write, but out comes foam,
I want to say so much and I freeze;   *
there is no spoken cipher which is not a sum,
there is no written pyramid, without a core.

I want to write, but I feel like a puma;   5
I want to laurel myself, but I stew in onions.
There is no spoken coughv, which doesn't end in mist,   *
there is no god nor son of god, without unfolding.

Let's go, then, through this, and eat grass,
the flesh of sobbing, the fruit of groaning,   10
our melancholy soul preserved in jam.

Let's go! Let's go! I'm wounded;
let's go drink that already drunk,
let's go, raven, and fecundate your rook.   *

Guitarra

El placer de sufrir, de odiar, me tiñe
la garganta con plásticos venenos,
mas la cerda que implanta su orden mágico,
su grandeza taurina, entre la prima
y la sexta
y la octava mendaz, las sufre todas.

El placer de sufrir . . . ¿Quién? ¿a quién?
¿quién, las muelas? ¿a quién la sociedad,
los carburos de rabia de la encía?
¿Cómo ser
y estar, sin darle cólera al vecino?

Vales más que mi número, hombre solo,
y valen más que todo el diccionario,
con su prosa en verso,
con su verso en prosa,
tu función águila,
tu mecanismo tigre, blando prójimo.

El placer de sufrir,
de esperar esperanzas en la mesa,
el domingo con todos los idiomas,
el sábado con horas chinas, belgas,
la semana, con dos escupitajos.

El placer de esperar en zapatillas,
de esperar encogido tras un verso,
de esperar con pujanza y mala poña;
el placer de sufrir: zurdazo de hembra
muerta con una piedra en la cintura
y muerta entre la cuerda y la guitarra,
llorando días y cantando meses.

28 Oct. 1937

Guitar

The pleasure of suffering, of hating, dyes my
throat with plastic venoms,
but the bristle that implants its magic order,
its taurine greatness, between the first string
and the sixth   5
and the mendacious eighth, suffers them all.   *

The pleasure of suffering . . . Who? Whom?
who, the molars? whom society,
the carbides of rage in the gums?
How to be   10
and to be here, without making one's neighbor angry?   *

You are worthier than my number, man alone,
and your eagle function,
your tiger mechanism, bland fellow man,
are worthier than all the dictionary,   15
with its prose in poetry,
with its poetry in prose.

The pleasure of suffering,
of waiting for hopes at the table,
on Sunday with all the languages,   20
on Saturday with Chinese, Belgian hours,
during the week, with two hockers.

The pleasure of waiting in slippers,
of waiting cowering behind a stanza,
of waiting empowered with a sick boner,   25*
the pleasure of suffering: hard left by a female
dead with a stone on her waist
and dead between the string and the guitar,
crying for days and singing for months.   *

```
      ×
   ×   ×
```

Oye a tu masa, a tu cometa, escúchalos; no gimas
de memoria, gravísimo cetáceo;
oye a la túnica en que estás dormido,
oye a tu desnudez, dueña del sueño.

Relátate agarrándote
de la cola del fuego y a los cuernos
en que acaba la crin su atroz carrera;
rómpete, pero en círculos;
fórmate, pero en columnas combas;
descríbete atmosférico, sér de humo,
a paso redoblado de esqueleto.

¿La muerte? ¡Opónle todo tu vestido!
¿La vida? ¡Opónle parte de tu muerte!
Bestia dichosa, piensa;
dios desgraciado, quítate la frente.
Luego, hablaremos.

29 Oct. 1937

X
X   X

Hear your mass, your comet, listen to them; don't moan   *
by heart, most ponderous cetacean;
hear the tunic in which you are asleep,
hear your nakedness, the owner of your dreams.

Relate to yourself grasping   5
the tail of the fire and the horns
where the mane ends its fierce race;
break apart, but in circles;
take form, but in curved columns;
describe yourself atmospheric, Being of smoke,   10
in the double time step of a skeleton.   *

Death? Oppose it with all you're wearing!
Life? Oppose it with part of your death!
Happy beast, think;
unhappy god, take off your forehead.   15
Then, we will talk.

×
× ×

¿Qué me da, que me azoto con la línea
y creo que me sigue, al trote, el punto?

¿Qué me da, que me he puesto
en los hombros un huevo en vez de un manto?

¿Que me ha dado, que vivo?
¿Qué me ha dado, que muero?

¿Qué me da, que tengo ojos?
¿Qué me da, que tengo alma?

¿Qué me da, que se acaba en mí mi prójimo
y empieza en mi carrillo el rol del viento?

¿Qué me ha dado, que cuento mis dos lágrimas,
sollozo tierra y cuelgo el horizonte?

¿Qué me ha dado, que lloro de no poder llorar
y río de lo poco que he reído?

¿Qué me da, que ni vivo ni muero?

30 Oct. 1937

×
× ×

What's got into me, that I am whipping myself with the line
and think that I am being followed, at a trot, by the period?

What's got into me, that I have placed
on my shoulders an egg instead of a mantle?

What's gotten into me, that I'm alive?   5
What's gotten into me, that I'm dying?

What's got into me, that I have eyes?
What's got into me, that I have a soul?

What's got into me, that my fellow man is ending in me
and the role of the wind is beginning in my cheek?   10

What's gotten into me, that I'm counting my two tears,
sobbing earth and hanging the horizon?   *

What's gotten into me, that I'm crying from not being able to cry
and laughing at the little I've laughed?

What's got into me, that I'm neither living nor dying?   15

Aniversario

¡Cuánto catorce ha habido en la existencia!
¡Qué créditos con bruma en una esquina!
¡Qué diamante sintético, el del casco!
¡Cuánta más dulcedumbre
a lo largo, más honda superficie:
¡cuánto catorce ha habido en tan poco uno!

¡Qué deber,
qué cortar y qué tajo,
de memoria a memoria, en la pestaña!
¡Cuánto más amarillo, más granate!
¡Cuánto catorce en un solo catorce!

Acordeón de la tarde, en esa esquina,
piano de la mañana, aquella tarde;
clarín de carne,
tambor de un solo palo,
guitarra sin cuarta ¡cuánta quinta,
y cuánta reunión de amigos tontos
y qué nido de tigres el tabaco!
¡Cuánto catorce ha habido en la existencia!

¿Qué te diré ahora,
quince feliz, ajeno, quince de otros?
¡Nada más que no crece ya el cabello,
que han venido por las cartas,
que me brillan los seres que he parido,
y que no hay nadie en mi tumba
y que me han confundido con mi llanto!

¡Cuánto catorce ha habido en la existencia!

31 Oct. 1937

Anniversary

How much 14 there has been in existence!   *
What credits with mist on a corner!
What a synthetic diamond the skull is!
The lengthier
the sweetness, the deeper the surface: 5
how much 14 there has been in such a small 1!

What a debt,
what a cut and what a slash,
from memory to memory, in an eyelash!
The more yellow, the more garnet!   10
How much 14 in a single 14!

Accordian of the afternoon, on this corner,
piano of the morning, that afternoon;
clarion of flesh,
drum with a single stick,   15
guitar without a fourth string, lots of fifth,
and how many gatherings of dumb friends!   *
and what a nest of tigers in tobacco!
How much 14 there has been in existence!

What will I say to you now,   20
15 happy, alien, 15 of others?
Just that my hair no longer grows,
that they have come for the letters,
that the beings I have given birth to are shining at me,
that there is no one in my tomb   25
and that they have taken me for my crying!

How much 14 there has been in existence!

Panteón

He visto ayer sonidos generales,
      mortuoriamente,
      puntualmente alejarse,
cuando oí desprenderse del ocaso
      tristemente
      exactamente un arco, un arcoíris

Ví el tiempo generoso del minuto,
      infinitamente
atado locamente al tiempo grande
pues que estaba la hora
      suavemente
premiosamente henchida de dos horas.

Dejóse comprender, llamar, la tierra
      terrenalmente;
negóse brutalmente así a mi historia,
y si ví, que me escuchen, pues, en bloque,
si toqué esta mecánica, que vean
      lentamente,
despacio, vorazmente, mis tinieblas.

Y si ví en la lesión de la respuesta,
      claramente,
la lesión mentalmente de la incógnita,
si escuché, si pensé en mis ventanillas
nasales, funerales, temporales,
      fraternalmente,
piadosamente echadme a los filósofos.

Mas no más inflexión precipitada
en canto llano, y no más
el hueso colorado, el son del alma
      tristemente
erguida ecuestramente en mi espinazo,
ya que, en suma, la vida es
      implacablemente,
imparcialmente horrible, estoy seguro.

31 Oct. 1937

Pantheon

Yesterday I saw general sounds,
  mortuarily,
  punctually recede,
when I heard rip loose from the sunset
  sadly,
  exactly a bow, a rainbow.   5
                                                               *

I saw the generous time of the minute,
  infinitely
tied insanely to large time
for the hour was
  softly   10
urgently swollen with two hours.

The earth earthlyly let itself be understood,
  and be called;
brutally it thus refused my history,
and if I saw, let them hear me, then, in bloc,   15
if I touched this mechanics, let them see
  slowly,
at leisure, voraciously, my Tenebrae.

And if I saw in the lesion of the response,   20
  clearly,
the lesion mentally of the unknown,
if I heard, if I thought about my funereal,
temporal nostrils,
  fraternally,
piously throw me to the philosophers.   25

But no more rash inflection
in Gregorian chant, and no more
the reddish bone, the sound of the soul
  sadly
straightened equestrianly in my spine,   30
since, in short, life is
  implacably,
impartially horrible, I am sure.

×
×　×

Un hombre está mirando a una mujer,
está mirándola inmediatamente,
con su mal de tierra suntuosa
y la mira a dos manos
y la tumba a dos pechos
y la mueve a dos hombros.

Pregúntome entonces, oprimiéndome
la enorme, blanca, acérrima costilla:
Y este hombre
¿no tuvo a un niño por creciente padre?
¿Y esta mujer, a un niño
por constructor de su evidente sexo?

Puesto que un niño veo ahora,
niño ciempiés, apasionado, enérgico:
veo que no le ven
sonarse entre los dos, colear, vestirse;
puesto que los acepto,
a ella en condición aumentativa,
a él en la flexión del heno rubio.

Y exclamo entonces, sin cesar ni uno
de vivir, sin volver ni uno
a temblar en la justa que venero:
¡Felicidad seguida
tardíamente del Padre,
del Hijo y de la Madre!
¡Instante redondo,
familiar, que ya nadie siente ni ama!
¡De qué deslumbramiento áfono, tinto,
se ejecuta el cantar de los cantares!
¡De qué tronco, el florido carpintero!
¡De qué perfecta axila, el frágil remo!
¡De qué casco, ambos cascos delanteros!

2 Nov. 1937

×
× ×

A man is looking at a woman,
is looking at her immediately,
with her earth sumptuous sickness
and he watches her two-handedly
and he fells her two-chestedly   5
and he moves her two-shoulderly.

I ask myself then, pressing down
my enormous, white, most pungent rib:
And this man
hasn't he had a child as a growing father?   10
And this woman, a child
as a builder of her evident sex?

Because I see a child now,
an energetic, impassioned, centipede child:
I see that they do not see him   15
blowing his nose between them, wagging his tail, getting dressed;
because I accept them,
her in augmentative condition,
him in the flexion of the gold hay.

And I cry out then, without ceasing even one   20
to live, without turning even one
to tremble in the joust I worship:
Happiness followed
belatedly by the Father,
by the Son and by the Mother!   25
Perfect, familiar
instant, that no one any longer feels or loves!
From what an aphonic, deep red dazzle
the Song of Songs is executed!
From what a trunk, the florid carpenter!   30
From what a perfect axilla, the fragile oar!
From what a hoof, both forehoofs!

Dos niños anhelantes

No. No tienen tamaño sus tobillos; no es su espuela
suavísima, que da en las dos mejillas.
Es la vida no más, de bata y yugo.

No. No tiene plural su carcajada,
no por haber salido de un molusco perpétuo, aglutinante,
ni por haber entrado al mar descalza,
es la que piensa y marcha, es la finita.
Es la vida no más; sólo la vida.

Lo sé, lo intuyo cartesiano, autómata,
moribundo, cordial, en fin, espléndido.
Nada hay
sobre la ceja cruel de su esqueleto;
nada, entre lo que dió y tomó con guante
la paloma, y con guante,
la eminente lombriz aristotélica;
nada delante ni detrás del yugo;
nada de mar en el océano
y nada
en el orgullo grave de la célula.
Sólo la vida; así: cosa bravísima.

Plenitud inextensa,
alcance abstracto, venturoso, de hecho,
glacial y arrebatado, de la llama;
freno del fondo, rabo de la forma.
Pero aquello
para lo cual nací ventilándome
y crecí con afecto y drama propios,
mi trabajo rehúsalo,
mi sensación y mi arma lo involucran.
Es la vida y no más, fundada, escénica.

Y por este rumbo,
su serie de órganos extingue mi alma
y por este indecible, endemoniado cielo,
mi maquinaria da silbidos técnicos,
paso la tarde en la mañana triste
y me esfuerzo, palpito, tengo frío.

2 Nov. 1937

Two yearning children

No. Their ankles have no size; it is not their softest   *
spur, that touches their two cheeks.
It is just life, with robe and yoke.

No. Their guffaw has no plural,   *
not even for having come out of a perpetual, agglutinating mollusk,   5
not even for having entered the sea barefoot,
it is what thinks and walks, it is finite.
It is just life; only life.

I know it, I intuit it Cartesian, robot-like,   *
moribund, cordial, in short, magnificent.   10
Nothing is
over the cruel brow of its skeleton;
nothing, between what the dove with kid gloves gave
and took back, and with kid gloves,
the eminent Aristotelian earthworm;   15
nothing before or behind the yoke;
nothing of sea in the ocean
and nothing
in the grave pride of the cell.
Only life; that is: a hell of a tough thing.   20*

Unextended plenitude,
abstract reach, fortunate, in fact,   *
glacial and impetuous, of the flame;
restrainer of depth, tail of form.
But that   25
for which I was born ventilating myself
and grew up with my own tenderness and drama,
is rejected by my work,
is jumbled by my feelings and my weapon.
It is life and that's all, grounded, scenic.   30

And in this way,
my soul extinguishes its series of organs
and in this inexpressible, demonized sky,
my machinery emits technical whistles,
I spend my afternoon in the sad morning   35
and I struggle, I throb, I am cold.

Los nueve monstruous

  I, desgraciadamente,
el dolor crece en el mundo a cada rato,
crece a treinta minutos por segundo, paso a paso,
y la naturaleza del dolor, es el dolor dos veces
y la condición del martirio, carnívoro, voraz,
es el dolor, dos veces
y la función de la yerba purísima, el dolor
dos veces
y el bien de sér, dolernos doblemente.

  ¡Jamás, hombres humanos,
hubo tánto dolor en el pecho, en la solapa, en la cartera,
en el vaso, en la carnicería, en la aritmética!
¡Jamás tánto cariño doloroso,
jamás tan cerca arremetió lo lejos,
jamás el fuego nunca
jugó mejor su rol de frío muerto!
¡Jamás, señor ministro de salud, fué la salud
más mortal
y la migrana extrajo tánta frente de la frente!
y el mueble tuvo en su cajón, dolor,
el corazón, en su cajón, dolor,
la lagartija, en su cajón, dolor.

  ¡Crece la desdicha, hermanos hombres,
más pronto que la máquina, a diez máquinas, y crece
con la res de Russeau, con nuestras barbas;
  crece el mal por razones que ignoramos
y es una inundación con propios líquidos,
con propio barrio y propia nube sólida!
Invierte el sufrimiento posiciones, da función
en que el humor acuoso es vertical
al pavimento,
el ojo es visto y esta oreja oída,
y esta oreja da nueve campanadas a la hora
del rayo, y nueve carcajadas
a la hora del trigo, y nueve sones hembras
a la hora del llanto, y nueve cánticos
a la hora del hambre, y nueve truenos
y nueve látigos, menos un grito.

The nine monsters

AND, unfortunately,   *
pain grows in the world every moment,
grows thirty minutes a second, step by step,
and the nature of the pain, is the pain twice
and the condition of the martyrdom, carnivorous, voracious,   5
is the pain, twice
and the function of the purest grass, the pain
twice
and the good of Being, to hurt us doubly.

Never, human men,   10
was there so *much* pain in the chest, in the lapel, in the wallet,
in the glass, in the butcher-shop, in arithmetic!
Never so much painful affection,
never did far away charge so close,
never did the fire ever   15
play better its role of dead cold!
Never, mister secretary of health, was health
more mortal,
and did the migraine extract so much forehead from the forehead!
And the cabinet have in its drawer, pain,   20
the heart, in its drawer, pain,
the wall lizard, in its drawer, pain.

Misfortune grows, brother men,
faster than the machine, at ten machines, and grows
with each head of Russeau cattle, with our beards;   25*
 evil grows for reasons we know not
and is a flood with its own liquids,
its own mud and its own solid cloud!   *
Suffering inverts positions, it acts making
the watery humour appear vertical   30
to the pavement,
the eye seen and this ear heard,
and this ear sounds nine strokes at the hour   *
of lightning, and nine guffaws
at the hour of wheat, and nine female sounds   35
at the hour of crying, and nine canticles
at the hour of hunger, and nine thunderclaps
and nine lashes, minus a scream.

El dolor nos agarra, hermanos hombres,
por detrás, de perfil,
y nos aloca en los cinemas
nos clava en los gramófonos,
nos desclava en los lechos, cae perpendicularmente
a nuestros boletos, a nuestras cartas;
y es muy grave sufrir, puede uno orar . . .
Pues de resultas
del dolor, hay algunos
que nacen, otros crecen, otros mueren,
y otros que nacen y no mueren, otros
que sin haber nacido, mueren, y otros
que no nacen ni mueren (Son los más).
Y también de resultas
del sufrimiento, estoy triste
hasta la cabeza, y más triste hasta el tobillo,
de ver al pan, crucificado, al nabo,
ensangrentado,
llorando, a la cebolla,
al cereal, en general, harina,
a la sal, hecha polvo, al agua, huyendo,
al vino, un ecce-homo,
tan pálida a la nieve, al sol tan ardio!
        ¡Cómo, hermanos humanos,
no deciros que ya no puedo y
ya no puedo con tánto cajón,
tánto minuto, tánta
lagartija y tánta
inversión, tánto lejos y tánta sed de sed!
Señor Ministro de Salud: ¿qué hacer?
¡Ah! desgraciadamente, hombres humanos,
hay, hermanos, muchísimo que hacer.

3 Nov. 1937

The pain grabs us, brother men,
from behind, in profile,   40
and drives us wild in the movies,
nails us into the gramophones,
denails us in bed, falls perpendicularly
to our tickets, to our letters;
and it is very serious to suffer, one might pray . . .   45
For as a result
of the pain, there are some
who are born, others grow, others die,
and others who are born and do not die, others
who without having been born, die, and others   50
who neither are born nor die (The most).
And also as a result
of suffering, I am sad
up to my head, and sadder down to my ankle,
from seeing bread, crucified, the turnip,   55
bloodied,
the onion, crying,
cereal, in general, flour,
salt, ground to dust, water, fleeing,
wine, an ecce-homo,   60
such pallid snow, such an arduent sun!   *
    How, human brothers,
not to tell you that I can no longer stand and
can no longer stand so much drawer,
so much minute, so much   65
wall lizard and so much
inversion, so much far away and so much thirst for thirst!
Mr. Secretary of Health: what to do?
Ah, unfortunately, human men,
there is, brothers, much too much to do.   70

Un hombre pasa con un pan al hombro.
¿Voy a escribir, después, sobre mi doble?

Otro se sienta, ráscase, extrae un piojo de su axila, mátalo.
¿Con qué valor hablar del psicoanálisis?

Otro ha entrado a mi pecho con un palo en la mano.
¿Hablar luego de Sócrates al médico?

Un cojo pasa dando el brazo a un niño.
¿Voy, despúes, a leer a André Breton?

Otro tiembla de frío, tose, escupe sangre.
¿Cabrá aludir jamás al Yo profundo?

Otro busca en el fango huesos, cáscaras.
¿Cómo escribir, después, del infinito?

Un albañil cae de un techo, muere y ya no almuerza.
¿Innovar, luego, el tropo, la metáfora?

Un comerciante roba un gramo en el peso a un cliente.
¿Hablar, después, de cuarta dimensión?

Un banquero falsea su balance.
¿Con qué cara llorar en el teatro?

Un paria duerme con el pie a la espalda.
¿Hablar, después, a nadie de Picasso?

Alguien va en un entierro sollozando.
¿Cómo luego ingresar a la Academia?

Alguien limpia un fusil en su cocina.
¿Con qué valor hablar del más allá?

Alguien pasa contando con sus dedos.
¿Cómo hablar del no-yó sin dar un grito?

5 Nov. 1937

A man walks by with a stick of bread on his shoulder.
Am I going to write, after that, about my double?   *

  Another sits, scratches, extracts a louse from his armpit, kills it.
How dare one speak about psychoanalysis?

  Another has entered my chest with a stick in hand.   5
To talk then about Socrates with the doctor?

  A lame man passes by holding a child's hand.
After that am I going to read André Breton?

  Another trembles from cold, coughs, spits blood.
Will it ever be possible to allude to the profound I?   10*

  Another searches in the mud for bones, rinds.
How write, after that, about the infinite?

  A bricklayer falls from a roof, dies and no longer eats lunch.
To innovate, then, the trope, the metaphor?

  A merchant cheats a customer out of a gram.   15
To speak, after that, about the fourth dimension?

  A banker falsifies his balance sheet.
With what face to cry in the theater?

  An outcast sleeps with his foot on his back.
To speak, after that, to anyone about Picasso?   20

  Someone goes to a burial sobbing.
How then become a member of the Academy?

  Someone cleans a rifle in his kitchen.
How dare one speak about the beyond?

  Someone passes by counting with his fingers.   25
How speak of the not-*i* without screaming?   *

×
×   ×

Me viene, hay días, una gana ubérrima, política,
de querer, de besar al cariño en sus dos rostros,
y me viene de lejos un querer
demostrativo, otro querer amar, de grado o fuerza,
al que me odia, al que rasga su papel, al muchachito,
a la que llora por el que lloraba,
al rey del vino, al esclavo del agua,
al que ocultóse en su ira,
al que suda, al que pasa, al que sacude su persona en mi alma.
Y quiero, por lo tanto, acomodarle
al que me habla, su trenza; sus cabellos, al soldado;
su luz, al grande; su grandeza, al chico.
Quiero planchar directamente
un pañuelo al que no puede llorar
y, cuando estoy triste o me duele la dicha,
remendar a los niños y a los genios.

Quiero ayudar al bueno a ser su poquillo de malo
y me urge estar sentado
a la diestra del zurdo, y responder al mudo,
tratando de serle útil en
lo que puedo, y también quiero muchísimo
lavarle al cojo el pie,
y ayudarle a dormir al tuerto próximo.

¡Ah querer, éste, el mío, éste, el mundial,
interhumano y parroquial, provecto!
Me viene a pelo,
desde el cimiento, desde la ingle pública,
y, viniendo de lejos, da ganas de besarle
la bufanda al cantor,
y al que sufre, besarle en su sartén,
al sordo, en su rumor craneano, impávido;
al que me da lo que olvidé en mi seno,
en su Dante, en su Chaplin, en sus hombros.

×
× ×

For several days, I have felt an exuberant, political need
to love, to kiss affection on its two cheeks,
and I have felt from afar a demonstrative
desire, another desire to love, willingly or by force,
whoever hates me, whoever rips up his paper, a little boy,   5
the woman who cries for the man who was crying,
the king of wine, the slave of water,
whoever hid in his wrath,
whoever sweats, whoever passes, whoever shakes his person in my soul.
And I want, therefore, to adjust   10
the braid of whoever talks to me; the hair of the soldier;
the light of the great one; the greatness of the little one.
I want to iron directly
a handkerchief for whoever is unable to cry
and, when I am sad or happiness hurts me,   15
to mend the children and the geniuses.

I want to help the good one become a little bit bad
and I badly need to be seated
on the right-hand of the left-handed, and to respond to the mute,
trying to be useful to him as   20
I can, and also I want very much
to wash the lame man's foot,   *
and to help the nearby one-eyed man sleep.

Ah love, this one, my own, this one, the world's,
interhuman and parochial, maturely aged!   25
It comes, perfectly timed,
from the foundation, from the public groin,
and, coming from afar, makes me want to kiss
the singer's muffler,
and whoever suffers, to kiss him on his frying pan,   30
the deaf man, on his cranial murmur, undaunted;
whoever gives me what I forgot in my breast,
on his Dante, on his Chaplin, on his shoulders.

Quiero, para terminar,
cuando estoy al borde célebre de la violencia
o lleno de pecho el corazón, querría
ayudar a reír al que sonríe,
ponerle un pajarillo al malvado en plena nuca,
cuidar a los enfermos enfadándolos,
comprarle al vendedor,
ayudarle a matar al matador—cosa terrible—
y quisiera yo ser bueno conmigo
en todo.

6 Nov. 1937

I want, finally,
when I am at the celebrated edge of violence   35
or my heart full of chest, I would like
to help whoever smiles laugh,   *
to put a little bird right on the evil man's nape,
to take care of the sick annoying them,
to buy from the vendor,   40
to help the killer kill—a terrible thing—
and I would like to be kind to myself
in everything.

×
×   ×

Hoy le ha entrado una astilla.
Hoy le ha entrado una astilla cerca, dándole
cerca, fuerte, en su modo
de ser y en su centavo ya famoso.
Le ha dolido la suerte mucho,
todo;
le ha dolido la puerta,
le ha dolido la faja, dándole
sed, aflixión
y sed del vaso pero no del vino.
Hoy le salió a la pobre vecina del aire,
a escondidas, humareda de su dogma;
hoy le ha entrado una astilla.

La inmensidad persíguela
a distancia superficial, a un vasto eslabonazo.
hoy le salió a la pobre vecina del viento,
en la mejilla, norte, y en la mejilla, oriente;
hoy le ha entrado una astilla.

¿Quién comprará, en los días perecederos, ásperos,
un pedacito de café con leche,
y quién, sin ella, bajará a su rastro hasta dar a luz?
¿Quién será, luego, sábado, a las siete?
¡Tristes son las astillas que le entran
a uno,
exactamente ahí precisamente!
Hoy le entró a la pobre vecina de viaje,
una llama apagada en el oráculo;
hoy le ha entrado una astilla.

Le ha dolido el dolor, el dolor joven
el dolor niño, el dolorazo, dándole
en las manos
y dándole sed, aflixión
y sed del vaso, pero no del vino.
¡La pobre pobrecita!

6 Nov. 1937

×
×   ×

Today a splinter has gotten into her.
Today a splinter has gotten into her close, striking her
close, hard, in her disposition
and in her now famous centavo.
Luck has hurt her a lot,   5
all over;
the door has hurt her,
her girdle has hurt her, giving her
thirst, aflixion   *
and thirst for the glass but not for the wine.   10
Today, on the sly, the smoke of her dogma
poured out of the poor air neighbor;   *
today a splinter has gotten into her.

Immensity pursues her   *
at a superficial distance, at a vast flint spark.   15
Today, on the cheek of the poor wind neighbor,
north came out, and on the cheek, orient;
today a splinter has gotten into her.

Who will buy, in these harsh, perishable days,
a little piece of coffee with cream, .   20
and who, without her, will descend to her trail until casting light?
Who will it be, then, a Saturday, at seven?
Sad are the splinters that get into
one,
exactly there precisely!   25
Today, a quenched flame has gotten into the oracle
of the poor traveling companion;
today a splinter has gotten into her.

Hurt has hurt her, young hurt,
child hurt, tremendous hurt, striking her   30
in her hands
and giving her thirst, aflixion
and thirst for the glass, but not for the wine.
The poor, poor little thing!

Palmas y guitarra

Ahora, entre nosotros, aquí,
ven conmigo, trae por la mano a tu cuerpo
y cenemos juntos y pasemos un instante la vida
a dos vidas y dando una parte a nuestra muerte.
Ahora, ven contigo, hazme el favor
de quejarte en mi nombre y a la luz de la noche teneblosa
en que traes a tu alma de la mano
y huímos en puntillas de nosotros.

Ven a mí, sí, y a ti, sí,
con paso par, a vernos a los dos con paso impar,
marcar el paso de la despedida.
¡Hasta cuando volvamos! ¡Hasta la vuelta!
¡Hasta cuando leamos, ignorantes!
¡Hasta cuando volvamos, despidámonos!

¿Qué me importan los fusiles,
escúchame;
escúchame, ¿qué impórtanme,
si la bala circula ya en el rango de mi firma?
¿Qué te importan a ti las balas,
si el fusil está humeando ya en tu olor?
Hoy mismo pesaremos
en los brazos de un ciego nuestra estrella
y, una vez que me cantes, lloraremos.
Hoy mismo, hermosa, con tu paso par
y tu confianza a que llegó mi alarma,
saldremos de nosotros, dos a dos.
¡Hasta cuando seamos ciegos!
¡Hasta
que lloremos de tánto volver!

Ahora,
entre nosotros, trae
por la mano a tu dulce personaje
y cenemos juntos y pasemos un instante la vida
a dos vidas y dando una parte a nuestra muerte.
Ahora, ven contigo, hazme el favor
de cantar algo
y de tocar en tu alma, haciendo palmas.
¡Hasta cuando volvamos! ¡Hasta entonces!
¡Hasta cuando partamos, despidámonos!

8 Nov. 1937

Clapping and guitar

Now, between ourselves, right here,
come with me, bring your body by the hand
and let's dine together and spend our life for a moment
in two lives, giving a part to our death.
Now, come with yourself, do me the favor   5
of complaining in my name and by the light of the teneblous night   *
in which you bring your soul by the hand
and we flee on tiptoes from ourselves.

Come to me, yes, and to you, yes,
in even step, to see the two of us out of step,
stepping in place to farewell.   10
Until we return! I'll see you then!
Until we read, ignoramuses!
Until we return, let's say goodbye!

What are the rifles to me,
listen to me;   15
listen to me, what's it to me
if the bullet is already circulating in my signature's rank?
What are the bullets to you,
if the rifle is already smoking in your odor?
This very day we will weigh   20
in the arms of a blindman our star
and, once you sing to me, we will cry.
This very day, beautiful woman, with your even step
and your trust reached by my alarm,
we will come out of ourselves, two by two.   25
Until we both become blind!
Until
we cry from so *much* returning!

Now,
between ourselves, bring   30
your sweet person by the hand
and let's dine together and spend our life for a moment
in two lives, giving a part to our death.
Now, come with yourself, do me the favor   35
of singing something
and playing on your soul, clapping hands.
Until we return! Until then!
Until we part, let's say goodbye!

El alma que sufrió de ser su cuerpo

Tu sufres de una glándula endocrínica, se ve,
o, quizá,
sufres de mí, de mi sagacidad escueta, tácita.
Tú padeces del diáfano antropoide, allá, cerca,
donde está la tiniebla tenebrosa.
Tú das la vuelta al sol, agarrándote el alma,
extendiendo tus juanes corporales
y ajustándote el cuello; eso se ve.
Tú sabes lo que te duele,
lo que te salta al anca,
lo que baja por ti con soga al suelo.
Tú, pobre hombre, vives; no lo niegues,
si mueres; no lo niegues,
si mueres de tu edad! ¡ay! y de tu época.
Y, aunque llores, bebes,
y, aunque sangres, alimentas a tu híbrido colmillo,
a tu vela tristona y a tus partes.
Tú sufres, tú padeces y tú vuelves a sufrir horriblemente,
desgraciado mono,
jovencito de Darwin,
alguacil que me atisbas, atrocísimo microbio.
Y tú lo sabes a tal punto,
que lo ignoras, soltándote a llorar.
Tú, luego, has nacido; eso
también se ve de lejos, infeliz y cállate,
y soportas la calle que te dió la suerte
a tu ombligo interrogas: ¿dónde? ¿cómo?

Amigo mío, estás completamente,
hasta el pelo, en el año treinta y ocho,
nicolás o santiago, tal o cual,
estés contigo o con tu aborto o con-
migo
y cautivo en tu enorme libertad,
arrastrado por tu hércules autónomo . . .
Pero si tú calculas en tus dedos hasta dos,
es peor; no lo niegues, hermanito.

¿Que nó? ¿Que sí, pero que nó?
¡Pobre mono! . . . ¡Dame la pata! . . . No. La mano, he dicho.
¡Salud! ¡Y sufre!

8 Nov. 1937

The soul that suffered from being its body

You suffer from an endocrine gland, it's obvious,
or, perhaps,
you suffer from me, from my tacit, stark sagacity.
You endure the diaphanous anthropoid, over there, nearby,   *
where the tenebrous darkness is.   5
You revolve around the sun, grabbing on to your soul,
extending your corporal juans   *
and adjusting your collar; that's obvious.
You know what aches you,
what leaps on your rump,   10
what descends through you by rope to the ground.
You, poor man, you live; don't deny it,
if you die; don't deny it,
if you die from your age! ah! and from your epoch.
And, even if you cry, you drink,   15
and, even if you bleed, you nourish your hybrid eyetooth,
your wistful candle and your private parts.
You suffer, you endure and again you suffer horribly,
miserable ape,   *
Darwin's little man,   20
bailiff prying on me, most atrocious microbe.
And you know this so well,
that you ignore it, bursting into tears.
You, then, were born; that
too is obvious at a distance, poor devil and shut up,   25
and you put up with the street that luck gave you
you question your navel: where? how?   *

My friend, you are completely,
up to your hair, in the 38th year,
nicolas or santiago, this one or that one,   30
either with yourself or with your abortion or with
me
and captive in your enormous liberty,
dragged on by your autonomous hercules . . .
But if you calculate on your fingers up to two,   35
it's worse; don't deny it, pal.

Why *no*? Why yes, but why *no*?
Poor ape! . . . Gimme your paw! . . . No. The hand, I meant.
To your health! Keep suffering!

Yuntas

Completamente. Además, ¡vida!
Completamente. Además, ¡muerte!

Completamente. Además, ¡todo!
Completamente. Además, ¡nada!

Completamente. Además, ¡mundo!
Completamente. Además, ¡polvo!

Completamente. Además, ¡Dios!
Completamente. Además, ¡nadie!

Completamente. Además, ¡nunca!
Completamente. Además, ¡siempre!

Completamente. Además, ¡oro!
Completamente. Además, ¡humo!

Completamente. Además, ¡lágrimas!
Completamente. Además, ¡risas! . . .

Completamente!

9 Nov. 1937

Couplings

Completely. Furthermore, life!
Completely. Furthermore, death!

Completely. Furthermore, everything!
Completely. Furthermore, nothing!

Completely. Furthermore, world!   5
Completely. Furthermore, dust!

Completely. Furthermore, God!
Completely. Furthermore, no one!

Completely. Furthermore, never!
Completely. Furthermore, always!   10

Completely. Furthermore, gold!
Completely. Furthermore, smoke!

Completely. Furthermore, tears!
Completely. Furthermore, laughs! . . .

Completely!   15

×
× ×

Acaba de pasar el que vendrá
proscrito, a sentarse en mi triple desarrollo;
acaba de pasar criminalmente.

Acaba de sentarse más acá,
a un cuerpo de distancia de mi alma,
el que vino en un asno a enflaquecerme;
acaba de sentarse de pie, lívido.

Acaba de darme lo que está acabado,
el calor del fuego y el pronombre inmenso
que el animal crió bajo su cola.

Acaba
de expresarme su duda sobre hipótesis lejanas
que él aleja, aún más, con la mirada.

Acaba de hacer al bien los honores que le tocan
en virtud del infame paquidermo,
por lo soñado en mí y en él matado.

Acaba de ponerme (no hay primera)
su segunda aflixión en plenos lomos
y su tercer sudor en plena lágrima.

Acaba de pasar sin haber venido.

12 Nov. 1937

×
×   ×

He has just passed by, the one who will come
banished, to sit down on my triple unfolding;
he has just passed by criminally.

He has just sat down nearer,
a body away from my soul,   5
the one who came on an ass to make me gaunt;
he has just sat down standing up, livid.

He has just given me what is finished,
the heat of fire and the immense pronoun
that the animal reared under its tail.   10

He has just
expressed his doubts about remote hypotheses
which he distances, even further, with his gaze.

He has just bestowed on the good its rightful honors
by virtue of the infamous pachyderm,   15
through what is dreamed in me and in him killed.

He has just fixed (there is no first)
his second aflixion right in my shoulders   *
and his third sweat right in my tear.

He has just passed by without having come.   20*

×
×   ×

¡Ande desnudo, en pelo, el millonario!
¡Desgracia al que edifica con tesoros su lecho de muerte!
¡Un mundo al que saluda;
un sillón al que siembra en el cielo;
llanto al que da término a lo que hace, guardando los comienzos;
ande el de las espuelas;
poco dure muralla en que no crezca otra muralla;
dése al mísero toda su miseria,
pan, al que ríe;
hayan perder los triunfos y morir los médicos;
haya leche en la sangre;
añádase una vela al sol,
ochocientos al veinte;
pase la eternidad bajo los puentes!
¡Desdén al que viste,
corónense los pies de manos, quepan en su tamaño;
siéntese mi persona junto a mí!
¡Llorar al haber cabido en aquel vientre,
bendición al que mira aire en el aire,
muchos años de clavo al martillazo;
desnúdese el desnudo,
vístase de pantalón la capa,
fulja el cobre a expensas de sus láminas,
magestad al que cae de la arcilla al universo,
lloren las bocas, giman las miradas,
impídase al acero perdurar,
hilo a los horizontes portátiles,
doce ciudades al sendero de piedra,
una esfera al que juega con su sombra;
un día hecho de una hora, a los esposos;
una madre al arado en loor al suelo,
séllense con dos sellos a los líquidos,
pase lista el bocado,
sean los descendientes,
sea la codorniz,
sea la carrera del álamo y del árbol;
venzan, al contrario del círculo, el mar a su hijo
y a la cana el lloro;
dejad los áspides, señores hombres,
surcad la llama con los siete leños,
vivid,
elévese la altura,
baje el hondor más hondo,
conduzca la onda su impulsión andando,
tenga éxito la tregua de la bóveda!

×
× ×

Let the millionaire go naked, stark naked!   *
Disgrace for whoever builds his death bed with treasures!
A world for whoever greets;
an armchair for whoever sows in the sky;
tears for whoever finishes what he does, keeping the beginnings;   5
let the spur-wearer walk;
let the wall crumble on which another wall is not growing;
let the miserable man have all his misery,
bread, for whoever laughs;
let the triumphs lose and the doctors die;   10
let milk be in our blood;
let a candle be added to the sun,
eight hundred to twenty;
let eternity pass under the bridges!
Scorn for whoever puts on clothes,   15
let our feet be crowned with hands, be fit in their size;
let my person sit next to me!
To cry having fit in that womb,
grace for whoever sees air in the air,
many years of nail for the hammer stroke;   20
let the naked man be stripped naked,
let the cape put on pants,
let the copper gleam at the expense of its plates,
magesty for whoever falls from the clay to the universe,   *
let the mouths weep, let the glances groan,   25
let us stop the steel from enduring,
thread for the portable horizons,
twelve cities for the stone path,
a sphere for whoever plays with his shadow;
a day made of an hour, for married people;   30
a mother at the plow in praise of the soil,
let the liquids be sealed with two seals,
let the mouthful call the roll,
let the descendants be,
let the quail be,   35
let the poplar and the tree have their race;
let the sea, contrary to the circle, defeat his son
and the crying, grey hair;
leave the asps alone, gentle sirs,
furrow your flame with the seven logs,   40
live,
let the height be raised,
let the deepness descend deeper,   *
let the wave drive its impulse walking,
let the vault's truce be a success!   45

¡Muramos;
lavad vuestro esqueleto cada día;
no me hagáis caso,
una ave coja al déspota y a su alma;
una mancha espantosa, al que va solo;
gorriones al astrónomo, al gorrión, al aviador!
¡Lloved, solead,
vigilad a Júpiter, al ladrón de ídolos de oro,
copiad vuestra letra en tres cuadernos,
aprended de los cónyuges cuando hablan, y
de los solitarios, cuando callan;
dad de comer a los novios,
dad de beber al diablo en vuestras manos,
luchad por la justicia con la nuca,
igualaos,
cúmplase el roble,
cúmplase el leopardo entre dos robles,
seamos,
estémos,
sentid cómo navega el agua en los océanos,
alimentaos,
concíbase el error, puesto que lloro,
acéptese, en tanto suban por el risco, las cabras y sus crías;
desacostumbrad a Dios a ser un hombre,
creced . . . !
Me llaman. Vuelvo.

19 Nov. 1937

Let us die;
wash your skeleton every day;
pay no attention to me,
let a bird grasp the despot and his soul;
an awful stain, for whoever walks around alone;   50
sparrows for the astronomer, for the sparrow, an aviator!
Give off rain, give off sun,
keep an eye on Jupiter, on the thief of your gold idols,
copy your hand-writing in three notebooks,
learn from the couples when they speak, and   55
from the lonely, when they are silent;
give food to the sweethearts,
give drink to the devil from your hands,
fight for justice with your nape,
make yourselves equal,   60
let the oak be fulfilled,
let the leopard be fulfilled between two oaks,
let us be,
let us be here,
let us feel how the water sails in the oceans,   65
take nourishment,
let the error be conceived, since I am crying,
accept it, while goats and their young climb along the cliff;
make God break the habit of being a man,
grow up . . . !   70
I am called. I am going back.

×
×　×

Viniere el malo, con un trono al hombro,
y el bueno, a acompañar al malo a andar;
dijeren "sí" el sermón, "no" la plegaria
y cortare el camino en dos la roca . . .

Comenzare por monte la montaña,
por remo el tallo, por timón el cedro
y esperaren doscientos a sesenta
y volviere la carne a sus tres títulos . . .

Sobrase nieve en la noción del fuego,
se acostare el cadáver a mirarnos,
la centella a ser trueno corpulento
y se arquearen los saurios a ser aves . . .

Faltare excavación junto al estiércol,
naufragio al río para resbalar,
cárcel al hombre libre, para serlo
y una atmósfera al cielo, y hierro al oro . . .

Mostraren disciplina, olor, las fieras,
se pintare el enojo de soldado,
me dolieren el junco que aprendí,
la mentira que inféctame y socórreme . . .

Sucediere ello así y así poniéndolo,
¿con qué mano despertar?
¿con qué pie morir?
¿con qué ser pobre?
¿con qué voz callar?
¿con cuánto comprender, y luego, a quién?

No olvidar ni recordar
que por mucho cerrarla, robáronse la puerta,
y de sufrir tan poco estoy muy resentido,
y de tánto pensar, no tengo boca.

19 Nov. 1937

×
×   ×

That the evil man might come, with a throne on his shoulder,   *
and the good man, to walk with the evil man for company;
that the sermon might say "yes," the prayer "no"
and that the path might cut the rock in two . . .

That the mountain might begin as a hill,   5
the stalk as an oar, the cedar as a tiller
and that two hundred might wait for sixty
and that the flesh might return to its three titles . . .

That there might be too much snow in the notion of fire,   *
that the corpse might lay down to watch us,   10
the flash might be corpulent thunder
and that the saurians might arch to become birds . . .

That the dung might lack an excavation nearby,   *
the river a shipwreck so to slide,
the free man a jail, so to be free   15
and the sky an atmosphere, and gold iron . . .   *

That wild beasts might show discipline, odor,
that anger might disguise itself as a soldier,
that the reed I learned might ache me,
the lie that infects and helps me . . .   20

That it might happen this way and thus stating it,
with what hand to awake?
with what foot to die?
with what to be poor?   *
with what voice to keep quiet?   25
with how much to understand, and then, whom?

Not to forget nor to remember
that from closing it too often, they stole the door,
and from suffering so little I am very resentful,
and from so *much* thinking, I have no mouth.   30*

×
× ×

Al revés de las aves del monte,
que viven del valle,
aquí, una tarde,
aquí, presa, metaloso, terminante,
vino el Sincero con sus nietos pérfidos,
y nosotros quedámonos, que no hay
más madera en la cruz de la derecha,
ni más hierro en el clavo de la izquierda,
que un apretón de manos entre zurdos.

Vino el Sincero, ciego, con sus lámparas.
Se vió al Pálido, aquí, bastar
al Encarnado;
nació de puro humilde el Grande;
la guerra,
esta tórtola mía, nunca nuestra,
diseñóse, borróse, ovó, matáronla.

Llevóse el Ebrio al labio un roble, porque
amaba, y una astilla
de roble, porque odiaba;
trenzáronse las trenzas de los potros
y la crin de las potencias;
cantaron los obreros; fuí dichoso.

El Pálido abrazóse al Encarnado
y el Ebrio, saludónos, escondiéndose.
Como era aquí y al terminar el día,
¡qué más tiempo que aquella plazoleta!
¡qué año mejor que esa gente!
¡qué momento más fuerte que ese siglo!

Pues de lo que hablo no es
sino de lo que pasa en esta época, y
de lo que ocurre en China y en España, y en el mundo.
(Walt Whitman tenía un pecho suavísimo y res-
piraba y nadie sabe lo que él hacía cuando lloraba en su comedor.)

×
× ×

Contrary to the mountain birds,
that live off the valley,
here, one afternoon,   *
here, imprisoned, the Sincere,
metalous, decisive, came with his perfidious grandchildren,   5*
and we remained, because there is no
more wood in the cross to the right,
nor more iron in the nail to the left,
than a handshake between the lefthanded.

The Sincere came, blind, with his lamps.   10
The Pale was seen, here, to be enough
for the Flesh-colored;
by sheer humbleness the Great was born;   *
the war,
this turtledove of mine, never ours,   15
sketched itself, erased itself, laid eggs, it was killed.

The Inebriated raised an oak to his lip, because
he loved, and a splinter
of oak, because he hated;
the colts' braids and the mane of the powers   20
braided themselves;
the workers sang; I was happy.

The Pale embraced the Flesh-colored
and the Inebriated, greeted us, hiding.
Since it was here and when the day ended,   25
how much more time than that small plaza!
what year better than those people!
what moment stronger than that century!

For what I am talking about is
nothing other than what is taking place in our time, and   30*
what is taking place in China and in Spain, and in the world.
(Walt Whitman had a very soft chest and breathed and nobody knows
what he was doing when he was crying in his dining room.)

Pero, volviendo, a lo nuestro,
y al verso que decía, fuera entonces
que ví que el hombre es malnacido,
mal vivo, mal muerto, mal moribundo,
y, naturalmente,
el tartufo sincero desespérase,
el pálido (es el pálido de siempre)
será pálido por algo,
y el ebrio, entre la sangre humana y la leche animal,
abátese, da, y opta por marcharse.

Todo esto
agítase, ahora mismo,
en mi vientre de macho entrañamente.

20 Nov. 1937

But, getting back to our subject,
and to the line that I wrote, it was then   35
I saw that man is evilborn,
evil alive, evil dead, evil dying,
and, naturally,
the sincere tartuffe despairs,
the pale (the one who is always pale)   40
will be for some reason pale,
and the inebriated, between human blood and animal milk,
slumps, gives up, and decides to take off.

   All this
stirs, right now,   45
in my male belly surprisingly.   *

×
×　×

Ello es que el lugar donde me pongo
el pantalón, es una casa donde
me quito la camisa en alta voz
y donde tengo un suelo, un alma, un mapa de mi España
Ahora mismo hablaba
de mí conmigo, y ponía
sobre un pequeño libro un pan tremendo
y he, luego, hecho el traslado, he trasladado,
queriendo canturrear un poco, el lado
derecho de la vida al lado izquierdo;
más tarde, me he lavado todo, el vientre,
briosa, dignamente;
he dado vuelta a ver lo que se ensucia,
he raspado lo que me lleva tan cerca
y he ordenado bien el mapa que
cabeceaba o lloraba, no lo sé.

Mi casa, por desgracia, es una casa,
un suelo por ventura, donde vive
con su inscripción mi cucharita amada,
mi querido esqueleto ya sin letras,
la navaja, un cigarro permanente.
De veras, cuando pienso
en lo que es la vida,
no puedo evitar de decírselo a Georgette,
a fin de comer algo agradable y salir,
por la tarde, comprar un buen periódico,
guardar un día para cuando no haya,
una noche también, para cuando haya
(así se dice en el Perú—me excuso);
del mismo modo, sufro con gran cuidado,
a fin de no gritar o de llorar, ya que los ojos
poseen, independientemente de uno, sus pobrezas,
quiero decir, su oficio, algo
que resbala del alma y cae al alma.

Habiendo atravesado
quince años; después, quince, y, antes, quince,
uno se siente, en realidad, tontillo,
es natural, por lo demás, ¡que hacer!
¿Y qué dejar de hacer, que es lo peor?
Sino vivir, sino llegar
á ser lo que es uno entre millones
de panes, entre miles de vinos, entre cientos de bocas,
entre el sol y su rayo que es de luna
y entre la misa, el pan, el vino y mi alma.

×
× ×

The fact is that the place where I put on
my pants, is a house where
I take off my shirt out loud
and where I have a ground, a soul, a map of my Spain.
Just now I was speaking   5
about me with myself and placing
on top of a little book a tremendous loaf of bread
and I have, then, made the move, I have moved,
trying to hum a little, the right
side of life to the left side;   10
later, I have washed all of me, my belly,
vigorously, with dignity;
I have turned around to see what gets dirty,
I have scraped what takes me so near
and I have properly ordered the map that   15
was nodding off or crying, I don't know.

My house, unfortunately, is a house,
a ground fortunately, where with its
inscription my beloved little spoon lives,
my dear skeleton now unlettered,   20
the pocket knife, a permanent cigar.
Truthfully, when I think
what life is,
I cannot help saying it to Georgette,   *
to be able to eat something nice and go out,   25
in the afternoon, to buy a good newspaper,
to save a day for when there isn't one,
a night too, for when there is
(that is a Peruvian saying—my apologies);
in the same way, I suffer with great care,   30
in order not to shout or cry, since our eyes
have, independent of oneself, their poverties,
I mean, their trade, something
that slips from the soul and falls to the soul.

Having gone through   35
fifteen years; fifteen years, after, and, fifteen years, before,   *
one feels, really, a little dumb,
it's natural, on the other hand, what can one do!
And what can one stop doing, that's even worse!
But to live, but to become   40
what one is among millions
of loaves, among thousands of wines, among hundreds of mouths,
between the sun and its beam, a moonbeam
and among the Mass, the bread, the wine and my soul.

Hoy es domingo y, por eso,
me viene a la cabeza la idea, al pecho el llanto
y a la garganta, así como un gran bulto.
Hoy es domingo, y esto
tiene muchos siglos; de otra manera,
sería, quizá, lunes, y vendríame al corazón la idea,
al seso, el llanto
y a la garganta, una gana espantosa de ahogar
lo que ahora siento,
como un hombre que soy y que he sufrido.

21 Nov. 1937

   Today is Sunday and, for this reason,   45
the idea comes to my mind, the crying to my chest
and to my throat, something like a big lump.
Today is Sunday, and this fact
is many centuries old; otherwise,
it would be, perhaps, Monday, and the idea would have come to my heart,   50
the crying to my brain
and to my throat, an awful desire to drown
what I now feel,
like a man that I am and who has suffered.

×
×   ×

Algo te identifica con el que se aleja de ti, y es la facultad
común de volver: de ahí tu más grande pesadumbre.

Algo te separa del que se queda contigo, y es la esclavitud
común de partir: de ahí tus más nimios regocijos.

Me dirijo, en esta forma, a las individualidades colectivas,
tanto como a las colectividades individuales y a los que, entre
unas y otras, yacen marchando al son de las fronteras o, simplemente,
marcan el paso inmóvil en el borde del mundo.

Algo típicamente neutro, de inexorablemente neutro, interpónese
entre el ladrón y su víctima. Esto, asimismo, puede discernirse
tratándose del cirujano y del paciente. Horrible medialuna, convexa
y solar, cobija a unos y otros. Porque el objeto hurtado tiene tam-
bién su peso indiferente, y el órgano intervenido, también su grasa
triste.

¿Qué hay de más desesperante en la tierra, que la imposibilidad
en que se halla el hombre feliz de ser infortunado y el hombre bue-
no, de ser malvado?

¡Alejarse! ¡Quedarse! ¡Volver! ¡Partir! Toda la mecánica social cabe
en estas palabras.

×
× ×

Something identifies you with the one who leaves you, and it is
your common power to return: thus your greatest sorrow.
Something separates you from the one who remains with you,
and it is your common slavery to depart: thus your meagerest
rejoicing.   5
I address myself, in this way, to collective individualities,
as well as to individual collectivities and to those who, between them
both, lie marching to the sound of the frontiers or, simply, mark
time without moving at the edge of the world.
Something typically neuter, inexorably neuter, stands between   10
the thief and his victim. This, likewise, can be noticed in the relation
between a surgeon and his patient. A horrible halfmoon, convex and
solar, covers all of them. For the stolen object has also its indifferent
weight, and the operated on organ, also its sad fat.
What on earth is more exasperating, than the impossibility for   15
the happy man to become unhappy, and the good man to become wicked?
To leave! To remain! To return! To depart! The whole social
mechanism fits in these words.

$$\times$$
$$\times \quad \times$$

En suma, no poseo para expresar mi vida sino mi muerte.

Y, después de todo, al cabo de la escalonada naturaleza y del gorrión en bloque, me duermo, mano a mano con mi sombra.

Y, al descender del acto venerable y del otro gemido, me reposo pensando en la marcha impertérrita del tiempo.

¿Por qué la cuerda, entonces, si el aire es tan sencillo? ¿Para qué la cadena, si existe el hierro por sí sólo?

César Vallejo, el acento con que amas, el verbo con que escribes, el vientecillo con que oyes, sólo saben de ti por tu garganta.

César Vallejo, póstrate, por eso, con indistinto orgullo, con tálamo de ornamentales áspides y exagonales ecos.

Restitúyete al corpóreo panal, a la beldad; aroma los floridos corchos, cierra ambas grutas al sañudo antropoide; repara, en fin, tu antipático venado; tente pena.

¡Que no hay cosa más densa que el odio en voz pasiva, ni más mísera ubre que el amor!

¡Que ya no puedo andar sino en dos harpas!

¡Que ya no me conoces, sino porque te sigo instrumental, prolijamente!

¡Que ya no doy gusanos, sino breves!

¡Que ya te implico tánto, que medio que te afilas!

¡Que ya llevo unas tímidas legumbres y otras bravas!

Pues el afecto que quiébrase de noche en mis bronquios, lo trajeron de día ocultos deanes y, si amanezco pálido, es por mi obra; y si anochezco rojo, por mi obrero. Ello explica, igualmente, estos cansancios míos y estos despojos, mis famosos tíos. Ello explica, en fin, esta lágrima que brindo por la dicha de los hombres.

¡César Vallejo, parece
mentira que así tarden tus parientes,
sabiendo que ando cautivo,
sabiendo que yaces libre!
¡Vistosa y perra suerte!
¡César Vallejo, te odio con ternura!

25 Nov. 1937

×
× ×

In short, I have nothing with which to express my life except my   *
death.
    And, after all, at the end of graded nature and the sparrow in
bloc, I sleep, hand in hand with my shadow.
    And, upon descending from the venerable act and from the other   5
groan, I rest thinking about the inexorable march of time.
    Why the rope, then, if air is so simple? What is the chain for,
if iron exists on its own?
    César Vallejo, the accent with which you love, the language with
which you write, the soft wind with which you hear, only know of you   10
through your throat.
    César Vallejo, fall on your knees, therefore, with indistinct pride,
with a bridal bed of ornamental asps and hexagonal echoes.
    Return to the corporeal honey comb, to Beauty; aromatize the
blossomed corks, close both caves to the enraged anthropoid; mend,   15
finally, your unpleasant stag; feel sorry for yourself.
    For there is nothing denser than hate in the passive voice, no
stingier udder than love!
    For I am no longer able to walk, except on two harps!
    For you no longer know me, unless instrumentally, fastidiously   20
I follow you!
    For I no longer issue worms, but breves!
    For I now implicate you so much, you almost become sharp!
    For I now carry some timid vegetables and others that are fierce!
    Because the affection that ruptures at night in my bronchia, was brought   25
during the day by hidden deacons and, if when my morning begins I am pale,
it is because of my work; and if when my night begins I am red, because of
my worker. This equally explains this weariness of mine and these spoils, my
famous uncles. This explains, finally, this tear that I offer as a toast to the
happiness of men.   30
    César Vallejo, it is hard
to believe that your relatives are so late,
knowing that I walk imprisoned,
knowing that you lie free!
What dazzling and shitty luck!   35
César Vallejo, I hate you with tenderness!

×
× ×

Otro poco de calma, camarada;
un mucho inmenso, septentrional, completo,
feroz, de calma chica,
al servicio menor de cada triunfo
y en la audaz servidumbre del fracaso.

Embriaguez te sobra, y no hay
tanta locura en la razón, como este
tu raciocinio muscular, y no hay
más racional error que tu experiencia.

Pero, hablando más claro
y pensándolo en oro, eres de acero.
a condición que no seas
tonto y rehuses
entusiasmarte por la muerte tánto
y por la vida, con tu sola tumba.

Necesario es que sepas
contener tu volúmen sin correr, sin afligirte,
tu realidad molecular entera
y más allá, la marcha de tus vivas
y más acá, tus mueras legendarios.

Eres de acero, como dicen,
con tal que no tiembles y no vayas
a reventar, compadre
de mi cálculo, enfático ahijado
de mis sales luminosas!

Anda, no más; resuelve,
considera tu crisis, suma, sigue,
tájala, bájala, ájala;
el destino, las energías íntimas, los catorce
versículos del pan; ¡cuántos diplomas
y poderes, al borde fehaciente de tu arranque!
¡Cuánto detalle en síntesis, contigo!
¡Cuánta presión idéntica, a tus pies!
¡Cuánto rigor y cuánto patrocinio!

×
× ×

A little more calm, comrade;
an immense much, northern, complete,
ferocious, of small calm,
at the minor service of each triumph
and in the audacious servitude of defeat.   5

You have intoxication to spare, and there is not
so much craziness in reason, as in this
your muscular reasoning, and there is no
more rational error than your experience.

But, saying it more clearly   10
and thinking it in gold, you are made of steel,
on condition that you are not
dumb and refuse
to become so enthusiastic about death
and about life, with your sole tomb.   15

It is necessary for you to learn
how to contain your volume without running, without grieving,   *
your entire molecular reality
and beyond, the march of your long live
and closer, your legendary death to.   20

You are made of steel, as it is said,
providing you do not tremble and do not start
exploding, godfather
of my calculation, emphatic godson
of my luminous salts!   25

Go right ahead; decide,
think about your crisis, add, carry,
cut it up, humble it, crumble it;
destiny, the intimate energies, the fourteen
verses of bread; how many diplomas   30
and powers, at the trustful edge of your start!
How much synthesized detail, in you!
How much identical pressure, at your feet!
How much rigor and how much patronage!

Es idiota
ese método de padecimiento,
esa luz modulada y virulenta,
si con sólo la calma haces señales
serias, características, fatales.

Vamos a ver, hombre;
cuéntame lo que me pasa,
que yo, aunque grite, estoy siempre a tus órdenes.

28 Nov. 1937

It is idiotic 35
that method of suffering,
that modulated and virulent light,
if with only calm you flash serious,
characteristic, fatal, signals.

Come on, man; 40
tell me what is happening to me,
for I, even when shouting, am always at your command.

Los desgraciados

Ya va a venir el día; da
cuerda a tu brazo, búscate debajo
del colchón, vuelve a pararte
en tu cabeza, para andar derecho.
Ya va a venir el día, ponte el saco.

Ya va a venir el día; ten
fuerte en la mano a tu intestino grande, reflexiona,
antes de meditar, pues es horrible
cuando le cae a uno la desgracia
y se le cae a uno a fondo el diente.

Necesitas comer, pero, me digo,
no tengas pena, que no es de pobres
la pena, el sollozar junto a su tumba;
remiéndate, recuerda,
confía en tu hilo blanco, fuma, pasa lista
a tu cadena y guárdala detrás de tu retrato.
Ya va a venir el día, ponte el alma.

Ya va a venir el día; pasan,
han abierto en el hotel un ojo,
azotándolo, dándole con un espejo tuyo . . .
¿tiemblas? Es el estado remoto de la frente
y la nacion reciente del estómago.
Roncan aún . . . ¡Qué universo se lleva este ronquido!
¡Cómo quedan tus poros, enjuiciándolo!
¡Con cuántos doses, ¡ay! estás tan solo!
Ya va a venir el día, ponte el sueño.

Ya va a venir el día, repito
por el órgano oral de tu silencio
y urge tomar la izquierda con el hambre
y tomar la derecha con la sed; de todos modos,
abstente de ser pobre con los ricos,
atiza
tu frío, porque en él se integra mi calor, amada víctima.
Ya va a venir el día, ponte el cuerpo.

The miserable

The day is about to come; wind
up your arm, look for yourself under
the mattress, stand again
on your head, to walk straight.
The day is about to come, put on your coat.   5

The day is about to come; grip
your large intestine tight in your hand, reflect,
before you meditate, for it is horrible
when misfortune falls on one
and one's tooth falls thoroughly.   10

You have to eat, but, I tell myself,
do not grieve, for grief and graveside
sobbing do not belong to the poor;
mend yourself, remember,
trust your white thread, smoke, call roll   15
on your chain and keep it behind your portrait.
The day is about to come, put on your soul.

The day is about to come; they go by,
they have opened an eye in the hotel,
lashing it, beating it with one of your mirrors . . .   20
are you trembling? It is the remote state of your forehead
and the recent nation of your stomach.
They're still snoring . . . What a universe is carried away by this snore!
And in what state your pores are left, on judging it!
With so many twos, my god! how alone you are!   25
The day is about to come, put on your dream.

The day is about to come, I repeat
through the oral organ of your silence
and it is urgent to take the left with your hunger
and to take the right with your thirst; in any case,   30
abstain from being poor with the rich,
stir
your cold, for my warmth becomes part of it, beloved victim.
The day is about to come, put on your body.

Ya va a venir el día;
la mañana, la mar, el meteoro, van
en pos de tu cansancio, con banderas,
y, por tu orgullo clásico, las hienas
cuentan sus pasos al compás del asno,
la panadera piensa en ti,
el carnicero piensa en ti, palpando
el hacha en que están presos
el acero y el hierro y el metal; jamás olvides
que durante la misa no hay amigos.
Ya va a venir el día, ponte el sol.

Ya viene el día; dobla
el aliento, triplica
tu bondad rencorosa
y da codos al miedo, nexo y énfasis,
pues tú, como se observa en tu entrepierna y siendo
el malo, ¡ay! inmortal,
has soñado esta noche que vivías
de nada y morías de todo . . .

   The day is about to come;   35
the morning, the sea, the meteor, go
after your weariness, with banners,
and, because of your classic pride, the hyenas
count their steps to the beat of the jackass,
the baker's wife thinks about you,   40
the butcher thinks about you, groping
the ax in which the steel
and the iron and the metal are imprisoned; never forget
that during Mass there are no friends.
The day is about to come, put on your sun.   45

   The day is now coming; double
your breath, triple
your rancorous goodness
and scorn fear, nexus and emphasis,
for you, as one can observe in your crotch, the evil man   50
being, god! immortal,
have dreamed tonight that you were living
on nothing and dying from everything . . .

Sermón sobre la muerte

Y, en fin, pasando luego al dominio de la muerte,
que actúa en escuadrón, previo corchete,
párrafo y llave, mano grande y diéresis,
¿a qué el pupitre asirio? ¿a qué el cristiano púlpito,
el intenso jalón del mueble vándalo
o, todavía menos, este esdrújulo retiro?

¿Es para terminar,
mañana, en prototipo del alarde fálico,
en diabetes y en blanca vacinica,
en rostro geométrico, en difunto,
que se hacen menester sermón y almendras,
que sobran literalmente patatas
y este espectro fluvial en que arde el oro
y en que se quema el precio de la nieve?
¿Es para eso, que morimos tánto?
¿Para sólo morir
tenemos que morir a cada instante?
¿Y el párrafo que escribo?
¿Y el corchete deísta que enarbolo?
¿Y el escuadrón en que falló mi casco?
¿Y la llave que va a todas las puertas?
¿Y la forense diéresis, la mano,
mi patata y mi carne y mi contradicción bajo la sábana?

¡Loco de mí, lovo de mí, cordero
de mí, sensato, caballísimo de mí!
¡Pupitre, sí, toda la vida; púlpito,
también, toda la muerte!
Sermón de la barbarie: estos papeles;
esdrújulo retiro: este pellejo.

De esta suerte, cogitabundo, aurífero, brazudo,
defenderé mi presa en dos momentos,
con la voz y también con la laringe,
y del olfato físico con que oro
y del instinto de inmovilidad con que ando,
me honraré mientras viva—hay que decirlo;
se enorgullecerán mis moscardones,
porque, al centro, estoy yo, y a la derecha,
también, y, a la izquierda, de igual modo.

8 Dic. 1937

Sermon on death

And, finally, going now into the domain of death,
which works in squadron, former bracket,
paragraph and brace, piece brace and dieresis,   *
for what the Assyrian writing desk? for what the Christian pulpit?
the violent jerk of Vandal furniture   5
or, even less, this proparoxytonic retreat?

Is it in order to end,
tomorrow, as a prototype of phallic boasting,
as diabetes and a white bedpan,
as a geometric face, as a deadman,   10
that sermon and almonds become necessary,
that there are literally too many potatoes   *
and this watery spectre in which gold burns
and in which the price of snow is set on fire?
Is it for this, that we die so much?   15
Only to die,
must we die every second?
And the paragraph that I write?
And the deistic bracket that I raise on high?
And the squadron in which my skull failed?   20
And the brace that fits all doors?
And the forensic dieresis, the hand,
my potato and my flesh and my contradiction under the bedsheet?   *

Out of my mind, out of my wolve, out of   *
my lamb, sensible, out of my absolute equinity!   25
Writing desk, yes, my whole life; pulpit,
likewise, my whole death!
Sermon on barbarism: these papers;
proparoxytonic retreat: this skin.

In this way, cognitive, auriferous, thick armed,   30*
I will defend my catch in a couple of moments,
with voice and also with larynx,
and of the physical smell with which I pray
and of the instinct for immobility with which I walk,
I will be proud while I live—it must be said;   35
my horseflies will engorge on their own pride,
because, in the middle, I am, and to the right,
also, and, to the left, likewise.

ESPAÑA, APARTA DE MÍ ESTE CÁLIZ

(1937–1938)

SPAIN, TAKE THIS CUP FROM ME

HIMNO A LOS VOLUNTARIOS DE LA REPÚBLICA

Voluntario de España, miliciano
de huesos fidedignos, cuando marcha a morir tu corazón,
cuando marcha a matar con su agonía
mundial, no sé verdaderamente
qué hacer, dónde ponerme; corro, escribo, aplaudo,
lloro, atisbo, destrozo, apagan, digo
a mi pecho que acabe, al bien, que venga,
y quiero desgraciarme;
descúbrome la frente impersonal hasta tocar
el vaso de la sangre, me detengo,
detienen mi tamaño esas famosas caídas de arquitecto
con las que se honra el animal que me honra;
refluyen mis instintos a sus sogas,
humea ante mi tumba la alegría
y, otra vez, sin saber qué hacer, sin nada, déjame,
desde mi piedra en blanco, déjame,
solo,
cuadrumano, más acá, mucho más lejos,
al no caber entre mis manos tu largo rato extático,
quiebro contra tu rapidez de doble filo
mi pequeñez en traje de grandeza!

Un día, diurno, claro, atento, fértil
¡oh bienio, el de los lóbregos semestres suplicantes,
por el que iba la pólvora mordiéndose los codos!
¡oh dura pena y más duros pedernales¡
¡oh frenos los tascados por el pueblo!
Un día prendió el pueblo su fósforo cautivo, oró de cólera
y soberanamente pleno, circular,
cerró su natalicio con manos electivas;
arrastraban candado ya los déspotas
y en el candado, sus bacterias muertas . . .

¿Batallas? ¡No! Pasiones Y pasiones precedidas
de dolores con rejas de esperanzas,
de dolores de pueblos con esperanzas de hombres!
¡Muerte y pasión de paz, las populares!
¡Muerte y pasión guerreras entre olivos, entendámonos!
Tal en tu aliento cambian de agujas atmosféricas los vientos
y de llave las tumbas en tu pecho,
tu frontal elevándose a primera potencia de martirio.

El mundo exclama: "¡Cosas de españoles!" Y es verdad. Consideremos,
durante una balanza, a quema ropa,
a Calderón, dormido sobre la cola de un anfibio muerto,
o a Cervantes, diciendo: "Mi reino es de este mundo, pero
también del otro": ¡punta y filo en dos papeles!

HYMN TO THE VOLUNTEERS FOR THE REPUBLIC

Spanish volunteer, civilian-fighter   *
with veritable bones, when your heart marches to die,
when it marches to kill with its world-wide
agony, I don't know truly
what to do, where to place myself: I run, write, applaud,   5
cry, glimpse, tear apart, they extinguish, I tell
my chest to end, good, to come,
and I want to ruin myself;
I bare my impersonal forehead until I touch
the vessel of blood, I stop,   10
my size is checked by those famous falls of the architect
with which the animal that honors me honors itself;
my instincts flow back to their ropes,
joy smokes before my tomb
and, without knowing what to do, without anything, leave me,   15
from my blank stone, leave me,
alone,
quadrumane, closer, much more distant,
since your long ecstatic instant won't fit between my hands,   *
I swirl my tininess costumed in greatness   20
against your double-edged speed!

One fertile, attentive, clear, diurnal day
oh biennial, those lugubrious half-years of begging,   *
through which the gunpowder went biting its elbows!
oh hard sorrow and harder flints!   25
oh those bits champed by the people!
One day the people struck their captive match, prayed with anger
and supremely full, circular,
closed their birthday with elective hands;
the despots were already dragging padlock   30
and in the padlock, their dead bacteria . . .

Battles? No! Passions And passions preceded
by aches with bars of hopes,
by aches of nations with hopes of men!
Death and passion for peace, of common people!   35
Death and passion for war among olive trees, let's get it straight!
Thus in your breath the winds change atmospheric needles
and the tombs change key in your chest,
your frontal rising to the first power of martyrdom.

The world exclaims: "A Spanish matter!" And it's true. Consider,   40
in a balance, point-blank,
Calderón, asleep on the tail of a dead amphibian,
or Cervantes, saying: "My kingdom is of this world, but
also of the next one": point and edge in two roles!

Contemplemos a Goya, de hinojos y rezando ante un espejo,
a Coll, el paladín en cuyo asalto cartesiano
tuvo un sudor de nube el paso llano,
o a Quevedo, ese abuelo instantáneo de los dinamiteros,
o a Cajal, devorado por su pequeño infinito, o todavía
a Teresa, mujer, que muere porque no muere,
o a Lina Odena, en pugna en más de un punto con Teresa . . .
(Todo acto o voz genial viene del pueblo
y va hacia él, de frente o transmitidos
por incesantes briznas, por el humo rosado
de amargas contraseñas sin fortuna.)
Así tu criatura, miliciano, así tu exangüe criatura,
agitada por una piedra inmóvil,
se sacrifica, apártase,
decae para arriba y por su llama incombustible sube,
sube hasta los débiles,
distribuyendo españas a los toros
toros a las palomas . . .

   Proletario que mueres de universo, ¡en qué frenética armonía
acabará tu grandeza, tu miseria, tu vorágine impelente,
tu violencia metódica, tu caos teórico y práctico, tu gana
dantesca, españolísima, de amar, aunque sea a traición, a tu enemigo!
Liberador ceñido de grilletes,
sin cuyo esfuerzo hasta hoy continuaría sin asas la extención,
vagarían acéfalos los clavos,
antiguo, lento, colorado, el día,
¡nuestros amados cascos, insepultos!
Campesino caído con tu verde follaje por el hombre,
con la inflexión social de tu meñique,
con tu buey que se queda, con tu física,
también con tu palabra atada a un palo
y tu cielo arrendado
y con la arcilla inserta en tu cansancio
y la que estaba en tu uña, caminando!
¡Constructores
agrícolas, civiles y guerreros,
de la activa, hormigueante eternidad: estaba escrito
que vosotros haríais la luz, entornando
con la muerte vuestros ojos;
que, a la caída cruel de vuestras bocas,
vendrá en siete bandejas la abundancia, todo
en el mundo será de oro súbito
y el oro,
fabulosos mendigos de vuestra propia secreción de sangre,
y el oro mismo será entonces de oro!

   ¡Se amarán todos los hombres
y comerán tomados de las puntas de vuestros pañuelos tristes

Contemplate Goya, on his knees and praying before a mirror,   45
Coll, the palatine in whose cartesian assault   *
a slow walk had the sweat of a cloud,
or Quevedo, that instantaneous grandfather of the dynamiters,   *
or Cajal, devoured by his little infinite, or even   *
Teresa, a woman, dying because she was not dying,   50*
or Lina Odena, in conflict with Teresa on more than one point . . .   *
(Every act or brilliant voice comes from common people
and goes toward them, directly or conveyed
by incessant filaments, by the rosy smoke
of bitter watchwords which failed.)   55
Thus your creation, civilian-fighter, thus your anaemic child,
stirred by a motionless stone,
sacrifices itself, stands apart,
decays upward and through its incombustible flame rises,
rises to the weak,   60
distributing spains to the bulls,
bulls to the doves . . .

  Proletarian who dies of universe, in what frantic harmony
your grandeur will end, your extreme poverty, your impelling whirlpool,
your methodical violence, your theoretical and practical chaos, your Dantesque   65
wish, so very Spanish, to love, even treacherously, your enemy!
Liberator wrapped in shackles,
without whose labor extension would continue up to this day without handles,
the nails would wander headless,
the day, ancient, slow, reddish,   70
our beloved skulls, unburied!
Peasant fallen with your green foliage for man,
with the social inflection of your little finger,
with your ox that does not move, with your physics,
also with your word tied to a stick   75
and your rented sky
and with the clay inserted in your fatigue
and with that under your fingernail, walking!
Agricultural
builders, civilian and military,   80
of the active, swarming eternity: it was written
that you will create the light, half-closing
your eyes in death;
that, at the cruel fall of your mouths,
abundance will come on seven trays, everything   85
in the world will be of sudden gold
and the gold,
fabulous beggars for your own secretion of blood,
and the gold itself will then be made of gold!

  All men will love each other   90
and they will eat holding the corners of your sad handkerchiefs

y beberán en nombre
de vuestras gargantas infaustas!
Descansarán andando al pie de esta carrera,
sollozarán pensando en vuestras órbitas, venturosos
serán y al son
de vuestro atroz retorno, florecido, innato,
ajustarán mañana sus quehaceres, sus figuras soñadas y cantadas!

  ¡Unos mismos zapatos irán bien al que asciende
sin vías a su cuerpo
y al que baja hasta la forma de su alma!
¡Entrelazándose hablarán los mudos, los tullidos andarán!
¡Verán, ya de regreso, los ciegos
y palpitando escucharán los sordos!
¡Sabrán los ignorantes, ignorarán los sabios!
¡Serán dados los besos que no pudísteis dar!
¡Sólo la muerte morirá! ¡La hormiga
traerá pedacitos de pan al elefante encadenado
a su brutal delicadeza; ¡volverán
los niños abortados a nacer perfectos, espaciales
y trabajarán todos los hombres,
engendrarán todos los hombres
comprenderán todos los hombres!

  Obrero, salvador, redentor nuestro,
¡perdónanos, hermano, nuestras deudas!
Como dice un tambor al redoblar, en sus adagios:
qué jamás tan efímero, tu espalda!
qué siempre tan cambiante, tu perfil!

  ¡Voluntario italiano, entre cuyos animales de batalla
un león abisinio va cojeando!
¡Voluntario soviético, marchando a la cabeza de tu pecho universal!
¡Voluntarios del sur, del norte, del oriente
y tú, el occidental, cerrando el canto fúnebre del alba!
¡Soldado conocido, cuyo nombre
desfila en el sonido de un abrazo!
¡Combatiente que la tierra criara, armándote
de polvo,
calzándote de imanes positivos,
vigentes tus creencias personales,
distinto de carácter, íntima tu férula,
el cutis inmediato,
andándote tu idioma por los hombros
y el alma coronada de guijarros!
¡Voluntario fajado de tu zona fría,
templada o tórrida,
héroes a la redonda,
víctima en columna de vencedores:

and they will drink in the name
of your ill-fated throats!
They will rest walking at the edge of this course,
they will sob thinking about your orbits, fortunate   95
they will be and to the sound
of your atrocious, burgeoned, inborn return,
tomorrow they will adjust their chores, the figures they've dreamt and sung!

The same shoes will fit whoever climbs
without trails to his body   100
and whoever descends to the form of his soul!
Entwining one another the mutes will speak, the paralyzed will walk!
The blind, upon coming back, will see
and throbbing the deaf will hear!
The ignorant will be wise, the wise ignorant!   105
Kisses will be given that you could not give!
Only death will die! The ant
will bring breadcrumbs to the elephant chained
to his brutal gentleness; the aborted children
will be born again perfect, spacial   110
and all men will work,
all men will beget,
all men will understand!

Worker, our savior and redeemer,
forgive us, brother, our trespasses!   115
As a drum says on rolling, in its proverbs:
what an ephemeral never, your back!
what a changing always, your profile!

Italian volunteer, among whose animals of battle
an Abyssinian lion is limping!   120*
Soviet volunteer, marching at the head of your universal chest!
Volunteers from the South, from the North, from the Orient
and you, the Westerner, closing the funereal song of the dawn!
Known soldier, whose name
files by in the sound of an embrace!   125
Fighter that the land had raised, arming you
with dust,
shoeing you with positive magnets,
your personal beliefs in force,
your character distinct, your ferule intimate,   130*
your complexion immediate,
your language moving about your shoulders
and your soul crowned with cobblestones!
Volunteer bruised by your cold zone,
temperate or torrid,   135
roundabout heroes,
victims in a column of conquerors:

en España, en Madrid, están llamando
a matar, voluntarios de la vida!

¡Porque en España matan, otros matan
al niño, a su juguete que se pára,
a la madre Rosenda esplendorosa,
al viejo Adán que hablaba en alta voz con su caballo
y al perro que dormía en la escalera.
Matan al libro, tiran a sus verbos auxiliares,
a su indefensa página primera!
Matan el caso exacto de la estatua,
al sabio, a su bastón, a su colega,
al barbero de al lado—me cortó posiblemente,
pero buen hombre y, luego, infortunado;
al mendigo que ayer cantaba enfrente,
a la enfermera que hoy pasó llorando,
al sacerdote a cuestas con la altura tenaz de sus rodillas . . .

¡Voluntarios,
por la vida, por los buenos, matad
a la muerte, matad a los malos!
¡Hacedlo por la libertad de todos,
del explotado y del explotador,
por la paz indolora—la sospecho
cuando duermo al pie de mi frente
y más cuando circulo dando voces—
y hacedlo, voy diciendo,
por el analfabeto a quien escribo,
por el genio descalzo y su cordero,
por los camaradas caídos,
sus cenizas abrazadas al cadáver de un camino!

Para que vosotros,
voluntarios de España y del mundo, viniérais,
soñé que era yo bueno, y era para ver
vuestra sangre, voluntarios . . .
De esto hace mucho pecho, muchas ansias,
muchos camellos en edad de orar.
Marcha hoy de vuestra parte el bien ardiendo,
os siguen con cariño los reptiles de pestaña inmanente
y, a dos pasos, a uno,
la dirección del agua que corre a ver su límite antes que arda.

in Spain, in Madrid, the command
is to kill, volunteers who fight for life!

  Because they kill in Spain, others kill   140
the child, his toy that stops,
radiant mother Rosenda,
old Adam who talked out loud with his horse
and the dog that slept on the stairs.
They kill the book, they fire at its auxiliary verbs,   145
at its defenseless first page!
They kill the exact case of the statue,
the sage, his cane, his colleague,
the barber next door—maybe he cut me,
but a good man and, besides, unlucky;   150
the beggar who yesterday was singing before us,
the nurse who passed by crying,
the priest burdened with the stubborn highness of his knees . . .

  Volunteers,
for life, for the good people, kill   155
death, kill the bad people!
Do it for the freedom of everyone,
of the exploited and the exploiter,
for painless peace—I glimpse it
when I sleep at the base of my forehead   160
and even more when I circulate shouting—
and do it, I keep saying,
for the illiterate to whom I write,
for the barefoot genius and his lamb,
for the fallen comrades,   165
their ashes clasped to the corpse of a road!

  So that you,
volunteers for Spain and for the world, would come,
I dreamt that I was good, and it was to see
your blood, volunteers . . .   170
Since then there has been much chest, much anxiety,
many camels at the age of prayer.
Today good on your behalf marches in flames,
reptiles with immanent eyelashes follow you affectionately
and, at two steps, at one,   175
the direction of the water that runs to see its limit before it burns.

BATALLAS

II

Hombre de Estremadura,
oigo bajo tu pie el humo del lobo,
el humo de la especie,
el humo del niño,
el humo solitario de dos trigos,
el humo de Ginebra, el humo de Roma, el humo de Berlín
y el de París y el humo de tu apéndice penoso
y el humo que, al fin, sale del futuro.
¡Oh vida! ¡oh tierra! ¡oh España!
¡Onzas de sangre,
metros de sangre, líquidos de sangre,
sangre a caballo, a pie, mural, sin diámetro,
sangre de cuatro en cuatro, sangre de agua
y sangre muerta de la sangre viva!

Estremeño, ¡oh no ser aún ese hombre
por el que te mató la vida y te parió la muerte
y quedarse tan solo a verte así, desde este lobo,
cómo sigues arando en nuestros pechos!
¡Estremeño, conoces
  el secreto en dos voces, popular y táctil,
del cereal: ¡que nada vale tanto
como una gran raíz en trance de otra!
¡Estremeño acodado, representando al alma en su retiro,
acodado a mirar
el caber de una vida en una muerte!

¡Estremeño, y no haber tierra que hubiere
  el peso de tu arado, ni más mundo
que el color de tu yugo entre dos épocas; no haber
el orden de tus póstumos ganados!
¡Estremeño, dejásteme
verte desde este lobo, padecer,
pelear por todos y pelear
para que el individuo sea un hombre,
para que los señores sean hombres,
para que todo el mundo sea un hombre, y para
que hasta los animales sean hombres,
el caballo, un hombre,
el reptil, un hombre,
el buitre, un hombre honesto,
la mosca, un hombre, y el olivo, un hombre
y hasta el ribazo, un hombre
y el mismo cielo, todo un hombrecito!

BATTLES

II

Man from Estremadura,
I hear under your foot the smoke of the wolf,   *
the smoke of the species,   *
the smoke of the child,
the solitary smoke of two wheats,   5
the smoke of Geneva, the smoke of Rome, the smoke of Berlin
and that of Paris and the smoke of your painful appendix
and the smoke that, finally, comes out of the future.
Oh life! oh earth! oh Spain!
Ounces of blood,   10
meters of blood, liquids of blood,
blood on horseback, on foot, mural, without diameter,
blood four by four, blood of water
and dead blood from the living blood!   *

Estremanian, oh not yet to be that man   15
for whom life killed you and death gave birth to you   *
and to stay on only to see you like this, from this wolf,
how you go on plowing in our chests!   *
Estremanian, you know
the secret in both voices, the popular and the tactile,   20
of the cereal! That nothing is worth as much
as a big root at the point of another!
Estremanian bent on an elbow, picturing the soul in its retreat,   *
on an elbow to look at
the fitting of a life in a death!   25

Estremanian, and not to have land that would have
the weight of your plow, nor other world
than the color of your yoke between two epochs; not to have
the order of your posthumous herds!
Estremanian, you allowed me   30
to see you from this wolf, to endure,
to fight for everyone and to fight
so that the individual can become a man,
so that masters can become men,
so that everyone can become a man, and so   35
that even animals can become men,
the horse, a man,
the reptile, a man,
the vulture, an honest man,
the fly, a man, and the olive tree, a man   40
and even the riverbank, a man
and the very sky, a whole little man!   *

Luego, retrocediendo desde Talavera,
en grupos de a uno, armados de hambre, en masas de a uno,
armados de pecho hasta la frente,
sin aviones, sin guerra, sin rencor,
el perder a la espalda
y el ganar
más abajo del plomo, heridos mortalmente de honor,
locos de polvo, el brazo a pie,
amando por las malas,
ganando en español toda la tierra,
retroceder aún, y no saber
dónde poner su España,
dónde ocultar su beso de orbe,
dónde plantar su olivo de bolsillo!

Mas desde aquí, más tarde,
desde el punto de vista de esta tierra,
desde el duelo al que fluye el bien satánico,
se ve la gran batalla de Guernica.
¡Lid a priori, fuera de la cuenta,
lid en paz, lid de las almas débiles
contra los cuerpos débiles, lid en que el niño pega,
sin que le diga nadie que pegara,
bajo su atroz diptongo
y bajo su habilísimo pañal,
y en que la madre pega con su grito, con el dorso de una lágrima
y en que el enfermo pega con su mal, con su pastilla y su hijo
y en que el anciano pega
con sus canas, sus siglos y su palo
y en que pega el presbítero con dios!
¡Tácitos defensores de Guernica!
¡oh débiles!
¡oh suaves ofendidos,
que os eleváis, crecéis y llenáis de poderosos débiles el mundo!

Then, retreating from Talavera,   *
in groups of one, armed with hunger, in masses of one,
armed with chest up to the forehead,   45
without planes, without war, without rancor,
their loss over their backs   *
and their gain
lower than the lead, mortally wounded by honor,
crazed by dust, their arms on foot,   50
loving unwillingly,   *
conquering the whole earth in a Spanish way,   *
to still retreat, and not to know
where to put their Spain,
where to hide their orbital kiss,   55
where to plant their pocket-size olive tree!   *

But from here, later,   *
from the viewpoint of this land,
from the sorrow to which the satanic good flows,
the great battle of Guernica can be seen.   60*
An a priori combat, unheard of,
combat in peace, combat of weak souls
against weak bodies, combat in which the child strikes,
without anyone telling him to strike,
beneath his atrocious dipthong   65
and beneath his very clever diaper,
and in which a mother strikes with her scream, with the backside of a tear
and in which the sick man strikes with his disease, with his pill and his son
and in which the old man strikes
with his white hair, his centuries and his stick   70
and in which the priest strikes with God!
Tacit defenders of Guernica,   *
oh weak ones!
oh offended gentle ones,
who rise up, grow up and fill up the world with powerful weak ones! 75

En Madrid, en Bilbao, en Santander,
los cementerios fueron bombardeados,
y los muertos inmortales,
de vigilantes huesos y hombro eterno, de las tumbas,
los muertos inmortales, de sentir, de ver, de oír
tan bajo el mal, tan muertos a los viles agresores,
reanudaron entonces sus penas inconclusas,
acabaron de llorar, acabaron
de esperar, acabaron
de sufrir, acabaron de vivir,
acabaron, en fin, de ser mortales!

¡Y la pólvora fué, de pronto, nada,
cruzándose los signos y los sellos,
y a la explosión salióle al paso un paso,
y al vuelo a cuatro patas, otro paso
y al cielo apocalíptico, otro paso
y a los siete metales, la unidad,
sencilla, justa, colectiva, eterna.

¡Málaga sin padre ni madre,
ni piedrecilla, ni horno, ni perro blanco!
¡Málaga sin defensa, donde nació mi muerte dando pasos
y murió de pasión mi nacimiento!
¡Málaga caminando tras de tus pies, en éxodo,
bajo el mal, bajo la cobardía, bajo la historia cóncava, indecible,
con la yema en tu mano: tierra orgánica!
y la clara en la punta del cabello: ¡todo el caos!
¡Málaga huyendo
de padre a padre, familiar, de tu hijo a tu hijo,
a lo largo del mar que huye del mar,
a través del metal que huye del plomo,
al ras del suelo que huye de la tierra
y a las órdenes ¡ay!
de la profundidad que te quería!
¡Málaga a golpes, a fatídico coágulo, a bandidos, a infiernazos,
a cielazos,
andando sobre duro vino, en multitud,
sobre la espuma lila, de uno en uno,
sobre huracán estático y más lila,
y al compás de las cuatro órbitas que aman
y de las dos costillas que se matan!
¡Málaga de mi sangre diminuta

In Madrid, in Bilbao, in Santander,
the cemeteries were bombed,   *
and the immortal dead,
with vigilant bones and eternal shoulder, from their tombs,
the immortal dead, upon feeling, upon seeing, upon hearing   80
how low the evil, how dead the miserable aggressors,
then resumed their unconcluded sentences,
they finished crying, finished
hoping, finished
aching, finished living,   85
finished, finally, being mortal!

And the gunpowder was, suddenly, nothing,
signs and seals crossing each other,
and before the explosion a step appeared,
and before the flight on all fours, another step   90
and before the apocalyptic sky, another step
and before the seven metals, the unity,
simple, just, collective, eternal.   *

Málaga without father nor mother,   *
nor pebble, nor oven, nor white dog!   95
Málaga defenseless, where my death was born taking steps
and my birth died of passion!
Málaga walking after your feet, in exodus,
under evil, under cowardice, under the concave inexpressible history,
with the yolk in your hand: organic earth!   100
and the white in your hair tips: the whole chaos!
Málaga fleeing
from father to father, familiar, from your son to your son,
along the sea which flees from the sea,
through the metal which flees from the lead,   105
level with the ground which flees from the dirt
and to the orders, my god!
of the profundity that loved you!
Málaga beaten up, fatidically clotted, bandit infested, hellstruck,
heavenslashed,   110
walking over hard wine, crowded,
over the lilac scum, one by one,
over a more lilac and static hurricane,
and to the rhythm of the four orbits that love
and of the two ribs that kill each other!   115
Málaga of my minute blood

y mi coloración a gran distancia,
la vida sigue con tambor a tus honores alazanes,
con cohetes, a tus niños eternos
y con silencio a tu último tambor,
con nada, a tu alma,
y con más nada, a tu esternón genial!
¡Málaga, no te vayas con tu nombre!
¡Que si te vas,
te vas
toda, hacia ti, infinitamente toda en son total,
concorde con tu tamaño fijo en que me aloco,
con tu suela feraz y su agujero
y tu navaja antigua atada a tu hoz enferma
y tu madero atado a un martillo!
¡Málaga literal y malagüeña,
huyendo a Egipto, puesto que estás clavada,
alargando en sufrimiento idéntico tu danza,
resolviendo en ti el volumen de la esfera,
perdiendo tu botijo, tus cánticos, huyendo
con tu España exterior y tu orbe innato!
¡Málaga por derecho propio
y en el jardín biológico, más Málaga!
¡Málaga en virtud
del camino, en atención al lobo que te sigue
y en razón del lobezno que te espera!
¡Málaga que estoy llorando!
¡Málaga, que lloro y lloro!

and my coloration at a great distance,
life follows with a drum your sorrel-draped honors,
with rockets, your eternal children,
and with silence, your last drum,   120
with nothing, your soul,
and with more nothing, your brilliant breastbone!
Málaga, don't go away with your name!
For if you go,
you go   125
wholly, toward yourself, infinitely whole in its whole,
equal to your fixed size in which I go mad,
with your fertile sole and its hole
and your pocket-knife tied to your sick sickle
and your beam tied to a hammer!   130
Literal and Malagüeñan Málaga,   *
fleeing to Egypt, since you are nailed
prolonging in identical suffering your dance,
reducing to yourself the volume of the sphere,
losing your water-jug, your canticles, fleeing   135
with your exterior Spain and your inborn world!
Málaga by its own right
and in the biological garden, more Málaga!
Málaga by virtue
of the road, in view of the wolf that follows you   140
and because of the wolf-cub that awaits you!
Málaga how I am crying!
Málaga, how I cry and cry!

III

Solía escribir con su dedo grande en el aire:
"¡Viban los compañeros! Pedro Rojas",
de Miranda de Ebro, padre y hombre,
marido y hombre, ferroviario y hombre,
padre y más hombre, Pedro y sus dos muertes.

Papel de viento, lo han matado: ¡pasa!
Pluma de carne, lo han matado: ¡pasa!
"¡Abisa a todos compañeros pronto!"

Palo en el que han colgado su madero,
lo han matado:
¡lo han matado al pie de su dedo grande!
¡Han matado, a la vez, a Pedro, a Rojas!

¡Viban los compañeros
a la cabecera de su aire escrito!
¡Viban con esta b del buitre en las entrañas
de Pedro
y de Rojas, del héroe y del mártir!

Registrándole, muerto, sorprendiéronle
en su cuerpo un gran cuerpo, para
el alma del mundo,
y en la chaqueta una cuchara muerta.

Pedro también solía comer
entre las criaturas de su carne, asear, pintar
la mesa y vivir dulcemente
en representación de todo el mundo
y esta cuchara anduvo en su chaqueta,
despierto o bien cuando dormía, siempre,
cuchara muerta viva, ella y sus símbolos.
¡Abisa a todos compañeros pronto!
¡Viban los compañeros al pie de esta cuchara para siempre!

Lo han matado, obligándole a morir
a Pedro, a Rojas, al obrero, al hombre, a aquél
que nació muy niñín, mirando al cielo,
y que luego creció, se puso rojo
y luchó con sus células, sus nos, sus todavías, sus hambres, sus pedazos.
Lo han matado suavemente
entre el cabello de su mujer, la Juana Vásquez,
a la hora del fuego, al año del balazo
y cuando andaba cerca ya de todo.

III

He used to write with his big finger in the air:
"Long live all combanions! Pedro Rojas,"
from Miranda de Ebro, father and man,
husband and man, railroad-worker and man,
father and more man, Pedro and his two deaths.   5

    Wind paper, he was killed: pass on!
Flesh pen, he was killed: pass on!
"Advise all combanions quick!"

    Stick on which they've hanged his beam,
he was killed;
he was killed at the base of his big finger!   10*
They've killed, in one blow, Pedro and Rojas!

    Long live all combanions
written at the head of his air!
Let them live with this buzzard b in Pedro's   15
and in Rojas'
and in the hero's and in the martyr's guts!

    Searching him, dead, they surprised
in his body a greater body, for
the soul of the world,   20
and in his jacket a dead spoon.

    Pedro too used to eat
among the creatures of his flesh, to clean up, to paint
the table and to live sweetly
as a representative of everyone,   25
and this spoon was in his jacket,
awake or else when he slept, always,
dead alive spoon, this one and its symbols.
Advise all combanions quick!
Long live all combanions at the foot of this spoon forever!   30

    He was killed, they forced him to die,
Pedro, Rojas, the worker, the man, the one
who was born a wee baby, looking at the sky,
and who afterwards grew up, blushed
and fought against his cells, his nos, his yets, his hungers, his pieces.   35*
He was killed softly
in his wife's hair, Juana Vásquez by name,
at the hour of fire, in the year of the gunshot
and when he was already close to everything.   *

Pedro Rojas, así, después de muerto,
se levantó, besó su catafalco ensangrentado,
lloró por España
y volvió a escribir con el dedo en el aire:
"¡Viban los compañeros! Pedro Rojas."
Su cadáver estaba lleno de mundo.

    Pedro Rojas, thus, after being dead,   40
got up, kissed his bloodsmeared casket,
cried for Spain
and again wrote with his finger in the air:
"Long live all combanions! Pedro Rojas."
His corpse was full of world.   45

IV

Los mendigos pelean por España,
mendigando en París, en Roma, en Praga
y refrendando así, con mano gótica, rogante,
los pies de los Apóstoles, en Londres, en New York, en México.
Los pordioseros luchan suplicando infernalmente
a Dios por Santander,
la lid en que ya nadie es derrotado.
Al sufrimiento antiguo
danse, encarnízanse en llorar plomo social
al pie del individuo,
y atacan a gemidos, los mendigos,
matando con tan solo ser mendigos.

Ruegos de infantería,
en que el arma ruega del metal para arriba,
y ruega la ira, más acá de la pólvora iracunda,
Tácitos escuadrones que disparan
con cadencia mortal, su mansedumbre,
desde un umbral, desde sí mismos, ¡ay!, desde sí mismos.
Potenciales guerreros
sin calcetines al calzar el trueno,
satánicos, numéricos,
arrastrando sus títulos de fuerza,
migaja al cinto,
fusil doble calibre: sangre y sangre.
!El poeta saluda al sufrimiento armado!

IV

The beggars fight for Spain,
begging in Paris, in Rome, in Prague
and thus authenticating, with an imploring Gothic hand,
the Apostles' feet, in London, in New York, in Mexico.
The beggars fight begging God   5*
satanically for Santander,
that combat in which no longer is anyone defeated.
They deliver themselves to
the old suffering, they mercilessly cry social lead
at the foot of the individual,   10*
and with moans those beggars attack,   *
killing by merely being beggars.

  Pleas of the infantry,   *
in which the weapon pleads from the metal up,
and the wrath pleads, this side of the raging gunpowder.   15
Tacit squadrons which fire,
with mortal cadence, their gentleness,
from a doorway, from themselves, alas! from themselves.
Potential warriors
without socks to cannon thunder,   20*
satanic, numerical,
dragging their titles of strength,
crumb under belt,   *
double caliber rifle: blood and blood.
The poet hails armed suffering!   25

× ×
× × V

¡Ahí pasa¡ ¡Llamadla! ¡Es su costado!
Ahí pasa la muerte por Irún:
sus pasos de acordeón, su palabrota,
su metro del tejido que te dije,
su gramo de aquel peso que he callado . . . ¡si son ellos!

¡Llamadla! ¡Daos prisa! Va buscándome en los rifles,
como que sabe bien dónde la venzo,
cuál es mi maña grande, mis leyes especiosas, mis códigos terribles.
¡Llamadla!, ella camina exactamente como un hombre, entre las fieras,
se apoya de aquel brazo que se enlaza a nuestros pies
cuando dormimos en los parapetos
y se pára a las puertas elásticas del sueño.

¡Gritó! ¡Gritó! ¡Gritó su grito nato, sensorial!
Gritara de vergüenza, de ver cómo ha caído entre las plantas,
de ver cómo se aleja de las bestias,
e oír cómo decimos: ¡Es la muerte!
¡De herir nuestros más grandes intereses!

(Porque elabora su hígado la gota que te dije, camarada;
porque se come el alma del vecino.)

¡Llamadla! Hay que seguirla
hasta el pie de los tanques enemigos,
que la muerte es un sér sido a la fuerza,
cuyo principio y fin llevo grabados
a la cabeza de mis ilusiones,
por mucho que ella corra el peligro corriente
que tú sabes
y que haga como que hace que me ignora.

¡Llamadla! No es un sér, muerte violenta,
sino, apenas, lacónico suceso;
más bien su modo tira, cuando ataca,
tira a tumulto simple, sin órbitas ni cánticos de dicha;
más bien tira su tiempo audaz, a céntimo impreciso
y sus sordos quilates, a déspotas aplausos.
¡Llamadla!, que en llamándola con saña, con figuras,
se la ayuda a arrastrar sus tres rodillas,
como, a veces,
a veces duelen, punzan fracciones enigmáticas, globales,
como, a veces, me palpo y no me siento.

×
× × V

There she goes! Call her! It's her side!
There goes Death through Irún:
her accordion steps, her curse,
her meter of cloth that I've mentioned,
her gram of that weight that I've not mentioned . . . they're the ones!   5

Call her! Hurry! She is searching for me among the rifles,
since she well knows where I defeat her,
what my great trick is, my deceptive laws, my terrible codes.
Call her! she walks exactly like a man, among wild beasts,
she leans on that arm which entwines our feet   10
when we sleep on the parapets
and she stops at the elastic gates of dream.

She shouted! She shouted! She shouted her born sensorial shout!
She shouted from shame, from seeing how she's fallen among the plants,
from seeing how she withdraws from the beasts,   15
from hearing how we say: It's Death!
From wounding our greatest interests!

(Because her liver manufactures the drop that I've mentioned, comrade;
because she eats the soul of our neighbor.)

Call her! We must follow her   20
to the foot of the enemy tanks,
for Death is a Being been by force,
whose beginning and end I carry engraved
at the head of my illusions,
even though she would run the normal risk   25
that you know
and though she would pretend to pretend to ignore me.

Call her! Violent Death is not a Being,
but, hardly, a laconic event;
rather her way aims, when she attacks,   30
aims at simple tumult, without orbits or joyous canticles;
rather her audacious time aims, at an imprecise penny
and her deaf carats, at despotic applause.
Call her! for by calling her with fury, with figures,
you help her drag her three knees,   35
as, at times,
at times, global enigmatic fractions hurt, pierce,
as, at times, I touch myself and don't feel myself.

¡Llamadla! ¡Daos prisa! Va buscándome,
con su coñac, su pómulo moral,
sus pasos de acordeón, su palabrota.
¡Llamadla! No hay que perderle el hilo en que la lloro.
De su olor para arriba, ¡ay de mi polvo, camarada!
De su pus para arriba, ¡ay de mi férula, teniente!
De su imán para abajo, ¡ay de mi tumba!

Imagen española de la muerte

 Call her! Hurry! She is searching for me,
with her cognac, her moral cheekbone,   40
her accordion steps, her curse.
Call her! The thread of my tears for her must not be lost.
From her smell up, oh god my dust, comrade!
From her pus up, oh god my ferule, lieutenant!
From her magnet down, oh god my tomb!   45

Spanish image of death

VI

Cortejo tras la toma de Bilbao

Herido y muerto, hermano,
criatura veraz, republicana, están andando en tu trono,
desde que tu espinazo cayó famosamente;
están andando, pálido, en tu edad flaca y anual,
laboriosamente absorta ante los vientos.

Guerrero en ambos dolores,
siéntate a oír, acuéstate al pie del palo súbito,
inmediato de tu trono;
voltea;
están las nuevas sábanas, extrañas;
están andando, hermano, están andando.

Han dicho: "Cómo! Dónde! . . .", expresándose
en trozos de paloma,
y los niños suben sin llorar a tu polvo.
Ernesto Zúñiga, duerme con la mano puesta,
con el concepto puesto,
en descanso tu paz, en paz tu guerra.

Herido mortalmente de vida, camarada,
camarada jinete,
camarada caballo entre hombre y fiera,
tus huesecillos de alto y melancólico dibujo
forman pompa española, pompa
laureada de finísimos andrajos!

Siéntate, pues, Ernesto,
oye que están andando, aquí, en tu trono,
desde que tu tobillo tiene canas.
¿Qué trono?
¡Tu zapato derecho! ¡Tu zapato!

13 Set. 1937

VI

Cortege after the capture of Bilbao

*

Wounded and dead, brother,
truthful creature, Loyalist, they are walking over your throne,   *
ever since your backbone fell famously;
they are walking, pale, over your lean and yearly age,
laboriously entranced before the winds.   5

Warrior in both sorrows,
sit down and listen, lie down at the foot of the sudden stick,
next to your throne;
turn around;
the new bedsheets there, extraneous;   10
they are walking, brother, they are walking.

They've said: "How! Where! . . ." stating it
in hunks of dove,
and the children go up to your dust without crying.
Ernesto Zúñiga, sleep with your hand on,   15
with your concept on,
your peace at rest, your war at peace.

Mortally wounded by life, comrade,
comrade rider,
comrade horse between man and wild beast,
your delicate bones of high and melancholy design   20
form Spanish pomp, pomp
laureled with the finest rags!

Sit down, then, Ernesto,
listen how they are walking, here, over your throne,
ever since your ankle got grey hair.   25
What throne?
Your right shoe! Your shoe!

×
× ×   VII

Varios días el aire, compañeros,
muchos días el viento cambia de aire,
el terreno, de filo,
de nivel el fusil republicano.
Varios días España está española.

Varios días el mal
mobiliza sus órbitas, se abstiene,
paraliza sus ojos escuchándolos.
Varios días orando con sudor desnudo,
los milicianos cuélganse del hombre.
Varios días, el mundo, camaradas,
el mundo está español hasta la muerte.

Varios días ha muerto aquí el disparo
y ha muerto el cuerpo en su papel de espíritu
y el alma es ya nuestra alma, compañeros.
Varios días el cielo,
éste, el del día, el de la pata enorme.

Varios días, Gijón;
muchos días, Gijón;
mucho tiempo, Gijón;
mucha tierra, Gijón;
mucho hombre, Gijón;
y mucho dios, Gijón,
muchísimas Españas ¡ay!, Gijón.

Camaradas,
varios días el viento cambia de aire.

5 Nov. 1937

×
× × VII

  For several days the air, companions,
for many days the wind changes air,
the ground, its edge,
its level, the Loyalist rifle.
For several days Spain looks Spanish.   5

  For several days evil
movilizes its orbits, abstains,   *
paralyzes its eyes listening to them.
For several days praying with naked sweat,
the civilian-fighters hang from man.   10
For several days, the world, comrades,
the world looks Spanish unto death.

  For several days the shooting here has died
and the body has died in its spiritual role
and the soul, companions, has become our soul.   15
For several days the sky,
this one, the one with a day, the one with an enormous paw.

  For several days, Gijón;   *
for many days, Gijón;
for much time, Gijón;   20
for much land, Gijón;
for much man, Gijón;
and for much God, Gijón,
for very many Spains, ay! Gijón.   *

  Comrades,   25
  for several days the wind changes air.

×
×   ×   VIII

Aquí,
Ramón Collar,
prosigue tu familia soga a soga,
se sucede,
en tanto que visitas, tú, allá, a las siete espada, en Madrid,
en el frente de Madrid.

¡Ramón Collar, yuntero
y soldado hasta yerno de su suegro,
marido, hijo limítrofe del viejo Hijo del Hombre!
Ramón de pena, tú, Collar valiente,
paladín de Madrid y por cojones; Ramonete,
aquí,
los tuyos piensan mucho en tu peinado!

¡Ansiosos, ágiles de llorar, cuando la lágrima!
¡Y cuando los tambores, andan; hablan
delante de tu buey, cuando la tierra!

¡Ramón! ¡Collar! ¡A ti! Si eres herido,
no seas malo en sucumbir; ¡refrénate!
Aquí,
tu cruel capacidad está en cajitas;
aquí,
tu pantalón oscuro, andando el tiempo,
sabe ya andar solísimo, acabarse;
aquí, Ramón, tu suegro, el viejo,
te pierde a cada encuentro con su hija!

Te diré que han comido aquí
tu carne, sin saberlo,
tu pecho, sin saberlo,
tu pie;
pero cavilan todos en tus pasos coronados de polvo!

¡Han rezado a Dios,
aquí;
se han sentado en tu cama, hablando a voces
entre tu soledad y tus cositas;
no sé quien ha tomado tu arado, no sé quien
fué a ti, ni quién volvió de tu caballo!

Aquí, Ramón Collar, en fin, tu amigo.
¡Salud, hombre de Dios, mata y escribe!

10 Set. 1937

×
× × VIII

Back here,   *
Ramón Collar,   *
your family goes forward from rope to rope,
it continues,
while you visit, you, out there, the seven swords, in Madrid,   5
at the Madrid front.

Ramón Collar, ox-driver
and soldier up to being son-in-law of his father-in-law,
husband, bordering son of the old Son of Man!
Ramón of sorrow, you, brave Collar,   10*
palatine of Madrid and by sheer balls. Ramonete,
back here,
your people give much thought to the way your hair is combed!

Anxious, quick to cry, at the time of the tear!
And at the time of the drums, they walk; they speak   15
before your ox, at the time of the soil!

Ramón! Collar! To you! If you are wounded,
don't act up when you succumb; refrain yourself!
Back here,
your cruel capacity is in little boxes;   20
back here,
your dark trousers, after a while,
finally know how to walk in utter solitude, how to wear out;
back here, Ramón, your father-in-law, the old man,
loses you at each encounter with his daughter!   25

I tell you that they've eaten
your flesh, without realizing it,
your chest, without realizing it,
your foot;
but they all brood over your steps crowned with dust!   30

They've prayed to God,
back here;
they've sat on your bed, talking loudly
between your solitude and your little things;
I don't know who has taken hold of your plow, I don't know who   35
went after you, nor who returned from your horse!

Back here, Ramon Collar, at last, your friend.
Greetings, my good man, kill and write!

IX

Pequeño responso a un héroe de la República

Un libro quedó al borde de su cintura muerta,
un libro retoñaba de su cadáver muerto.
Se llevaron al héroe,
y corpórea y aciaga entró su boca en nuestro aliento;
sudamos todos, el hombligo a cuestas;
caminantes las lunas nos seguían;
también sudaba de tristeza el muerto.

Y un libro, en la batalla de Toledo,
un libro, atrás un libro, arriba un libro, retoñaba del cadáver.

Poesía del pómulo morado, entre el decirlo
y el callarlo,
poesía en la carta moral que acompañara
a su corazón.
Quedóse el libro y nada más, que no hay
insectos en la tumba,
y quedó al borde de su manga el aire remojándose
y haciéndose gaseoso, infinito.

Todos sudamos, el hombligo a cuestas,
también sudaba de tristeza el muerto
y un libro, yo lo ví sentidamente,
un libro, atrás un libro, arriba un libro
retoñó del cadáver ex abrupto.

10 Set. 1937

IX

Short prayer for a Loyalist hero

A book remained at the edge of his dead waist,
a book was sprouting from his dead corpse.   *
The hero was carried off,   *
and corporeal and ominous his mouth entered our breath;
we all sweated, under the load of our navells;   5
the moons were following us on foot;
the dead man was also sweating from sadness.

And a book, during the battle for Toledo,
a book, a book behind, a book above, was sprouting from the corpse.

Poetry of the purple cheekbone, between saying it   10*
and not saying it,
poetry in the moral map that had accompanied
his heart.
The book remained and nothing else, for there are no
insects in his tomb,   15
and at the edge of his sleeve the air remained soaking
and becoming gaseous, infinite.

We all sweated, under the load of our navells,
the dead man was also sweating from sadness
and a book, I saw it feelingly,   20
a book, a book behind, a book above
abruptly sprouted from the corpse.

X

Invierno en la batalla de Teruel

¡Cae agua de revólveres lavados!
Precisamente,
es la gracia metálica del agua,
en la tarde nocturna, en Aragón,
no obstante las construídas yerbas,
las legumbres ardientes, las plantas industriales.

Precisamente,
es la rama serena de la química,
la rama de explosivos en un pelo,
la rama de automóviles en frecuencias y adioses.

Así responde el hombre, así, a la muerte,
así mira de frente y escucha de costado,
así el agua, al contrario de la sangre, es de agua,
así el fuego, al revés de la ceniza, alisa sus rumiantes ateridos.

¿Quién va, bajo la nieve? ¿Están matando? No.
Precisamente,
va la vida coleando, con su segunda soga.

¡Y horrísima es la guerra, solivianta,
lo pone a uno largo, ojoso;
da tumba la guerra, da caer,
da dar un salto extraño de antropoide!
Tú lo hueles, compañero, perfectamente,
al pisar
por distracción tu brazo entre cadáveres;
tú lo ves; pues tocaste tus testículos, poniéndote rojísimo;
tú lo oyes en tu boca de soldado natural.

Vamos, pues, compañero;
nos espera tu sombra apercibida,
nos espera tu sombra acuartelada,
mediodía capitán, noche soldado raso . . .
Por eso, al referirme a esta agonía,
aléjome de mí gritando fuerte:
¡Abajo mi cadáver! . . . Y sollozo.

X

Winter during the battle for Teruel

Water falls from washed revolvers!
It is precisely
the metalic grace of the water,
in the nocturnal afternoon, of Aragón,
in spite of the constructed grasses,   5
the burning vegetables, the industrial plants.

It is precisely
the serene branch of Chemistry,   *
the branch of explosives in one hair,
the branch of automobiles in frequencies and goodbyes.   10

This is how man responds, like this, to death,
this is how he looks forward and listens sideways,
this is how water, contrary to blood, is made of water,
this is how fire, opposite of ash, smooths its frozen ruminants.

Who goes there, under the snow? Are they killing? No.   15
It is precisely
life going on wagging, with its second rope.

And war is utter horror, it incites,
it makes one long, eyey;
war gives tomb, gives falling,   20
gives giving an anthropoid leap!
You smell it, companion, perfectly,
on stepping
distractedly on your arm among the corpses;
you see it, for you touched your testicles, blushing intensely;   25
you hear it in your natural soldier's mouth.   *

Let's go, then, companion;
your alerted shadow awaits us,
your quartered shadow awaits us,
captain noon, common soldier night . . .
That is why, on referring to this agony,   30
I withdraw from myself shouting wildly:
Down with my corpse! . . . And I sob.

×
× × XI

Miré el cadáver, su raudo orden visible
y el desorden lentísimo de su alma;
le ví sobrevivir; hubo en su boca
la edad entrecortada de dos bocas.
Le gritaron su número: pedazos.
Le gritaron su amor: ¡más le valiera!
Le gritaron su bala: ¡también muerta!

Y su orden digestivo sosteníase
y el desorden de su alma, atrás, en balde.
Le dejaron y oyeron, y es entonces
que el cadáver
casi vivió en secreto, en un instante;
más le auscultaron mentalmente, ¡y fechas!
lloráronle al oído ¡y también fechas!

3 Set. 1937

×
× × XI

I looked at the corpse, at his visible swift order
and at the very slow disorder of his soul;
I saw him survive; there was in his mouth
the intermittent age of two mouths.
They shouted his number at him: pieces.   5
They shouted his love at him: it would be better for him!
They shouted his bullet at him: likewise dead!

And his digestive order stood still
and the disorder of his soul, behind, in vain.
They left him and listened, and it is then   10
that the corpse
almost lived secretly, for an instant;
but they auscultated him mentally—only dates!
they cried to his ear, and more dates!

XII

Masa

Al fin de la batalla,
y muerto el combatiente, vino hacia él un hombre
y le dijo: "¡No mueras; te amo tánto!"
Pero el cadáver ¡ay! siguió muriendo.

Se le acercaron dos y repitiéronle:
"¡No nos dejes! ¡Valor! ¡Vuelve a la vida!"
Pero el cadáver ¡ay! siguió muriendo.

Acudieron a él veinte, cien, mil, quinientos mil,
clamando: "Tánto amor, y no poder nada contra la muerte!"
Pero el cadáver ¡ay! siguió muriendo.

Le rodearon millones de individuos,
con un ruego común: "¡Quédate, hermano!"
Pero el cadáver ¡ay! siguió muriendo.

Entonces, todos los hombres de la tierra
le rodearon; les vió el cadáver triste, emocionado;
incorporóse lentamente,
abrazó al primer hombre; echóse a andar . . .

10 Nov. 1937

XII

Mass

    At the end of the battle,
and the combatant dead, a man came toward him
and said: "Don't die; I love you so much!"
But the corpse, alas! kept on dying.

    Two approached him and repeated: 5
"Don't leave us! Be brave! Return to life!"
But the corpse, alas! kept on dying.   *

    Twenty, a hundred, a thousand, five hundred thousand, came up to him,
crying out: "So *much* love and no power against death!"
But the corpse, alas! kept on dying.   10

    Millions of persons surrounded him,
with a common plea: "Do not leave us, brother!"
But the corpse, alas! kept on dying.

    Then, all the inhabitants of the earth
surrounded him; the corpse looked at them sadly, moved;   15
he sat up slowly,
embraced the first man; started to walk . . .

XIII

Redoble fúnebre a los escombros de Durango

Padre polvo que subes de España,
Dios te salve, libere y corone,
padre polvo que asciendes del alma.

Padre polvo que subes del fuego,
Dios te salve, te calce y dé un trono,
padre polvo que estás en los cielos.

Padre polvo, biznieto del humo,
Dios te salve y ascienda a infinito,
padre polvo, biznieto del humo.

Padre polvo en que acaban los justos,
Dios te salve y devuelva a la tierra,
padre polvo en que acaban los justos.

Padre polvo que creces en palmas,
Dios te salve y revista de pecho,
padre polvo, terror de la nada.

Padre polvo, compuesto de hierro,
Dios te salve y te dé forma de hombre,
padre polvo que marchas ardiendo.

Padre polvo, sandalia del paria,
Dios te salve y jamás te desate,
padre polvo, sandalia del paria.

Padre polvo que avientan los bárbaros,
Dios te salve y te ciña de dioses,
padre polvo que escoltan los átomos.

Padre polvo, sudario del pueblo,
Dios te salve del mal para siempre,
padre polvo español, ¡padre nuestro!

Padre polvo que vas al futuro,
Dios te salve, te guíe y te dé alas,
padre polvo que vas al futuro.

XIII

Funereal drumroll for the ruins of Durango

*

Father dust who rises from Spain,
God save you, liberate you and crown you,
father dust who ascends from the soul.

Father dust who rises from the fire,
God save you, shoe you and offer you a throne,   5
father dust who art in heaven.

Father dust, great grandson of the smoke,
God save you and raise you to infinity,
father dust, great grandson of the smoke.

Father dust in whom the just end,   10
God save you and return you to earth,
father dust in whom the just end.

Father dust who grows into palms,
God save you and invest you with chest,
father dust, terror of the void.   15

Father dust, made up of iron,
God save you and give you human form,
father dust, who marches burning.

Father dust, sandal of the pariah,
God save you and never unbind you,   20
father dust, sandal of the pariah.

Father dust who the barbarians winnow,
God save you and encircle you with gods,
father dust who the atoms escort.

Father dust, shroud of the people,   25
God save you from evil forever,
Spanish father dust, our father!

Father dust who goes into the future,
God save you, guide you and give you wings,
father dust who goes into the future.   30

XIV

¡Cúidate, España, de tu propia España!
¡Cúidate de la hoz sin el martillo,
cúidate del martillo sin la hoz!
¡Cúidate de la víctima apesar suyo,
del verdugo apesar suyo
y del indiferente apesar suyo!
¡Cúidate del que, antes de que cante el gallo,
negárate tres veces,
y del que te negó, después, tres veces!
¡Cúidate de las calaveras sin las tibias,
y de las tibias sin las calaveras!
¡Cúidate de los nuevos poderosos!
¡Cúidate del que come tus cadáveres,
del que devora muertos a tus vivos!
¡Cúidate del leal ciento por ciento!
¡Cúidate del cielo más acá del aire
y cúidate del aire más allá del cielo!
¡Cúidate de los que te aman!
¡Cúidate de tus héroes!
¡Cúidate de tus muertos!
¡Cúidate de la República!
¡Cúidate del futuro! . . .

XIV

*

Beware, Spain, of your own Spain!
Beware of the sickle without the hammer,
beware of the hammer without the sickle!
Beware of the victim in spite of himself,
of the hangman in spite of himself
and of the uncommitted in spite of himself!
Beware of the one who, before the cock crows,
will have denied you three times,
and of the one who denied you, afterwards, three times!
Beware of the skulls without tibias
and of the tibias without skulls!
Beware of the new potentates!
Beware of the one who eats your corpses,
of the one who devours dead your living!
Beware of the one hundred percent loyal!
Beware of the sky this side of the air
and beware of the air beyond the sky!
Beware of those who love you!
Beware of your heros!
Beware of your dead!
Beware of the Republic!
Beware of the future! . . .

XV

España, aparta de mi este cáliz

Niños del mundo,
si cae España—digo, es un decir—
si cae
del cielo abajo su antebrazo que asen,
en cabestro, dos láminas terrestres;
niños, ¡qué edad la de las sienes cóncavas!
¡qué temprano en el sol lo que os decía!
¡qué pronto en vuestro pecho el ruido anciano!
¡qué viejo vuestro 2 en el cuaderno!

¡Niños del mundo, está
la madre España con su vientre a cuestas;
está nuestra maestra con sus férulas,
está madre y maestra,
cruz y madera, porque os dió la altura,
vértigo y división y suma, niños;
está con ella, padres procesales!

Si cae—digo, es un decir—si cae
España, de la tierra para abajo,
niños, ¡cómo vais a cesar de crecer!
¡cómo va a castigar el año al mes!
¡cómo van a quedarse en diez los dientes,
en palote el diptongo, la medalla en llanto!
¡Cómo va el corderillo a continuar
atado por la pata al gran tintero!
¡Cómo vais a bajar las gradas del alfabeto
hasta la letra en que nació la pena!

Niños,
hijos de los guerreros, entre tanto,
bajad la voz, que España está ahora mismo repartiendo
la energía entre el reino animal,
las florecillas, los cometas y los hombres.
¡Bajad la voz, que está
con su rigor, que es grande, sin saber
qué hacer, y está en su mano
la calavera hablando y habla y habla,
la calavera, aquélla de la trenza,
la calavera, aquélla de la vida!

XV

Spain, take this cup from me   *

   Children of the world,
if Spain falls—I mean, it's just a thought—
if she falls
from the sky downward let her forearm be seized,
in a halter, by two terrestrial plates;   5
children, what age in those concave temples!   *
how early in the sun what I was telling you!
how soon in your chest the ancient noise!
how old your 2 in your notebook!

   Children of the world,
mother Spain is with her belly on her shoulders;
our teacher is with her ferules,
she appears as mother and teacher,
cross and wood, because she gave you the height,
vertigo and division and addition, children;   15
she is with herself, procedural fathers!

   If she falls—I mean, it's just a thought—if Spain
falls, from the earth downward,
children, how you are going to stop growing!
how the year is going to punish the month!   20
how you're never going to have more than ten teeth,
how the dipthong will remain in downstroke, the medal in tears!
How the little lamb is going to continue
bound by its leg to the great inkwell!
How you're going to descend the steps of the alphabet   25
to the letter in which pain was born!

   Children,
sons of warriors, meanwhile,
lower your voice, for Spain is right this moment distributing
energy among the animal kingdom,   30
little flowers, comets and men.
Lower your voice, for she is
with her rigor, which is great, not knowing
what to do, and she has in her hand
the talking skull and it talks and talks,   35
the skull, the one with the braid,
the skull, the one with life!

¡Bajad la voz, os digo;
bajad la voz, el canto de las sílabas, el llanto
de la materia y el rumor menor de las pirámides, y aún
el de las sienes que andan con dos piedras!
¡Bajad el aliento, y si
el antebrazo baja,
si las férulas suenan, si es la noche,
si el cielo cabe en dos limbos terrestres,
si hay ruido en el sonido de las puertas,
si tardo,
si no veis a nadie, si os asustan
los lápices sin punta, si la madre
España cae—digo, es un decir—
salid, niños del mundo; id a buscarla! . . .

Lower your voice, I tell you;
lower your voice, the song of syllables, the crying
of matter and the minor rumor of the pyramids, and even   40
that of your temples which walk with two stones!
Lower your breathing, and if
the forearm comes down,
if the ferules sound, if it is night,
if the sky fits into two terrestrial limbos,   45*
if there is noise in the sound of the doors,
if I am late,
if you don't see anyone, if the blunt pencils
frighten you, if mother
Spain falls—I mean, it's just a thought—   50
go out, children of the world, go and look for her! . . .

FACSIMILES OF VALLEJO'S WORKSHEETS

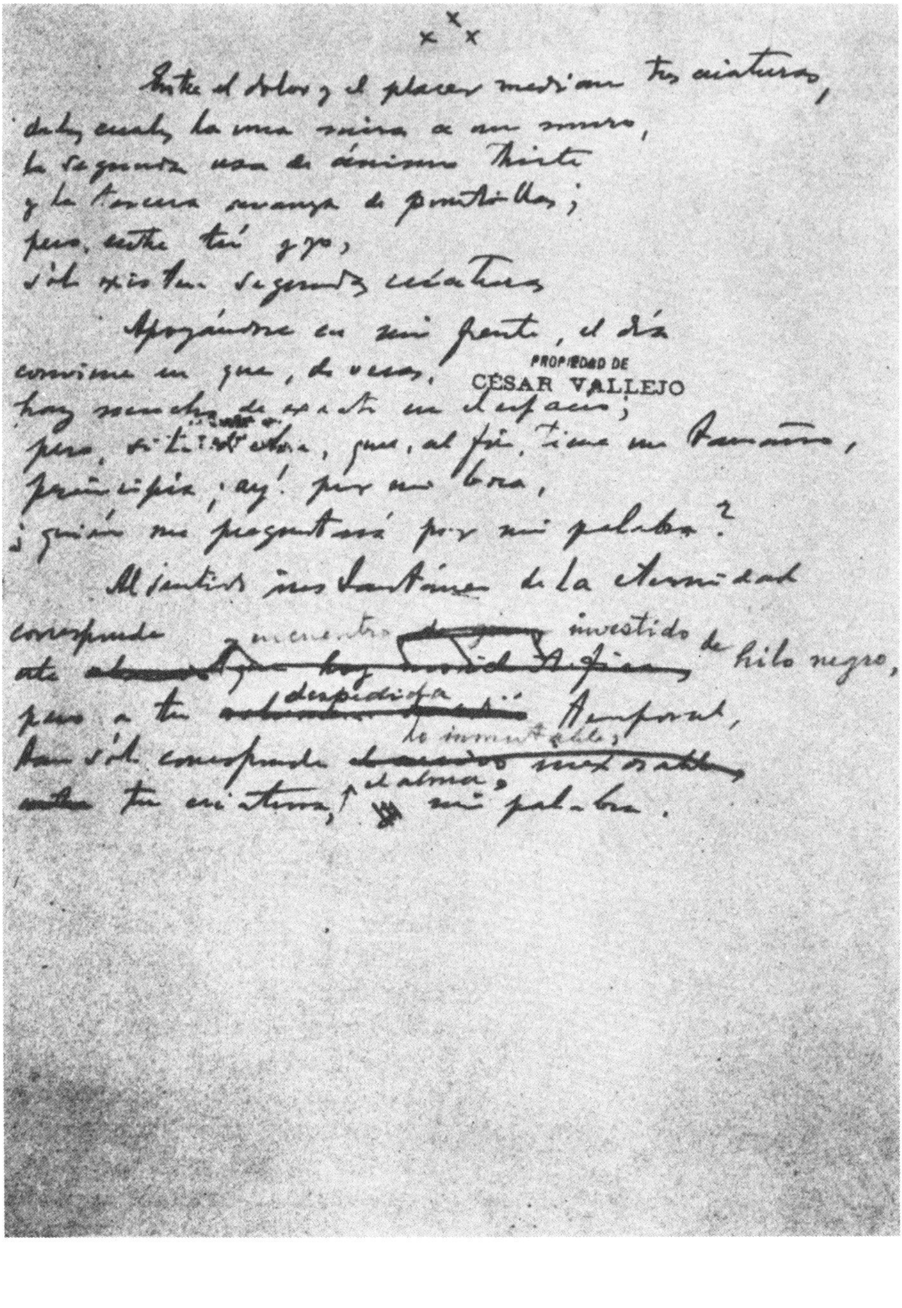

epístola a los transeuntes

~~unidad de verso~~

Reanudo mi día de conejo,
mi noche de elefante en descanso,

~~por el mi brazo llame~~
~~que~~

Y, entre mí, digo: *en virtù, a contraros?*
ésta es mi inmensidad ~~que~~
éste mi grato peso, que me buscara abajo para pájaro;
éste es mi brazo ~~que~~
que por ~~su~~cuenta rehusó ser ala,
éstas son mis sagradas escrituras, ~~~~
éstos mis ~~compuestos~~ alarmados *compañones.* PROPIEDAD DE

Lúgubre isla me alumbraré continental, CÉSAR VALLEJO
mientras el capitolio se apoya en mi íntimo derrumbe
y la asamblea en lanzas clausura mi desfile.

Pero cuando yo muera
de vida y no de tiempo, *¡ cuando lleguen a dar mis dos malitos;*
éste ha de ser mi estómago en que cupo mi lámpara en pedazos,
ésta aquella cabeza que expió los tormentos del círculo en mis pasos,
éstos esos gusanos, que el corazón contó por unidades,
éste ha de ser mi cuerpo solidario
por el que vela el alma individual; éste ha de ser
mi ombligo en que maté mis piojos ~~~~ *natos,*
ésta mi cosa cosa, mi cosa tremebunda.

En tanto, convulsiva, ~~~~ *ásperamente*
convalece mi ~~~~ *freno,*
sufriendo como sufro del lenguaje directo del león; *de ladrillo;*
~~y~~que he existido entre dos potestades ~~~~
convalezco, ~~~~ sonriendo de mis labios
~~~~

¡Mecánica sincera
¡Suelo teórico y práctico!
¡Surcos inteligentes; ejemplo
¡Papales, cebadales, alfalfares, cosa buena!
¡Cultivos que integran una asombrosa jerarquía de útiles
y que integran con viento los mujidos,
las aguas con su sorda antigüedad!

¡Cuaternarios maíces, de opuestos natalicios,
los oigo por los pies cómo se alejan,
los huelo retornar cuando la tierra
tropieza con la técnica del cielo!
¡Molécula exabrupto! ¡Atomo terso!

¡Oh campos humanos!
¡Oh climas encontrados dentro del   listos!
¡Oh campo intelectual
con religión, con campo
¡Paquidermos en prosa cuando pasán
¡Roedores que miran con sentimiento judicial en torno!
¡Oh patrióticos asnos de mi vida!
¡Oh luz que dista apenas un espejo de la sombra,
que es vida con el punto y, con la línea, polvo
y que por eso acato, subiendo por la idea a mi osamenta!

Guitarra

·El placer de sufrir, de odiar, tiñe
la garganta con plásticos venenos,
la cerda que implanta su orden mágico,
su grandeza taurina, entre la prima
y la sexta
y la octava mendaz, sufre

El placer de sufrir. ¿Quién? ¿a quién?
¿quién, las muelas? ¿a quién
los carburos de rabia de la encía?
¿Cómo ser
y estar,

Vales más que mi número, hombre solo,
y valen más que todo el diccionario,
con su prosa en verso,
con su verso en prosa,
tu función águila,
tu mecanismo tigre, blando prójimo.

El placer de sufrir,
de esperar esperanzas en la mesa,
el domingo con todos los idiomas,
el sábado con horas chinas, belgas,
la semana, con dos escupitajos.

El placer de esperar en zapatillas,
de esperar encogido tras de un verso,
de esperar
el placer de sufrir: zurdase de hembra
muerta con una piedra en la cintura
y muerta entre la cuerda y la guitarra,
llorando días y cantando meses.

28 Oct 1937

el gas del tren blindado, el gas del último tobillo,
la angosta excavación del alma.
tintín amarillo golpe de dedo usual en pleno tigre,
de Irún, cuando muere a dos pasos de la muerte,
el testículo en su pálido terreno!

Ola del Bidasoa, junto a Irún en fuego,
río a río con el hielo, a la altura del polvo,
río a río con la tierra,

cayendo, cayendo
agosto Irún detrás de enflaquecida inmensidad

todos

combatiendo todos
las penas dejar cuñas,
mangos,
que hau triunfado, todos

donde durmió la frente
que era frente en ambas facultades

cargados de balas
de la causa de la muerte!
en castellano: eso es torear!
triunfal, tambor y medio, delirante!

Retrocediendo desde Talavera,
grupos de a uno, armados de hambre, en masas de a uno,
de pecho hasta la frente,
sin guerra, sin rencor,   el perder a la espalda
del mismo, heridos mortalmente de honor,
el brazo a pie,

IX

Pequeño responso a un héroe de la República

Un litro quedó al borde de su cintura muerta,
un litro retoñaba de su cadáver ~~muerte~~.
~~Litro con mango de horta fibra o fil acarba~~
Se llevaron al héroe, ~~en su nostro entendido incredible~~,
y corpórea y aciaga entró su boca en nuestro aliento;
sudamos todos, el hombligo a cuestas;
caminantes las lunas nos seguían;
también sudaba de triste~~za~~ el muerto.

Y un litro, *en la batalla a felido,*
~~pues~~ un litro, atrás un litro, arriba un litro, retoñaba del cadáver.

Poesía del pómulo morado, entre el decirlo
y el callarlo, poesía en la carta moral que acompañara
a su corazón ~~...~~
~~...~~
Quedó el libro y ~~...~~ *nada más, y... no hay*
~~no hay~~ insectos en la tumba,
y quedó al borde de su manga el aire remojándose
y haciéndose ~~...~~ infinito.
Todos sudamos, el hombligo a cuestas,
también sudaba de tristeza el muerto
y un litro, yo lo vi, *sentado...,*
~~pues~~ un litro, atrás un litro, arriba un litro
retoñaba ~~...~~ del cadáver *... , ...*

PROPIEDAD DE
CÉSAR VALLEJO

10 Set. 1937

APPENDIX

BATTLES IN SPAIN

I

Under your foot I hear the smoke of the human wolf,
the smoke of the evolution of the species,
the smoke of the child,
the solitary smoke of two wheats,
the smoke of Geneva, the smoke of Rome, the smoke of Berlin
and that of Paris and the smoke that comes out, finally, from the soul.
Oh life! oh earth! oh Spain!
Ounces of blood,
meters of blood, liquids of blood,
blood on horseback, on foot, mural, without diameter,
blood four by four, blood of water
and living blood from the dead blood.
The blood has left me: the smoke
has left me listening to my jaws.

Estremanian, oh to still be that man
for whom death killed you and life gave birth to you
and to stay on only to see you like this, from this wolf,
how you go on plowing with your cross in our chests!
Estremanian, you know
the secret in both voices, the popular and the tactile,
of the cereal: that nothing is worth as much as two wheats together!
Estremanian bent on an elbow, picturing the soul in its retreat,
to listen to the dying of the dyings
and bent on an elbow to look at
the fitting of a life in a death!

Estremanian, and not to have land that would have
the weight of your plow, nor other world
than the color of your yoke between two epochs; not to have
the order of your posthumous herds!
Estremanian, you allowed me
to see you from my wolf, to endure,
to fight for everyone and to fight
so that the man can become a man,
so that masters themselves can become men,
so that everyone can become a man, and so
that even animals can become men,
the horse, a man,
the reptile, a man,
the vulture, an honest man,
the fly, a man, and the olive tree, a man
and even the riverbank, a man
and the very sky, a whole little man!

That is why, Estremanian man, you have fallen,
you have cleaned yourself up
and you have ended up dying from hope!

II

The bony darkness presses on, sketches moral cheekbones,
the gas of the armored train, the gas of the last ankle
the curve of evil, the narrow excavation of the soul.
A yellow tinkling, a blow of a usual finger in full tiger,
those of Irún, when two steps from death
the testicle dies, behind, on its pale ground!
A yellow tinkling, under the smell of the human
tooth, when metal ends up being metal!

Wave of the Bidasoa,
river to river with the sky, at the height of the dust,
and river to river with the earth, at the height of the inferno!
A toil that they had tackled on crutches,
falling down, falling;
narrow Irún behind an emaciated immensity,
when the imagined bone is made of bone!

A battle in which all had died
and all had fought
and in which all the sorrows leave wedges,
all the sorrows, handles,
all the sorrows, always wedge and handle!
A battle in which all had triumphed
and all had fought
and in which all the trees left one leaf,
not a single flower and one root, man!

Cheekbones! And they are moral cheekbones,
those of Irún, where the forehead went to sleep
and dreamt that they were a forehead in both faculties . . .
And a blow of a usual finger in full tiger,
the one at Irun, where the smell drew a noise of eyes
and where the tooth had slept
its tranquil geological dream . . .

Terrestrial and oceanic, infinite Irún!

III

    Loss of Toledo
due to rifles loaded with affectionate bullets!
Loss of the cause of death!
Loss in the Castilian language: or bullfighting!
And a triumphal loss, drum and a half, delirious!
Loss of the Spanish loss!

    Retreating from Talavera,
in groups of one, armed with hunger, in masses of one,
armed with chest up to the forehead,
without planes, without war, without rancor,
dying, their rotulas over their shoulders and their loss over their backs
and their gain
lower than lead, mortally wounded by honor,
crazed by dust, their arms on foot,
loving unwillingly, they forced Toledo to commit suicide,
conquering the whole earth in a Spanish way!

  And on the succeeding day, the third day,
as the African hooves resounded in the sad narrow alleys,
to still retreat, and not to know
where to put their Spain,
where to hide their orbital kiss,
where to plant their pocket-sized olive tree!

  What noon that noon between two afternoons! Something to be seen! . . .
Say it, Alcántara bridge,
you say it better,
better than the water
which flows sobbing on its way back!
It hurts, truly, that noon,
the exact size of a suicide; and remembering it,
no one any longer,
no one lies down outside his body . . .

IV

    From here, from this point,
from the point of this rectilinear line,
from the good to which the satanic good flows,
the great battle of Guernica can be seen.
An a priori combat, unheard of,
combat in peace, combat of weak souls
against weak bodies, combat in which the child strikes,
without anyone telling him to, beneath his atrocious dipthong

and beneath his very clever diaper,
and in which a mother strikes with her scream, with the backside of a tear
and in which the sick man strikes with his disease, with his pill and his son
and in which the old man strikes hard
with his white hair, his centuries and his stick
and in which the priest strikes with God!
Combat at Guernica in honor
of the bull and his pale animal: man!

From here, as I repeat,
from this viewpoint,
the defenders of Guernica can be perfectly seen!
weak ones, offended ones,
rising up, growing up, filling up the world with powerful weak ones!

V

The cemeteries were bombed, and another combat
took place with cadavers against cadavers:
combat of the dead dead who attacked
the immortal dead
with vigilant bones and eternal shoulder, with their tombs.
The immortal dead, upon feeling, upon seeing
how low the evil, then, aie!
completed their unfinished sentences,
they finished crying, finished
hoping, finished
aching, finished living,
finished, finally, being mortal!

And the gunpowder was, suddenly, gunpowder,
signs and seals crossing each other,
and before the explosion a step appeared,
and before the flight on all fours, another step
and before the apocalyptic sky, another step
and before the seven metals, the unity,
simple and one, collective and one!

Composition and strength of the fistful of nothingness, as they say,
the whole living death defended life,
fighting for the whole, which is dialectical
and for the butterfly, that seeks us,
for the free sky and the free chain! . . .

VI

He used to write with his big finger in the air:
"Long live all combanions! Pedro Rojas,"
from Miranda de Ebro, father and man,
husband and man, railroad-worker and man,
father and more man, Pedro and his two deaths.

Wind paper, he was killed: pass on!
Flesh pen, he was killed: pass on!
"Advise all combanions quick!"

Stick on which they've hanged his beam,
he was killed;
he was killed at the base of his big finger!
They've killed, in one blow, Pedro and Rojas!

Long live all combanions
written at the head of his air!
Let them live with this buzzard b in Pedro's
and in Rojas'
and in the hero's and in the martyr's guts!

Searching him, dead, they surprised
in his body a greater body, for
the soul of the world,
and in his jacket a dead spoon.

Pedro too used to eat
among the creatures of his flesh, and used to clean off
the table and used to live, at times,
as a representative of everyone together,
and this spoon was in his jacket, all his life,
awake or else when he slept, always,
dead alive spoon, this one and its symbols.
Advise all combanions quick!
Long live all combanions at the foot of this spoon forever!

He was killed, they forced him to die,
Pedro, Rojas, the worker, the man, the one
who was born so very tiny, looking at the sky
and who afterwards grew up, blushed
and fought against so many sad people as they were
his cells, his nos, his yets, his hungers, his pieces.
He was killed softly
in his wife's hair, Juana Vásquez by name,

at the hour of fire, in the year of gunshot
and when the poor man was after himself.

Pedro also used
to die at the foot of time and without lying down, a slave;
his corpse was full of world.
Pedro Rojas, thus, after being dead,
got up, kissed his casket,
cried for Spain
and again wrote with his finger in the air:
"Long live all combanions! Pedro Rojas."

VII

The beggars fight for Spain oh Marx! oh Hegel!
begging in Paris, in Rome, in Prague
and thus authenticating, with an aspiring, Gothic hand,
the Apostles' feet, in London, in New York, in Mexico.
The beggars fight Satanically begging
God, so that the poor win the battle
of Santander, that combat in which no longer is anyone defeated,
the campaign of the wheat, and its symbols.
They deliver themselves to
the old suffering, they mercilessly cry social lead
at the foot of the individual, on the mountain at the peak of the heart
and they attack with moans, because the beggars
kill at a distance merely from existing.
The beggars fight for the poor!

Troops of pleas on foot,
in which the weapon pleads from the metal up,
and the wrath pleads, this side of the raging gunpowder.
Tacit squadrons which fire,
with mortal cadence, their gentleness,
from a doorway, from themselves, alas! from themselves.
Potential warriors
without socks to cannon thunder,
satanic, numerical,
or on horseback on their titles of strength,
crumb under belt,
functional attack after their chests,
double caliber rifle: blood and blood.
The poet hails armed suffering!

VIII

Beware, Spain, of your own Spain!
Beware of the sickle without the hammer,
beware of the hammer without the sickle!
Beware of the victim in spite of himself,
of the hangman in spite of himself
and of the uncommitted in spite of himself!
Beware of the one who, before the cock crows,
will have denied you three times,
and of the one who denied you, afterwards, three times!
Beware of the skulls without tibias
and of the tibias without skulls!
Beware of the new potentates!
Beware of the one who eats your corpses,
of the one who devours dead your living!
Beware of the one hundred percent loyal!
Beware of the sky this side of the air
and beware of the air beyond the sky!
Beware of those who love you!
Beware of your heros!
Beware of your dead!
Beware of the Republic!
Beware of the future! . . .

NOTES

The following poem, bearing the same title as Vallejo's second book, was originally published in the Spanish magazine, *Alfar, #33*, October 1923. The poem was last reprinted by Juan Larrea in his book, *César Vallejo, héroe y mártir indo-hispano* (Biblioteca Nacional, Montevideo, 1973), p. 84. This poem is not included in the Moncloa *Obra Poética Completa*. However, since Vallejo himself did not make a final copy of either *Nómina de huesos* or *Sermón de la barbarie*, we do not know whether he would have included it or not. We feel that it is appropriate to make it available in these Notes as an interesting link between *Trilce* and the present manuscripts.

Trilce

There is a spot that I am sure of,
incredibly, in this world,
where we will never arrive.

Where, even if our foot
stepped on it for an instant
it will be, truly, as if we were not there.

It is that place that one sees
at every moment in this life,
while walking, walking in single file.

This side of myself and of
my pair of yolks, I have glimpsed it
always distant from our destinations.

It does not matter if you went on foot
or out of sheer sentiment on horseback,
since not even the stamps could reach it.

The tea color horizon
is dying to colonize it
for its great Any part.

But the spot that I am sure of,
incredibly, in this world,
strives to equal its opposites.

"Close that door which
is ajar in the entrails
of that mirror." "This one?" "No; its sister."

> It cannot be closed. One can
> never arrive at that place
> where the door-latches act unbound.
>
> Such is the spot that I am sure of.

*

Payroll of bones, p. 3

Title: in the facsimile, "Lista de huesos" (List of bones) is crossed out in favor
of the final title. According to Larrea, this poem and the seven following it, were
typed out between May 1925 and December 1926 (*Aula Vallejo,* #11−12−13, p. 91).

Line 6: the comma in Valleio's poetry sometimes expresses a guideline for read-
ing a line, e.g., emphasis or pause. We have kept the poet's original punctuation
intact throughout the translation.

*

Violence of the hours, p. 5

According to Larrea, this poem was written before Vallejo's father's death on
24 March 1924 (the assumption is, that he would have been mentioned in the
poem had it been written after his death). See *Aula Vallejo,* pp 90−91; *Poesía
completa,* p. 175.

Line 3: "burgo" is an archaic word in Spanish that meant "town" or "village."

Line 10: in response to our query, Larrea wrote that Vallejo's home in Santiago
de Chuco had two floors, with interior corridors encircling a small inner patio.
We have thus translated "corredores" in this poem, as well as in "We probably
already were of a compassionate age," as "interior corridors" or "interior corridor."

Line 16: after this line, there is a five line paragraph which has been crossed out:

> My horse Macachón died, no longer with us but with
> others. My father was informed of his death, one night, a long time
> ago, by the alfalfa farmer Manuel Benites, the peasant who shook the
> hair from his shoulders with the bristles of his climates.

*

Good sense, p. 7

Line 10: at the beginning of the paragraph following this line, Vallejo had origi-
nally written:

> My mother is successive of beings and alternative of hours.

Line 20: following this line, there is a paragraph crossed out:

> What is there, then, about me, that my father lacks and
> since my returning home, leaves my mother so pensive? My father is
> now losing his authority and home oscillates around me, with sleeves,
> fillet, galloon and lapels.

Line 33: there are a number of corrections from this point on, so we have trans-
lated Vallejo's original version:

> There resides her woman's illusion and the most sacred candor that
> becomes a brilliant melancholy in the depth of her face. In order to help
> her illusion and her candor, I say to her filially:
> —There is, mother, in the world a place called Paris. A
> very big place and very far off, where there are more men than women,
> more grown-ups than children. Corpulent beam! Cilicious stone!
> My mother, on hearing me, eats her lunch and shows in
> her mortal eyes the command of my personal life.

*

The gravest moment in life, p. 9

Title: "Acerca de la corrección de los actos" (Concerning the correctness of
actions) is crossed out in favor of the final title.

*

"The windows shuddered," pp. 11–15

Title: the following one is crossed out: "Complemento de tiempo del hospital de
Boyer" (Complement of time in the Boyer hospital). According to Larrea, the

piece was written while Vallejo was in the Charité hospital for a hemorrhoid operation in October 1924, or shortly after (See *Aula Vallejo*, pp. 91 and 252, *Poesía completa*, p. 175).

After this crossed out title, the following eight lines are also crossed out:

> The bedsheets still stink of expedience because of the death of a man.
> The mattress has been turned, according to regulations. Thus the stench
> of the last agony will not hit you in the face. As for the one now arriving,
> it would be better if they looked at him, if they put him to bed, if they
> asked him lots of questions, for if they leave him alert, he will handle
> the perilous density of his importance by himself. But he understands
> very well that there are other men crying here and that no one will know
> how to answer them, if his mouth looked at the mouth of the others, of
> us, the sick ones.

Line 9: the word "ay" often appears in Vallejo's poetry and we have resisted always translating it literally as "ay" or "alas." We have tried to pick up the emotional edge of the word in each Vallejo context in which we encounter it; thus it is translated in a number of ways in these poems.

Line 56: Larrea suggests that "nos perdonan pecho" might mean "they forgive us the sin of having chests" (and allow us, as a consequence, to breathe). "Pecho," depending on the context, can mean "chest," "breast," "heart," or even "courage." Larrea's interpretation is strengthened by the probability that the "mosca" (fly) in line 55 seems to be a religious person, e.g., a nun. Since Vallejo uses "pecho" often (especially in *Spain, take this cup from me*), and gives it a feeling of his own, we have decided to stick with its literal meaning in English.

Line 77: "azor" is a Peruvian expression for "azoro" and "azoramiento" and can mean "shyness" or "embarrassment" rather than its regular meaning, "goshawk."

Line 84: this line was originally the following three line paragraph:

> Blood runs wild in the thermometers. The order of the numbers
> reared on 22 and the following numbers exclaim central! central!
> central!

*

I am going to speak of hope, p. 17

After the second paragraph, the following paragraph has been crossed out:

> It is necessary to differentiate my present pain, from that
> pain which derives from not having a cause to feel pain. Today I suffer
> a pain that did not have a cause nor did it lack one. There are pains

like this in the bottomless kingdom, in the continent, without history or future, of the heart of man. I suffer, then, without conditions or consequences. Suspended in the air, I do not know if fragile or resistant, my pain has now such sufficiency and a courage so much its own, that before it men would feel religious and almost joyous respect. Because oh miracle of the maximum circles! this pain is not conditioned to come or to leave.

After the last paragraph, the following paragraph was crossed out:

And in this heart, that has neither had a cause nor the lack of one; in this heart, without back or chest, without state or name, without source or use, there is no room for hope or memory and what is even sadder, ah tremendous fall upward! how I now make my pain feel pain.

*

"We probably already were of a compassionate age," p. 19

This poem was not included in *Poemas humanos* editions prior to the *Obra poética completa*, and appears to originally have been part of *Contra el secreto professional* (written in the 20s, and first published by Mosca Azul, Lima, 1973). In the facsimile, the following title is crossed out: "Lánguidamente a su licor" (Languidly to their/his/her/its liquor).

Line 2: "Cura de amor" could be translated "as a cure of love" modifying "el yantar de oracion" instead of "mamà."

Line 5: "mi madre iba sentada" (my mother went sitting) is a typical construction in this piece, coherent and at the same time irrationally dense. We translate literally when a phrase is not idiomatic nor appears to have been invented, as a neologism, by Vallejo.

Lines 9/10: "tocar" means "to knock," "to touch," and "to play" and when connected to "trastos" (originally written as "trastes"), suggests the playing of a stringed musical instrument, with "entrails" taking the place of "heart" or "feelings." By altering one letter, Vallejo changed "trastes" (stops, frets) to "trastos" (junk, implements) and we have had to translate the word as if it were "trastes" since to render the latter word would eliminate the musical image.

Line 20: "me ha echado Miguel al pavo. A su paVO." A Peruvian idiomatic expression whose meaning to us is not clear, although we feel it is probably connected with "subírsele a uno el pavo" (to blush). A literal translation would be: "Miguel has thrown me to the turkey. To his turKEY." The Moncloa OPC treats the typographical oddity, "paVO," as an error, but we feel that it is intentional, thus we reproduce it in English.

Line 21: "padrE" is handled as "paVO" above.

Line 35: from this line on, the original version varies considerably with the final one:

> . . . the hen was widower of her children, the hen is the eternal bride of the mammalia. All the eggs were found empty. The brooder afterward had the verb and, in an elegant construction, past, present and chirping.
>
> One story, two stories, three stories.
>
> No one frightened her. And in case she was frightened, no one allowed himself to be lulled by her clucking nor by her viviparous chill.
>
> —Where are the old hen's children?
> —Where are the old hen's chickens?
> Afterwards botanical works were scarce in the hamlet.
> One small eye, two small eyes, three small eyes.

*

Discovery of life, p. 21

Before the first paragraph, the following paragraph has been crossed out:

> When was it that I savored for the first time the taste of life? When was it that I tested this impression of nature, that makes me ecstatic at this moment? Have I savored on another occasion the taste of life? Have I already tested at another time my impression of nature? I am completely convinced of not having tested it, of never having savored it, except now. This is extraordinary! Today is the first time that I have savored the taste of life; today is the first time that the impression of nature has made me ecstatic. This is extraordinary! This astonishes me and makes me brim with tears and happiness.

Line 9: "me haría desgraciado" (would make me miserable). This personal use of the conditional form places the previous thought in a mixed temporal zone, sharing reality and possibility.

Line 26: "inconocido" appears to be Vallejo's play on "desconocido" (unknown) and we have translated it accordingly.

After the fourth paragraph, the following paragraph has been crossed out:

> I am possessed by the emotion of this discovery. A discovery of the unexpected and a discovery of goodness. How much has this happiness cost me? How long have I awaited it?

Neither expectation nor price. Do you know the unexpected happiness?
Do you know the unpaid happiness? This is my happiness today. That
which makes me ecstatic and clothes me with an air so unused, that
people will take me for a foreigner on earth. Yes. Neither do I know any-
one nor does anyone know me.

After the last line, the following two sentences have been crossed out:

And I am now at the point of dying, before I am at the point of getting
old. I will die of life and not of time.

*

"Longing ceases," p. 25

Line 1: "rabo al aire" (tail to the air) has a colloquial meaning in Perú and we have
rendered it accordingly.

*

I am laughing, p. 31

For reasons unexplained, this poem and the two following it are without fac-
similes in the OPC. I am laughing and "Behold that today I salute" both appeared
in *Favorables-Paris-Poem*, a magazine published by Vallejo and Larrea in Paris, in
1926.

*

"Behold that today I salute," p. 33

Line 4: it appears as if the capital A in the word "distanciA" has been put there by
Vallejo to make fun of the rhyme and musicality of all of the quatrain up to that
point. By capitalizing the "a" in "distance" we intend to throw the accent onto
that syllable, creating a similar effect. From this point on, the poem is written
freely, as if that "A" released Vallejo from the regular/traditional shape.

Line 17: "hun" meaning "un" (a) is misspelled on purpose: the reason for doing
so is not clear. We have tried to create a similar effect in English with "aa" (hun)
and "ssssuch" for "ttttales" in line 11.

*

Spine of the scriptures, p. 35

This poem first appeared in *Mundial,* a Lima magazine, in 1927.

Line 1: Vallejo's first line is awkwardly written and we have not eliminated this awkwardness in the translation.

Line 3: "pecho," as noted before, can mean several things. We want to point out again that we feel it should be rendered literally when it appears in these poems. Feminine "breast," without such ambiguity, is "seno."

*

height and hair, p. 37

An earlier version of this poem, entitled "Actitud de excelencia" (Lofty attitude), was published in the Lima magazine, *Mundial,* on the 18th of November, 1927:

> Who doesn't own a blue suit
> and eat lunch and board the streetcar
> with his smoked cigarette and his pocket-sized pain?
>
> Who doesn't write a letter
> and talk about something very important?
> Ah, I was born so alone.
>
> Who isn't called Carlos
> and doesn't at least say kitty, kitty, kitty, kitty?
> Ah, I was born so alone.
>
> Ah, how I was born so alone.
> Ah, how I was born so alone.

*

"Between pain and pleasure there are three," p. 41

In the facsimile, the third stanza of this poem originally read:

> To the instantaneous meaning of eternity
corresponds
this absurdity that identifies us today,
but to your volume of goodbye,
corresponds solely what is inexorably harmful,
between your creature, and my word.

*

"The moment the tennis player masterfully serves," p. 43

Another version of this poem, written out as prose, has been published in the Mosca Azul edition of *Contra el secreto professional*, p. 13.

*

hat, overcoat, gloves, p. 45

Line 5: "jebe" (caoutchouc) is used to mean "goma" (rubber) in Perú. It also means "condom" in Perú.

*

epistle to those passing through, p. 49

Line 2: after this line, Vallejo had originally written the following three lines:

> just in case my brute calls out in great fables
> and the sky becomes human earth,
> a sky at full speed, mounted slowly on a sword.

Line 9: "compañones" is an archaic Spanish word for "testicles." We attempt to match it with a similarly archaic word for testicles in English.

Line 21: Vallejo misspells "ombligo" (navel) as "hombligo" (perhaps as a play on "hombre"—man). We render the word as "navell" as the sound is not changed by the added letter.

The last stanza originally read:

> Meanwhile, convulsive, continued,
> my soft quality convalesces,
> suffering like I suffer the direct language of the lion;
> and in that I have existed between two potentates with candles,
> I convalesce, I feel better, smiling at my lips,
> when my sex is sad
> and my destruction is good enough.

*

"And don't say another word," p. 51

In the facsimile, the following title has been crossed out: "grandeza de los trabajos vulgares" (the greatness of common works).

*

GLEBE, p. 53

The title: originally the Spanish word "gleba" meant "clod" (in modern Spanish, "terrón"), or "soil" (in modern Spanish, "suelo" or "tierra"), but today the word "gleba" persists only in the old expression "siervos de la gleba" (serfs of the soil, or slaves of the soil) and is always associated with the idea of the worst kind of serfdom or human slavery.

Line 2: "hombres a golpes" (men at blows) implies "hombres hechos a golpes de hacha" (men hacked out by ax blows).

Line 3: "a tiro de neblina" (within fog range) is also unusual, and appears to derive from such common expressions as "a tiro de escopeta" (within shotgun range), or "a tiro de cañón" (within cannon range).

Line 5: "reginas de los valles" sounds like the name of a common flower, "lirio de los valles" (lily of the valley). If "reginas" (queens) is a Peruvian variation on "lirio," we have not been able to trace it, so we have translated the phrase literally.

Line 34: Luis Taboada is the name of a famous Spanish humorist (1848–1906), but it is not entirely certain that Vallejo had him in mind when he used the name.

*

TUBEROUS SPRING, p. 55

Line 3: "picotón" appears to be an unusual augmentative of "pico" (beak, pick) and may in Vallejo's mind be connected with "azadón" (mattock). However, it is actually a Peruvian expression that means to strike hard, and in this context suggests the vulture using its beak as a mattock while eating.

Line 19: "deglucion" is misspelled as "deglusion," with the "s" underlined and a question mark penciled in the left margin of the facsimile.

*

Black stone on a white stone, p. 57

According to Carlos del Rio León (in *Caretas*, Lima, April 19, 1966, pp. 24–25), the title of this poem is based on the fact that one day, in Paris, Vallejo was very depressed and, while wearing a black overcoat, sat down on a white stone. The stone evoked a white sepulcher and his own appearance a black stone. This poem, like several others in *Payroll of bones* and *Sermon on barbarism*, is structurally a traditional sonnet.

Line 3: "correr" (to run) acquires a different meaning when used reflexively, mainly "to move" (forward to the right or left). The implication here appears to be that he will remain in Paris, in spite of his intuition that death awaits him there.

Line 7: "a la mala" could also be translated here as "unwillingly" (the phrase occurs in line 51 of "Battles" in *Spain, take this cup from me*, and there we have translated it as "unwillingly"). In this sonnet, Vallejo uses the phrase idiomatically *and* idiosyncratically, and its specific meaning remains mysterious.

*

"Sweetness through heartsown sweetness!" p. 59

Line 1: "corazona" is an arbitrary feminine, probably of the masculine noun "corazón" (heart), although it could also be the third person singular of a made-up verb based on "corazón," such as "corazonar." On the basis of the second possibility, the line could be rendered: "Sweetness through sweetness heartens!"

However, since we have "hearten" as an accepted English word, such a rendering does not translate the uniqueness of "corazona." So we have translated it as a noun, hoping to expose "heart's own," "heart sown," and "heart zone," in our rendering.

Line 2: the word "eras" could also mean "threshing floors" or "garden-plots" here.

Line 6: "tezón" appears to be a neologism, based on "tesón" (tenacity), and we have rendered it accordingly. However, it could also be a neologism based on "tez" (complexion).

Line 16: "perduroso" appears to be a neologism, based on "perdurar" (to last long), with a suffix such as one finds in "presuroso" (hasty) for which the verb would be "apresurar" (to hasten).

Lines 31/32: the two lines of French read: "When one has life and youth / that's already so much!"

Line 36: "haz" here is an intentional misspelling of "has" (second person singular, present tense, of "haber"—to have—used as an auxillary verb). If Vallejo had written: "has de besarme" we would have translated it as: "you will kiss me." "Haz" by itself could also mean "bundle" or "face."

*

"Life, this life," p. 65

Lines 9/10: these lines, before corrections, read:

> their sacred bones slanting ner the sewers,
> over an old screw, proclivitous, misfortunate.

"cabe" (near) is misspelled "cave" and we attempt to match the slight sound change with "ner" in English.

Line 13: "póbridas" is a neologism derived from "pobres" (poor ones) and perhaps "podrida" (rotten).

Line 18: originally read:

> if their loadstones then fell

Line 21: this line and the three following it originally read:

> sent forth dense smoke of thoughtful madmen, attacked
> by physics, and from pain half deaf.

>   Doves jumping from the depths,
>   doves fragrant to the affront of that day,

Line 25: the word "manferidas" is archaic, and once meant "forewarned" or "ready," and as a derivative, "cautioned."

Line 32: the word "nimal" could just be a misspelling of "animal" or a neologism (perhaps punning on "ni"—not—and "mal"—bad—).

*

"Today I like life much less," p. 67

Line 14: before being partially crossed out, this line was corrected by hand to read:

>   but entering five abreast, of course,

Line 29: originally read:

>   and always, much always, always in line under caneblows.

and then was changed to:

>   and always, much always, always lying down outside my body.

before it was corrected to the final version.

*

"Today I would like to be happy willingly," p. 69

Line 9: this line was originally different, and was followed by two lines which were crossed out after some rewriting. The original typewritten version read:

>   the wait for that which will never arrive
>   and the forgetting of the refused waiting.
>
>   I see everything this way, without adherence or bond.

The discarded corrections in pencil, limited to the first two lines, read:

>   the wait for the nevers they did not find
>   and the forgettings of the refused waiting.

Line 19: originally read:

> at what hour, then, would I desire that they love me?

Line 22: the last stanza originally read:

> Now I notice that I cross through my temples as a traveler:
> at the misericordias, comrade,
> my fellowman in rejection and observation, more mine,
> father through the friend,
> brother through the son, in whose neck rises and lowers,
> inactive, unseasoned, without thread, my hope . . .

*

"From disturbance to disturbance," p. 71

Line 16: because of the absence of commas before and after "en suma" (in short), the line is odd in Spanish. We have translated it literally, leaving out the commas in English too.

Line 25: "taco" here is a South American word for "tacón" (heel). From this line on the facsimile copy continues in handwriting.

*

"Considering coldly, impartially," p. 73

Line 29: originally read:

> and he knows how to mend himself with tears and songs . . .

Line 36: the last line of the poem was added by hand to the typewritten original.

*

'And if after so many words," p. 75

Line 6: "que se lo coman todo" literally means "for them to eat all of it," but we feel that the phrase was used by Vallejo in its common idiomatic meaning of "to blow something" e.g., to blow a fortune.

*

"Finally, without that good continuous aroma," p. 77

Line 10: "tristumbre" appears to contain "triste" (sad) and the kind of suffix one associates with pesa/pesadumbre, or manse/mansedumbre. However, the suffix "umbre" is never used with "triste" and the common way to express "sadness" in Spanish is "tristeza." Therefore, we have had to invent our own word.

*

"Idle on a stone," pp. 79–81

Line 16: originally read:

> his betrayed dice . . .

Line 19: after this line, the two following were crossed out:

> This is the one who bled through his side,
> who today drowns in his refused blood!

(when he wrote the above two lines, Vallejo had ended the line right before them with "undesired blood." After crossing out the two lines above, he changed "undesired"—no querida—to "refused.")

Line 44: originally read:

> and the nourishing bread that they don't need

Line 46: this and the following line originally read:

> how the lightning nails its headless nail into its clavicles

Line 48: this line and the three last lines were added by hand to the typewritten original.

Line 51: as an adjective, "padre" (father) is a common augmentative for almost everything, e.g., "una vida padre" (a great life), "un automóvil padre" (a great car). Here we have tried to translate the act of the lowest parasite being ironically elevated to a role of seminal importance.

*

"The miners came out of the mine," p. 83

The first three stanzas of the poem originally read:

> The miners came out
> climbing over their future forms,
> they greeted their health with pavilions
> and, elaborating their mental function,
> they closed with their voice
> the shaft, in the shape of a profound symptom.
>
> Ah, what dust their reclined dusts!
> Ah, what oxide their high oxides!
> Mouth wedges, mouth anvils, mouth apparatus (Tremendous!)
> Great joy following, head to head, their feelings.
>
> They imagine, writings on a femur,
> their plastic inductions, their choral replies,
> crowded at the base of fiery misfortunes
> and aerent yellowing was known by the saddened,
> the tristes, imbued
> with the metal that exhausts itself, the pallid and small metaloid.

(In the lines quoted above, in the 10th line, "head to head" was crossed out and "from saliva to saliva" penciled in, which was then rejected too.)

Line 13: "airente" appears to be a neologism, based on "aire" (air) to which has been attached the suffix "ente," which is a common suffix but which is normally never attached to "aire." In the same line, "amarillura" derives from "amarillo" (yellow) but is not of normal or frequent usage. Near the end of this same line, "trístidos," while based on "triste" (sad), appears to be a neologism, as "idos" is normally never attached to that word. Lastly, "tristes" could either be a plural of the adjective "triste" or possibly the word for a song that is a lover's lament (which would have no translation). We interpret it as the former.

Line 20: after this line, the following one was crossed out:

> the miners of the timbre of the voice of man;

Line 23: after this line, the rest of the poem is handwritten.

*

"But before all this," p. 85

Line 8: "falanjas" appears to be a neologism based on "falanges" (phalanges).

Line 17: the first four lines of the fourth stanza were originally five and read:

> Torso over the hill that I encircled,
> whistling at your death,
> hat rakishly tilted,
> feet over the shoulders,
> white, hillman swaying to win your battle among the fishes,

Line 18: "pedrada" is a blow or stone throw, but in this case, "sombrero a la pedrada" is a Peruvian idiom, and refers to a hat either adorned with a ribbon, or tilted at a rakish slant. In his book, *Vallejo y su tierra*, Francisco Izquierdo Ríos wrote about the poet's home town, Santiago de Chuco: "The horse-breakers with fine ponchos and 'sombreros a la pedrada' made the horses caracole."

Line 19: "blanco" can mean "white," "target," and "blank," and Vallejo may very well have had all three meanings in mind when he used the word in this line. In the 1967 Seghers edition of Vallejo's poetry translated by his widow, the French word chosen here is "cible" (target).

*

Telluric and magnetic, pp. 87–89

Title: the following title is crossed out: "Meditación agrícola" (Agricultural Meditation). The poem was originally much more modest in scope than it finally came to be, ending with line 27 and omitting some of the material in the final first 27 lines.

Line 1: the first four lines were originally three and read:

> Ascended and sincere mechanics!
> Theoretical and practical soil!
> Intelligent furrows, and with pyramid examples!

Line 2: in the same book by Izquierdo Ríos, one reads: "In Santiago de Chuco there exists a Reddish Hill."

Line 14: the poem originally ended with this stanza and read:

> Oh human fields!
> Oh climates found inside iron, ready!
> Oh intellectual field,
> with religion, and with peasant fields!
> Pachyderms in prose while passing!
> Rodents which look with judicial feeling all around!

Oh my life's patriotic asses!
Oh light which is hardly a mirror away from the shadow,
which is life with a period and, with a line, dust
and that is why I revere it, climbing through the idea to my skeleton!

(from this point on, the poem is handwritten.)

Line 28: "molle" is *Schinus molle,* a genus of tropical American trees of the sumac family, popularly known as the pepper tree. It was the sacred tree of the Incans, and the fruit is used to make an alcoholic beverage similar to chicha.

Line 30: "barreta" (small bar) is probably a miner's tool, a small straight bar with one sharpened end, used like a crowbar. Larrea wrote us that he is under the impression that the word is also Santiago de Chuco slang for "penis."

Line 33: "cuy" (cavy) is a short-tailed rough-haired South American rodent (guinea-pigs are from the same species). A "cuya" would be a female "cuy." We add a feminine ending to cavy—cavess—to imitate the commonplace Spanish ending.

Line 34: "rocoto" is a pepper, *Capsicum baccatum,* popularly known as the bird pepper. The red fruit are small, oblong and very pungent. The Spanish word probably derives from the Quechuan "rucuta."

Line 35: "Me friegan los cóndores!" could also be rendered as "Those condors make me sick!" and it is true that the verb is softer in Perú than it is in Mexico where it is a strong vulgar word. We feel that the fact that Vallejo used the word in the mid-thirties, when it was much more objectionable than today, justifies our present translation. Also: see the note on line 62—the same Mexican friend who apparently stimulated Vallejo to use "me las pelan," may also have stimulated his use of "friegan."

Line 42: these "four operations" probably allude to the four basic arithmetic operations. Another possibility, rather remote yet possible given the associative depth of Vallejo's mind, is an allusion to the abortions Georgette Vallejo is said to have had in the early 30s—such could be also thought of as operations. The verb "sustraer" (to remove, deduct, subtract) can be seen to reinforce the arithmetic interpretation, yet we feel that here it has a more ample meaning than the one pointing to arithmetic alone.

Line 44: "en infraganti" appears related to the commonly used adverbial expression "in fraganti" or "en flagrante," both meaning "in the very act." Vallejo's alteration seems simply odd. The idea seems to be that the "cuestas" (slopes) are being "caught in the act" of becoming slopes. And such a parthenogenesis is coherent in the context of the poem itself, which envisions Perú as a process of unceasing creation. The poem has the feel of a long string of couplets, or pieces of couplets, which ignite each other Chinese firecracker style.

Line 45: "auquenidos" is derived from "auquenia" which is the generic Latin form for certain South American animals of the camel family, such as llamas, vicuñas, alpacas and guanacos—all of which have big sad eyes.

Line 61: "quena" is a one-hole Indian flute that accompanies the yaravi songs in some parts of South America. Legend has it that it is carved out of the shinbone of a dead belovéd.

Line 62: in answer to our query about "me las pelan!," Larrea wrote: "In our Hispanoamerican group in Montparnasse in 1926, we often sang a kind of ballad, thanks to a good Mexican friend, which had a refrain which went: 'Pelame la pinga' (peel my foreskin down) and also repeated another expression: 'me la pelan' (they peel mine down). I would say that this is the origin of that line of Vallejo's. That he puts it in the plural surprises me—perhaps he does that out of modesty. It would translate something like 'me la menean' (they jack me off)."

*

Old asses thinking, p. 91

This poem was inspired by the death of Vallejo's close friend from his first days in Paris, Alfonso Silva, a Peruvian composer and writer who went back to Perú and died in Lima on May 7, 1937. Vallejo also wrote another poem in response to Silva's death, which begins: "Alfonso: you keep looking at me, I see."

Line 11: "boldo," a genus of Chilean evergreen shrubs, having as the only known species *B. boldus*, the boldo. It has sweet, edible fruit, and the dried leaves are hypnotic and diuretic.

Line 19: after this line the one following is crossed out:

I will call him at the margin of his encased river's name!

(Alfonso's name, which Vallejo might have heard as "a fondo," suggesting both thoroughness and depth, might have evoked the image of an "encased river.")

Line 21: in Spanish the word "jamases" (the plural of an adverb meaning "never") is grammatically impossible—but it does exist in popular speech.

*

The hungry man's wheel, p. 97

Line 15: "calcárida" appears to be a neologism based on "calcáreo" (calcareous) and "árida" (arid).

*

"Heat, tired I go with my gold," p. 99

Line 3: the French reads:

It's cooled off September,

Lines 5/6: these two lines originally read:

Paris, and 4, and 5, of dried anxiety,
hanged, in the heat, from cloud and owl.

Line 7: the French reads:

It's Paris, queen of the world!

Line 11: the French reads:

It's spring,

Line 15: the French reads:

It's life, death of the Death!

*

"One pillar holding up consolations," p. 101

Line 3: "pilaroso" appears to be a neologism, based on "pilar" (pillar), to which the common suffix "oso" has been added. To do this is like adding "oso" to "temer," turning "to fear" into timorous." Since "pilar" is not a verb, the "oso" acts as an intensifier, leading us to our "pillarous."

Line 17: this line and the three following originally read:

I am going to close my baptismal font, this edge,
this fright with a band in the form of wrath,
this finger without a hand,
directly tied to my skeleton.

Line 20: "corazonmente" is a neologism, based on "corazon" (heart) to which has been added the suffix "mente," usually translated as "ly" in English.

*

"Upon reflecting on life," p. 163

The first version of this poem, significantly different than the final version, read:

> Upon reflecting,
> existence feels better, settles us,
> condemns to death;
> and, wrapped in white rags, it falls,
> falls with a planet step,
> the nail boiled in grief.
> Official bitterness, that of my left,
> old pocket, in itself considered, in itself pocket,
> without situation, without number, this sword.

> Everything is joyful, except my joy
> and everything, long, except my furor,
> my incertitude!
> Through form, nevertheless, I go forward,
> limping,
> up to my encounter,
> and forget through my tears my eyes
> and climb to my feet from my star.

> I weave. From having spun, I am weaving . . .
> I search for what follows me and hides from me among archbishops,
> under my soul and behind the smoke that I've smoked.
> Such is death,
> that grew up by crushings, by gunshots,
> exhaling lethal petroleums,
> only yesterday, a Sunday of faces . . .

> Such is death, with ram and everything.

*

Poem to be read and sung, p. 105

Line 1: "persona" is a word that refers to both men and women, and in this poem a case can be made for it being translated as masculine (as an inner person of the poet) as well as feminine (a woman, perhaps the poet's wife, Georgette, according to Larrea, pp. 389–392).

Line 19: "tasa" (measure, appraisal) has been misread in all previous editions of these poems as "taza" (cup, bowl), for the latter word seems to make more ordinary sense in context. We stick with the way Vallejo typed it out. "Tasa" appears to be an unintentional misspelling when it appears on p. 10 in line 25.

*

"The tip of man," p. 109

Line 25: "dondoneo" appears to be a neologism, based on "contoneo" (strut). To match Vallejo's sound distortion, we take the word "sashay" and replace the two s/s with two z/s.

*

"Oh bottle without wine!" p. 111

Line 8: "penetratativa" seems to be an unintentional misspelling for "penetrativa."

Line 9: the adjective "jugarino" appears to be a neologism based on the verb "jugar" (to play) and the suffix "ino." The normal Spanish adjective would have been "juguetón." The "ino" gives the word an Italian flavor and also a lighter playfulness.

Line 23: our rendering of "zánganos de ala" (winged drones) is literal here, and we suspect that it might have meant something more to Vallejo. It could be a Santiago de Chuco Peruvianism which we have not been able to track down. On the other hand, the fact that he originally wrote "zánganos con ala," then crossed out "con" and put in "de," suggests that he might have been making up his own expression.

*

"He is running, walking, fleeing," p. 113

Line 11: originally read:

at an inkwell pace, flees

*

"My chest wants and does not want its color," pp. 117

Line 17: "perrazo" is an augmentative of "perro" (dog), and the thought here
seems to derive from the expression "tener vida de perro" (to live a dog's life).

Line 19: "cejón" appears to be a neologism, based on "ceja" (eyebrow). Vallejo
uses "ceja" in somewhat the same way that "cabezón" (headstrong) augments
"cabeza" (head).

Line 27: originally read:

>   anguish, yes, with all the nipple,

(nipple being here "tetilla," a male nipple).

*

"This," p. 119

Line 1: the poem originally began without this one word line, and its first two
lines read:

>   It happened between two flowers and two eyelids; I trembled
>   in my scabbard, with alkali, with anger,

Line 11: originally "of the sky" which ends this line and stanza, began a new line
which, along with another one, completed the stanza:

>   of the sky. (I would have dealt with other themes, but
>   I write them unsung, without my mouth)

Line 13: instead of "in my scabbard," this line originally began with "from fear of
death." "Vaina" (scabbard) appears to be intentionally misspelled as "vayna."

Line 16: this line and the one following it originally read:

>   (They say that sighs have
>   then regresses that do not want to go away;

Line 26: originally read:

>   the half-years revise me in their album

*

"I stayed on to warm up the ink in which I drown," p. 121

Line 2: originally read:

> I stayed on to listen also to my elbow,

Lines 7/8: these two lines originally read:

> And yet, this very day,
> I digest extremely sacred tenths,

Line 15: the last stanza was originally four typed lines to which Vallejo added four handwritten lines ("pens," in both cases, refers to writing pens):

> And yet,
> even now,
> warm, listener, he/earth, sun and he/moon,
> unknown I cross the cemetery,
> go off to the left, splitting
> the grass with a pair of hendecasyllables,
> years of port, liters of infinity,
> ink, pen, and adobe pens.

Line 19: Vallejo changes the normal endings of the words "tierra" (earth) and "luna" (moon) to make them unusual masculine nouns, possibly to be able to identify himself with them in fact as in appearance, or perhaps to stress the patriarchal saturation of nature. The word "sol" (sun) is already a masculine noun in Spanish.

Line 24: this line went through several changes before a final version was arrived at. Vallejo changed the line as translated above to:

> ink, pen, bricks, and spectacles.

At this point, "spectacles" was crossed out, and "pardons" put in its place.

*

"The peace, the whasp, the heel, the slopes," pp. 123

Line 1: "avispa" (wasp) appears to be intentionally misspelled as "abispa." The reader may have noticed that most of Vallejo's "misspellings" have to do with either adding a silent letter ("hun" for "un") or changing a "b" into a "v" or vice versa, as in the present case. That is, there is a pattern, and while we can indicate it by slightly warping the word in question, we cannot find a parallel predictable construction to match the Spanish. The point of this may be, in Vallejo's mind, to point up the arbitrariness of spelling in sounding the written word—and too, perhaps, to reinforce a feeling that language itself is highly unstable, especially in charged meditation, and may, as Dali's melting watches, give way at any moment.

Line 19: in Spanish, "tan" (so) is never used, in normal speech, followed by "nunca" (never).

*

"Overcome, solomonic, decent," p. 125

Line 1: instead of "decent," Vallejo had originally written "impelling."

*

"Well? Does the pallid metaloid heal you?" p. 127

Lines 15/16: these lines originally read:

> your soul bends passionately to the iron
> bone on which your temple marks time.

*

"It is so hot I feel cold," p. 129

Line 1: originally read:

> I am cold from heat,

Lines 8/9: these lines originally read:

> The caterpillar plays its inexistent
> voice, with its soul,

＊

"Confidence in the eyeglass," p. 131

In lines 1, 3, 5 and 7, Vallejo puts an accent mark over the "o" in "no." Since this is unusual, we have italicized these words in English.

＊

"Speaking of kindling," p. 133

In all typeset editions of Vallejo's poetry (including the typeset part of the Moncloa OPC), this poem is entitled "Terremoto" (Earthquake). On the facsimile page, however, the poem has no title. "Terremoto" is handwritten a couple of lines below the poem and underlined.

The proper names Atanacio (which is normally spelled Atanasio), Hermeregildo (normally spelled Hermenegildo), Isabel and Luis, have no particular meaning for a Spanish reader.

＊

"Mocked, acclimatized to goodness," pp. 135

Line 1: "urent" appears to be intentionally misspelled as "hurent." He used "hurente" in *Trilce XVII,* line 3.

Line 10: "with the whole ax" in this line was originally "or to delouse oneself;"

Lines 15/16: originally read:

> leap from the margin,
> from the daily margin of my mule that walks;

＊

"Alfonso: you keep looking at me," pp. 137–139

Line 9: originally read:

> and on the wire your last act to dawn,

Line 13: the French reads:

> wine, milk, counting the pennies

Lines 19/20: "amado sér" (beloved Being) and "amado estar" (beloved to be) cannot be fully translated (without interpretation, which would distort the actual meaning of the original), as "ser" (to be, as a verb) is not the same thing as "estar" (to be, as a verb). If the two verbs are matched, the meaning-distinction in English is more or less "to be" versus "to exist," as "ser" is less time-bound and temporary than "estar." However, Vallejo has turned "ser" into a noun by placing an accent over the "e," and in doing so seems to be stressing that which is or is idealized to always be versus that which has potential to be. To translate "estar" here as "existence" would be to lose the noun/verb relationship clearly established in the Spanish. Notice that the "double tomb" referred to in line 34 is merely a "tomb" with Silva's "Being," but a "mahogany one" with his "to be," which emphasizes the abstractness associated with "ser" and the materiality associated with "estar."

Line 34: originally read:

> in the opening of that horrible tomb without a corpse,

*

Stumble between two stars, pp. 141–143

Line 11: here the word "ay" seems to stress "pity for . . ." so we have slightly departed from an abstract exclamation to give that stress. The last word in line 11, "ellas" (them, feminine), is repeated, in the masculine form, "ellos," in the last line of the poem. There is no way to translate this difference in English.

Line 15: Meo Zilio makes an interesting observation about "las orejas sanchez" (the sanchez ears): if one says the phrase quickly pronounced with the common Spanish American "seseo," one can hear "las orejas anchas" (the wide ears) in place of a person's name.

*

Farewell remembering a goodbye, p. 145

Lines 7/8: originally read:

> and, as a last glass of blood, on its dramatic role,
> there is, and until the end, the practical dream of the soul.

*

"Chances are, I am another;" p. 147

Line 5: in Spanish, a "there is" is sensed before both "scarlet index" and "bronze cot" in a way that is less elliptic than in English, and less awkward too. But since it is not actually there, we have left it out.

Line 13: originally read:

> But another's sweat, but my metaphysical serum

*

The book of nature, p. 149

Line 6: the literal meaning of this line is: "his three of cups, his horse of golds." In American playing cards, these figures correspond to "hearts" and "diamonds," and the "horse" to the "queen." The cups are not really cups, but chalices and the "golds" figures of the sun.

*

Wedding March, p. 153

Title: this poem was originally called: "Batallón de dioses" (Battalion of gods). A second title, handwritten, was also rejected: "Séquito y Epitalamio" (Retinue and Epithalamion).

Line 3: "cuello" (neck) seems to be unintentionally misspelled as "cuelo" here.

Line 9: the last two tercets originally read:

> I will ignite, my ant will ignite,
> my key will ignite, my quarrel
> in which I lost the cause of my track.
>
> Then, making a wheat spike of the atom,
> I will ignite my sickles at its foot
> and the battalion will say: "Go on! Let him go on!"

At a latter stage of composition (perhaps after the first title had been eliminated), Vallejo rewrote the tercets as follows:

> I will extinguish, my ant will extinguish,
> my key will extinguish, the quarrel
> in which the undersigned won his cause.

> Then, making a wheat spike of the atom,
> I will extinguish my sickles at its foot
> and the spike will finally be a spike.

He then changed all the "extinguishes" back to "ignites," and the "won" to "lost" in making his final revisions. There is also a crossed out third version of the final line which reads: "And for the rest, I don't give . . ." (with the last two words entirely unintelligible).

*

Intensity and height, p. 157

Line 2: "me atollo" is a seldom used equivalent for "me atasco" (I get stuck, I freeze).

Line 7: "toz" appears to be a neologism, combining "tos" (cough) with "voz" (voice).

Line 14: since "cuerva" is not merely the female "cuervo" (raven, crow), we have made use of this possibility to avoid translating it into an anthropomorphical word.

*

Guitar, p. 159

Line 6: this line, and the one following it (crossed out and not reworked) originally read:

> and the mendacious eighth, suffers from an algebra
> more mendacious, more base, more metal.

Added by hand to this crossed out seventh line (and then also crossed out) was:

> gown, copper and boa.

Line 11: originally read:

> and to be here, between two treacherous days?

Line 25: the facsimile edition clearly says "poña" in a handwritten addition by Vallejo himself, instead of "saña," which has been printed instead of "poña" in all previous editions of these poems. The original typewritten line read: "de esperar pronunciando mal su nombre" (of waiting pronouncing his name badly); then the last four words were crossed out and to "de esperar" was probably added by hand: "con pujanza y paga y poña" (with might and salary and "poña"). We say "probably" because "paga" is crossed out in such a way that it could be "paja" (straw). When Vallejo later crossed out either "paga" or "paja" he inserted "mala" over it, to leave as the final version of the entire line: "de esperar con pujanza y mala poña." Our effort to establish an acceptable and clear meaning in Spanish for the expression "y mala poña" has been unsuccessful, although we have a sense, in the context of the stanza, of how the expression is functioning. After the publication of the hardback edition, Irene Vegas-García called our attention to the possible connection between the word "poña" and the Santiago de Chuco popular expression "no te apoñes" (don't be embarrassed), also mentioned by Izquierdo (op. cit., p. 188). The word "poña" nevertheless exists in the Spanish Galician language and perhaps was used as a euphemism by the two natural grandfathers of Vallejo and later on might have been spoken by members of his family at home while he was growing up. If this is true, he might have remembered the word for its strangeness, since he probably did not hear it elsewhere. Its equivalence in Spanish is "porra," which literally means a "strong stick," but figuratively, and when spoken as an exclamation, is a polite euphemism for "polla" (cock, i.e., slang for penis). "Mala poña" also suggests a parallelism with common Spanish expressions like "mala roña" (awful mange) and "mala saña" (terrible hatred). Since the speaker in the poem, at least in this stanza, seems to be anticipating a sexual encounter with considerable ambivalence, we have translated the line accordingly. We hope that the play on "hard left" (zurdazo)—to be left with an erection as well to be hit with a left-handed blow—in the following line will help reinforce Vallejo's meaning in English.

Line 29: after this line, the last one in the poem, Vallejo originally wrote:

> and added to the females of the dead.

*

"Hear your mass, your comet, listen to them;" p. 161

Lines 1/2: originally read:

> Hear your finger, listen to it: don't moan
> through your hand;

Line 11: originally read:

> to be carmine, to be in the double time step of a skeleton.

*

"What's got into me," p. 163

Line 12: this line, and the rest of the poem, originally read:

> crying earth and standing out in physics?
>
>> What's gotten into me, that I cry and do not cry,
> that I laugh and do not laugh?
>
>> Pity for me! pity for you! pity for him!

*

Anniversary, pp. 165

Line 1: we have used numerical numbers in this translation, rather than written ones, so that it is clear to the English reader that Vallejo means "1" at the end of the sixth line, not "one" (i.e., a person).

Lines 17/18: originally read:

> and how many Great Charmers
> and what a nest of tigers in the lamp,

*

Pantheon, p. 167

Line 6: an "arco" is more accurately an "arc" or "arch" instead of a "bow." However, since Vallejo's line runs "un arco, un arcoíris" we have used "bow" to imitate the way he moves into "rainbow."

*

Two yearning children, p. 171

Line 1: Vallejo's original first stanza read:

> No. The cock's aggresive jaw
> has no size

> nor is it sharpened on its ankle; it is not its teethed
> spur, that touches both cheeks.
> It is just life, with robe and yoke.

Line 4: originally read:

> No. Their erectile exodus has no plural,

Line 9: this line and the two following it originally read:

> I know it, I intuit it Cartesian,
> moribund, alive, dead, in short, magnificent.
> Nothing is over the capote of the inkwell,

Line 20: "cosa bravisíma" (literally, a very wild thing) is a Peruvianism meaning "a hell of a tough thing."

Line 22: this line and the two following it originally read:

> abstract reach, fortunate and anatomical, nevertheless,
> glacial and impetuous, of the flame;
> motor of the depth, restrainer of form.

*

The nine monsters, pp. 173–175

Line 1: "I" appears to be an intentional misspelling of "Y" (And). The two letters are pronounced the same way in Spanish. After this line, Vallejo originally wrote the following line, then crossed it out:

> I have already said this to Doña Genoveva,

Line 25: "Russeau" appears to be an unintentional misspelling of "Rousseau."

Line 28: the typewritten version ended here and was dated "5 Nov 1937." The rest of the poem is handwritten and was added after that date (which was then crossed out).

Line 33: beginning with this line, the number "nine" is repeated six times in the next six lines. Originally, Vallejo used "seven" each place that has "nine" now.

Line 61: "ardio" appears to be a metaplasm derived from "ardiente" (ardent) and "arduo" (arduous). It is possible that the word "ardido" (intrepid, angry) also figured into the construction.

*

"A man walks by with a stick of bread on his shoulder." p. 177

Line 2: originally read:

> Am I going to write, after that, of the profound I?

Line 10: originally read:

> Will it ever be possible to allude to the durable I?

Line 26: here we use a lower-case italicized "i" to parallel Vallejo's lowercase "yó," in contrast to the "Yo" (I) in line 10. It would be possible to translate the I/i as Ego/ego too. Since Vallejo criticizes psychoanalysis in line 4 we have not chosen to use Ego/ego.

*

"For several days," pp. 179–181

Line 22: after this line, the following one has been crossed out:

> the foot that he lacks,

Line 37: after this line, the following one has been crossed out:

> to help the elderly ones chew,

*

"Today a splinter has gotten into her." p. 183

Line 9: "aflixion" (aflixion) appears to be an intentional misspelling for "afliccion" (affliction). Perhaps the "x" suggested a tilted cross? The same situation is repeated in line 32.

Line 12: instead of "humareda" (a great deal of smoke), Vallejo wrote "humillo" (a thin smoke or vapor) in his original version. To avoid having to write "a great deal of smoke" in English, we have translated "humareda" as "smoke" and "salió" (came out) as "poured out."

Line 14: originally read:

> Immensity pillages her

*

Clapping and guitar, p. 185

Line 6: "teneblosa" appears to be a combination of "tiniebla" (darkness, obscurity) and "tenebrosa" (tenebrous, gloomy).

*

The soul that suffered from being its body, p. 187

Line 4: where the word "diaphanous" now occurs in this line, the word "carbon" originally occurred.

Line 7: "juanes" is the plural of the name Juan (John). Vallejo's use of it also evokes "juanetes" (bunions, high cheekbones).

Line 19: after this line, the following two originally read:

> barefoot, ashen cock; Darwin's little man,
> bailiff who urinates on me, most atrocious microbe.

Line 27: this line was originally a little different than the final version and was followed by two lines later crossed out:

> and you question your navel valiantly:
> where? how?
> and your sex with impetuosity: for how long?

*

"He has just passed by," p. 191

Line 18: "aflixion"—same situation as in "Today a splinter has gotten into her."

Line 20: after this line, the last one in the final version, Vallejo had originally written two more lines which were crossed out:

he will not forget me, in past time, when he returns,
to remember me, in future time, when he parts.

*

"Let the millionaire go naked," pp. 193–195

Line 1: "en pelo" (bareback) is normally used for riding a horse bareback. In Perú, when used in reference to a person, it suggests stark nakedness.

Line 24: "magestad" appears to be an unintentional misspelling of "majestad" (majesty).

Line 43: "hondor" is a neologism, based on "hondo" (deep) to which a suffix "r" has been added, as in "negro" (black) and "negror" (blackness).

*

"That the evil man might come," p. 197

Line 1: "viniere" (might come) is a future subjunctive, a tense seldom used in modern Spanish, especially as an independent tense, and there is no exact equivalent in English. The tense expresses uncertainty about future contingencies, although it is never based on causation or emotion.

Line 9: originally read:

That the notion of fire might lack snow,

Line 13: originally read:

That two would lack eleven for thirteen,

Line 16: originally read:

and the difficult an easy, and iron gold . . .

Line 24: this line was corrected, and the one following it crossed out:

with what to be poor, if I have nothing?
and, furthermore, with whom?

Line 31: after this line, the last one in the final version, the poem originally ended with:

> I'm not exaggerating.

*

"Contrary to those mountain birds," pp. 199–201

Lines 3/5: "una tarde" (one afternoon), is a feminine noun in Spanish and in the line following it carries "presa," (imprisoned). At that point, the gender of the adjectives changes, and "metaloso" (metalous) and "terminante" (decisive) belong to the masculine "Sincero."

Line 5: "metaloso" appears to be a neologism, constructed in the same way that "pilar" / "pilaroso" is.

Line 13: originally read:

> by half humbleness all of the Great was born;

Line 30: after this line to the end of the stanza, the original typewritten version read:

> in the world; Walt Whitman was almost completely right.
> Walt Whitman had a very soft chest and used
> to breathe and no one knows what he did do when he was crying in his
>   dining room;
> in my opinion, he could not count beyond one hundred and thirty,
> when trying to reach five hundred; it is probable.

Line 46: after this line, the following one was crossed out:

> Sad is the cause; the end, even happier.

*

"The fact is that the place where I put on," pp. 203–205

Line 24: "Georgette" is the name of Vallejo's surviving widow.

Line 36: Vallejo was forty-five years old when he dated this poem.

*

"Something identifies you with the one who leaves you," p. 207

Line 18: after this sentence, the following one was crossed out:

> That is why I lock myself, at times, in my hotel, to kill
> my corpse and hold a wake over it.

*

"In short, I have nothing with which to express," p. 209

Line 1: after this line, an original second line was crossed out:

> In short, I cure with death the sores of life.

*

"A little more calm," pp. 211–213

Line 17: originally read:

> how to contain your mental volume without grieving,

*

Sermon on death, p. 219

Line 3: "llave" is most commonly "key" but because of the context we have trans-
lated it as "brace," i.e., a musical indicator for two or more staves. For it is fol-
lowed by "mano grande," which is definitely a "piece brace," an expanded kind of
regular brace, or any of several type characters used with dashes inserted to form
braces of any required depth or length. Until now, Vallejo is perhaps suggesting,
death has acted, within life's sentence (or chorus), as a parenthetic force seemingly
capable of infinite extension. When "llave" appears again in line 21, we translate it
as "brace" for consistency, although at this point in the poem its "key" meaning-
possibility is stronger than above.

Line 12: Vallejo originally wrote "papas" instead of the revised "patatas," and he did this in line 23 as well. "Papa" could mean "potatoes" too, but also, as a Peruvianism, could refer to a lump of native silver (which would have connected this poem to the earlier piece beginning "At last, a hill,").

Line 23: originally read:

> And my lump of silver (or potato) and my flesh and my contradiction
> worthy of opprobrium?

Line 24: "lovo" appears to be an intentional misspelling for "lobo" (wolf).

Line 30: in place of "auriferous," Vallejo had originally written "elliptical." In the same line, "brazudo" appears to be a neologism, deriving from "brazo" (arm), with the suffix "udo" added to suggest "with big or strong arms." A parallel accepted word would be "forzudo" from "fuerza" (strength).

*

HYMN TO THE VOLUNTEERS FOR THE REPUBLIC, pp. 223–229

Line 1: "miliciano" is literally "militiaman." Because of current American connotations of this word we have decided that "civilian-fighter" conveys more accurately the meaning that "miliciano" acquired during the Spanish Civil War.

Lines 19/21: here Vallejo fully opens himself to the conflict, and thus to death, envisioning this act as a torero working against a bull's "double-edged speed." His "costumed in greatness" evokes the bullfighter's garb, his "traje de luces." Line 21 originally read:

> my tininess in the form of smoke from a fire.

Line 23: the biennial referred to here is the period 1934–36 called "el bienio negro" (the black biennial) which preceded the war.

Line 42: Pedro Calderón de la Barca (1600–81), famous Spanish playwright, author of *Life is a dream.* Lines 42 through 52 are an extraordinary weave of great Spanish figures of the past and contemporary war heroes and heroines.

Line 46: Antonio Coll, popular hero during the war. He appears to have been the first to, on foot, knock out Italian tanks with homemade hand grenades.

Line 48: Francisco de Quevedo (1580–1645), famous satirist, perhaps the Spanish poet most admired by Vallejo.

Line 49: Santiago Ramón y Cajal (1852–1934), famous histologist who shared the

Nobel Prize for medicine in 1906. He specialized in the microscopic study of cells in the nervous system.

Line 50: Teresa de Jesús (1515−82), famous writer and mystic, to whom is attributed the sonnet which begins: "I die because I am not dying."

Line 51: Lina Odena, popular heroine who died fighting Fascism on the southern front.

Line 120: an allusion to the Abyssinian "negus" or "Lion of Judea" exiled by the invading Mussolini forces. The Italians fought on both sides during the Spanish Civil War.

Line 130: "férula" (ferule), like "pecho," is a word that seems to have had a special significance for Vallejo. It is not, like "rod," commonly used, so we have once again not interpreted it. The word comes from the giant fennel stalks traditionally used in punishing school boys. Vallejo uses the word several times in *Spain, take this cup from me.*

*

BATTLES / II, pp. 231−237

Title: the original title was "BATALLAS DE ESPANA" (BATTLES IN SPAIN), followed by the Roman numeral I. Later sections of this poem have additional crossed out Roman numerals, and several later poems in the final *Spain, take this cup from me* sequence also have crossed out Roman numerals, which have been changed by hand. It appears that Vallejo originally intended an eight section poem called BATTLES IN SPAIN, some of which was crossed out, and all of which was reorganized in the construction of the final version. The original BATTLES IN SPAIN can be reconstructed from the facsimile, and since it is an excellent poem in itself, and contains considerable first-rate crossed out material, we have done so and present a translation of it as an Appendix to these Notes.

Line 1: The names "Extremadura" and "Extremeño" are misspelled in Spanish throughout the poem, written as "Estremadura" and "Estremeño." Extramadura, the western region of Spain, is known for its poverty and absentee landowners. The first important battle of the war took place there. The region was finally over-run by colonial Moorish troops brought to Spain to fight for the Fascist rebels.

Line 2: originally read:

I hear under your foot the smoke of the human wolf,

Line 3: originally read:

the smoke of the evolution of the species,

Line 14: originally read:

> and living blood from the dead blood!

and was followed by two later omitted lines which read:

> The blood has left me; the smoke
> has left me listening to my jaws.

Line 16: originally read:

> for whom death killed you and life gave birth to you

Line 18: originally read:

> how you go on plowing with your cross in our chests!

Line 23: after this line, the following one was crossed out:

> to listen to the dying of the dyings

("rencores"—rancors—was substituted for "dyings" at one point)

Line 42: after this line the following forty-one lines were crossed out:

> That is why, Estremanian man, you have fallen,
> you have cleaned yourself up
> and you have ended up dying from hope!

The part of the poem originally under Roman numeral I ended here. The following thirty-two lines made up what was originally section II of BATTLES IN SPAIN:

> The bony darkness presses on, sketches moral cheekbones,
> the gas of the armored train, the gas of the last ankle
> the cure of evil, the narrow excavation of the soul.
> A yellow tinkling, a blow of a usual finger in full tiger,
> those of Irún, when two steps from death
> the testicle dies, behind, on its pale ground!
> A yellow tinkling, under the smell of the human
> tooth, when metal ends up being metal!
>
> Wave of the Bidasoa,
> river to river with the sky, at the height of the dust,
> and river to river with the earth, at the height of the inferno!
> A toil that they had tackled on crutches,
> falling down, falling;
> narrow Irún behind an emaciated immensity,
> when the imagined bone is made of bone!

A battle in which all had died
and all had fought
and in which all the sorrows leave wedges,
all the sorrows, handles,
all the sorrows, always wedge and handle!
A battle in which all had triumphed
and all had fought
and in which all the trees left one leaf,
not a single flower and one root, man!

Cheekbones! And they are moral cheekbones,
those of Irún, where the forehead went to sleep
and dreamt that they were a forehead in both faculties . . .
And a blow of a usual finger in full tiger,
the one at Irún, where the smell drew a noise of eyes
and where the tooth had slept
its tranquil geological dream . . .

Terrestrial and oceanic, infinite Irún!

The part of the poem originally under Roman numeral II ended here. Irún, a Basque town very close to the French-Spanish border, was occupied by Fascist troops on September 5, 1936, after being ferociously attacked by land, sea and air. The Bidasoa is a river in Basque country, a part of the French-Spanish border. The following six lines made up what was originally the beginning of Section III of BATTLES IN SPAIN:

Loss of Toledo
due to rifles loaded with affectionate bullets!
Loss of the cause of death!
Loss in the Castilian language: or bullfighting!
And a triumphal loss, drum and a half, delirious!
Loss of the Spanish loss!

Retreating from Talavera,

This last line, with the addition of an initial "Then," became the first line of what is now the unnumbered second section of BATTLES / II i.e., line 43.

Line 43: Talavera de la Reina, a town in the province of Toledo, taken by Fascist troops on September 5, 1936, on their way toward Madrid.

Line 47: originally read:

dying, their rotulas over their shoulders and their loss over their backs

Line 51: originally read:

loving unwillingly, they forced Toledo to commit suicide,

Line 52: originally this line ended with a period and these two lines, later crossed out, followed:

> And on the succeeding day, the third day,
> as the African hooves resounded in the sad narrow alleys,

Line 56: after this line, the following ten lines were crossed out:

> What noon that noon between two afternoons! Something to be seen! . . .
> Say it, Alcántara bridge,
> you say it better,
> better than the water
> which flows sobbing on its way back!
> Sun and shadow of Spain over the world!
> It hurts, truly, that noon,
> the exact size of a suicide; and remembering it,
> no one any longer,
> no one lies down outside his body . . .

(in the sixth line of this deleted material, "Toledo" was substituted for "Spain" at one point)

Line 57: this line and the two following it originally read:

> From here, from this point,
> from the point of this rectilinear line,
> from the good to which the satanic good flows,

Line 60: Guernica, immortalized by the famous painting of Picasso, was the sacred town of the Basque people. German bombers, authorized by Franco, destroyed it completely on April 26, 1937, even though it had no military value.

Line 72: instead of this line and the three following it, the end of this section originally read:

> Combat at Guernica in honor
> of the bull and his pale animal: man!
>
> From here, as I repeat,
> from this viewpoint,
> the defenders of Guernica can be perfectly seen!
> weak ones, offended ones,
> rising up, growing up, filling up the world with powerful weak ones!

Line 77: this line and the six following it originally were eight and read:

> The cemeteries were bombed, and another combat
> took place with cadavers against cadavers:
> combat of the dead dead who attacked

the immortal dead
with vigilant bones and eternal shoulder, with their tombs.
The immortal dead, upon feeling, upon seeing
how low the evil, then, aie!
completed their unfinished sentences,

Line 93: this line was originally different and was followed by five lines later crossed out:

simple and one, collective and one!

Composition and strength of the fistful of nothingness, as they say,
the whole living death defended life,
fighting for the whole, which is dialectical
and for the butterfly, that seeks us,
for the free sky and the free chain! . . .

Line 94: this section was originally not part of BATTLES IN SPAIN; it appears to have been added later when Vallejo was organizing *Spain, take this cup from me*. Málaga was taken by the Italian General Roatta's troops on February 8, 1937. Thousands of the city's inhabitants fled along the coast toward Almeria and were slaughtered in great numbers by German naval fire and German and Italian bombers.

Line 131: originally read:

Literal Málaga, separation of posthumous grains of sand,

*

III "He used to write with his big finger in the air:" pp. 239—241

This poem was originally VI in BATTLES IN SPAIN. It was later taken out of that sequence, and turned into III in *Spain, take this cup from me*.

Line 2: Pedro Rojas appears to be a fictitious character, a symbol of the most humble and oppressed human beings. He has just learned to write a little, and hearing "avisa" as "abisa," misspells the word. We pick up the misspelling in "combanions" for "companions."

Line 10: this line originally was two lines:

he was killed; grow hearing his look; pass on!
stop, looking at his ears; pass on!

Lines 35/36: originally these two lines read:

and fought against so many sad people as they were
his cells, his nos, his yets, his hungers, his pieces.

Line 39: after this line, the three following it were crossed out:

> Pedro also used
> to die at the foot of time and without lying down, a slave;
> his corpse was full of world.

(this third line was later added at the end of the final version)

*

IV "The beggers fight for Spain," p. 243

This poem was originally section VII of BATTLES IN SPAIN.

Line 5: this line and the two following it were originally four lines:

> The beggars fight satanically begging
> God, so that the poor win the battle
> of Santander, that combat in which no longer is anyone defeated,
> the campaign of the wheat and its symbols.

Line 10: originally read:

> at the foot of the individual, on the mountain at the peak of the heart

Line 12: this line was originally followed by a crossed out line that read:

> The beggars fight for the poor!

Line 13: originally read:

> Troops of pleas on foot,

Line 20: "sin calcetines al calzar el trueno" does not have an equivalent in English. "Calzar un cañón" means "to load a cannon." The word "calcetines" means "socks," having lost its meaning as a diminutive of "calzas," (tights or long, loose trousers) or "calza" (wedge, or support). "Sin calcetines" (without socks) could also be translated as "barefoot."

Line 23: this line was originally followed by a crossed out line that read:

> functional attack after their chests,

*

V "There she goes!" pp. 245–247

This poem, originally untitled and unnumbered, is marked with the three small xs that Vallejo often used to indicate the beginning of an untitled poem in *Payroll of bones* and *Sermón on barbarism*. At the end of the poem, a few spaces below it, "Imagen española de la muerte" is written in by hand. Because of specific revisions and additions to this poem, we suspect that it was written earlier than most of the Spanish Civil War poems and/or at one point intended for inclusion in one of the two earlier manuscripts—for, in its original typed version, the poem is not connected to the war itself and, in our opinion, is a stronger piece than it finally became as Vallejo worked it into the fabric of the present book. Instead of indicating changes line by line, in this case we would like to present a translation of the poem based on the original version:

> There she goes! Call her! It's her side!
> There goes Death with her carbonic acid declivity,
> her accordion steps, her curse,
> her meter of cloth that I've mentioned,
> her gram of that weight that I've not mentioned . . . they're the ones!
>
> Call her! Hurry! She is searching for me,
> since she well knows where I defeat her,
> what my great trick is, my deceptive laws, my terrible codes.
> Call her! For Death walks exactly like a man,
> she leans on that arm which entwines our feet
> when we sleep
> and she stops at the elastic gates of dream.
>
> She shouted! She shouted! She shouted her born, sensorial shout!
> She shouted from shame, from seeing how she's fallen among the plants,
> from seeing how she withdraws from the beasts,
> from hearing how we say: It's Death!
> From wounding our greatest interests!
>
> (Because her liver manufactures the drop that I've mentioned,
> because she eats the soul of our neighbor.)
>
> Call her! We must follow her
> to her matriarchy and to her windows,
> for Death is a Being been by force,
> whose beginning and end I carry feverishly engraved in my meatus, the
>   glans penis,

even though she would run the normal risk
that you know
and though she would pretend to pretend to ignore me.

    Call her! She is not a Being,
but, hardly, a laconic event;
rather her way aims,
aims at simple tumult, without orbits or joyous canticles;
rather her audacious time aims, at an imprecise penny
and her deaf carats, at despotic applause.
    Call her, for by calling her with fury, with figures,
you help her drag her rapid sketch,
as, at times,
at times, global, enigmatic fractions hurt,
as, at times, I touch myself and don't feel myself.

    Call her! Hurry! She is searching for me,
with her side of road acid,
her accordion steps, her curse.
Call her! The thread and the fin in which I cry for her must not be lost.
From her smell up, oh god my dust!
From her pus up, oh god my ferule!
From her magnet down, oh god my chemistry!

In the above version, there are a few textual variations:

Line 2: "with her carbonic acid declivity" was crossed out in favor of "with her ink and inkwell," which was crossed out in favor of "through Teruel" which led to the final "through Irún."

Line 23: "the glans penis" is added by hand to the line in such a way that it appears as if it were originally not a correction for "my meatus," but rather an extension of it.

    *

VI / <u>Cortege after the capture of Bilbao, pp. 249</u>

Title: Bilbao, the greatest industrial city in northern Basque Spain, fell into Fascist hands on June 18, 1937.

Line 2: to translate "republicana" here as "Republican" would be misleading. "Loyalist" conveys the idea of one loyal to the existing government, the Spanish Republic.

*

VII "For several days the air, companions," p. 251

Line 7: "mobiliza" appears to be an intentional misspelling of "moviliza" (mobilizes).

Line 18: Gijón, industrial town in the nothern province of Asturias, which withstood Fascist attack for a long time before being evacuated on October 21, 1937.

Line 24: this line was originally followed by two lines later crossed out:

> For several days Spain
> ay! Spain looks Spain forever.

*

VIII "Back here," p. 253

Line 1: the first stanza originally read:

> Back here,
> Ramón Collar,
> your capacity tinged with foolishness
> continues, from rope to rope,
> while you visit, out there, your seven swords,
> standing, on the funereal crystal of January.

Line 2: Ramón Collar (pronounced Co-yár), probably a fictitious name, symbolizing a peasant-soldier in the defense of Madrid.

Line 10: originally read:

> Ramón of sorrow and with a Collar of abuses,

Line 37: originally this line and the last one were three and read:

> Back here, Ramón Collar,
> your work has only produced shadow!
>
> Greetings, Ramón Collar, and write to us!

*

IX Short prayer for a Loyalist hero, p. 255

Line 2: this line was originally followed by a line later crossed out:

a book with the quality of deep fiber or filament.

Line 3: originally read:

The hero was carried off, knees extended over his name,

Line 5: as before, "hombligo" appears to be an intentional misspelling of "ombligo" (navel).

Line 10: the third stanza originally read:

Poetry of the purple cheekbone, between saying it
and not saying it, poetry in the moral map that had accompanied
his heart; light membranes of the human stone:
the Christianity, the works, the great theme.
The book remained and that is all;
there are no insects in his tomb
and at the edge of his sleeve the air remained soaking
and becoming gaseous, infinite.

*

X Winter during the battle for Teruel, pp. 257

The title was originally typed "After the battle" and corrected in hand to its final state, with the exception that previous to the addition of "Teruel," another place name, too smudged to decipher, was considered. The battle for Teruel took place in terrible weather (the temperature got as low as 20 degrees below zero) from December 15, 1937, to February 22, 1938. It was perhaps the most ferocious battle of the war.

Line 8: following this line, there appears, crossed out:

with the swift precision of a verdict

Line 26: originally this line ended with a comma and was followed by:

while eating a moaning oyster.

*

XII <u>Mass</u>, p. 261

Line 7: after this line, a third stanza of three lines was crossed out:

> Four moved near the dead one:
> "To no longer be at your side, so you won't leave!"
> But the corpse, alas! kept on dying.

*

XIII <u>Funereal drumroll for the ruins of Durango</u>, p. 263

Durango, a town in the Basque province of Viscaya, was destroyed by repeated German air raids, at almost the same time Guernica was, on April 26, 1937. In the title, the word "drumroll" was originally "hymn." Since the original version of this poem is quite different than the final one (and in our opinion a stronger poem), we have decided once again to print the original in its entirety:

> Father dust who rises from Spain,
> God save you, liberate you and crown you,
> father dust who rises from the serf.
>
> Father dust who art in heaven,
> God save you, shoe you and offer you a throne,
> father dust who art in the soul.
>
> Father dust who lives off the furrow,
> God save you, clothe you and undress you,
> father dust who lives off men.
>
> Father dust who dresses the pariah,
> God save you, escort you and shelter you,
> father dust who art in jail.
>
> Father dust in whom the hungry man ends,
> God save you and return you to earth,
> father dust who haloes the poor.
>
> Father dust who flies on lances,
> God save you, hurt you and bury you,
> father dust who descends from the soul.

Father dust who has so much gold,
God save you, scatter you and give you form,
father dust who has so much soul.

Father dust who art in human temples,
God save you and decorate your atoms,
father dust who art in our steps.

Father dust who marches in smoke,
God save you and encircle you with gods,
father dust who marches burning.

Father dust who goes into the future,
God save you, guide you and give you wings,
father dust that blood has made you.

Father dust who art on earth,
God save you and nourish you with heaven,
father dust who art in the wheat spike.

Father dust who suffers from dust,
God save you, nail you and unnail you,
father dust who was a hammer.

(In revising this poem, Vallejo crossed out stanzas three and eight, and completely altered the lines and order of the others.)

*

XIV "Beware, Spain, of your own Spain!" p. 265

In the facsimile, this poem appears to have originally been section VIII, the final section of BATTLES IN SPAIN. VIII was then crossed out, and XIV written in by hand.

*

XV Spain, take this cup from me, pp. 267–269

Title: Jesus at Gethsemane: "My Father, if it be possible, let this cup pass away from me: nevertheless, not as I will, but as thou wilt." Matthew 26: 39. We have not felt bound to copy the Biblical version of the phrase, but have rendered it more actively. In the facsimile, there is a handwritten XIII which is crossed out in favor of a handwritten XV.

Line 6: as in line 41, "sienes" (temples) refers only to the human head. After this line, the following one was crossed out:

what a wheat spike on the agricultural thumb!

Line 45: originally read:

if heaven fits in terrestrial plates,

*